Introduction to

SOCIAL WORK

in the South African context

Rinie Schenck

Paul Mbedzi
Lulama Qalinge
Peter Schultz
Johannah Sekudu
Mimie Sesoko

T0347052

OXFORD

UNIVERSITY PRESS

SOUTHERN AFRICA

Oxford University Press is a department of the University of Oxford.
It furthers the University's objective of excellence in research, scholarship,
and education by publishing worldwide. Oxford is a registered trade mark of
Oxford University Press in the UK and in certain other countries.

Published in South Africa by
Oxford University Press Southern Africa (Pty) Limited

Vasco Boulevard, Goodwood, N1 City, Cape Town, South Africa, 7460
P O Box 12119, N1 City, Cape Town, South Africa, 7463

First published 2015
First impression 2015

Introduction to social work in the South African context

ISBN 978 0 19 907568 3

Typeset in Utopia Std Regular 9.5 pt on 12 pt
Printed on 80gsm Woodfree paper

Acknowledgements
Publishing manager: Alida Terblanche
Publisher / Commissioning editor: Lydia Reid / Marisa Montemarano
Project manager: Tanya Paulse
Editor: Jackie de Vos
Designer: Cindy Armstrong
Illustrator: Dedrè Fouquet
Typesetter: Baseline Publishing Services
Indexer: Tanya Paulse

Printed and bound by: Mega Digital (Pty) Ltd

Table of Contents

PART 2

PART 3

Paul (Rembuluwani) Mbedzi

Paul is a lecturer in the Department of Social Work at the University of South Africa. His research interests include the integration of the person-centred approach into practice, marriage and couple counselling, family functioning, and working with children. Paul has practised for many years as a social worker in the public service and in diverse non-governmental organisations.

Lulama (Lulu) Qalinge

Lulu has recently retired as Head of the Department of Social Work at the University of South Africa. Before joining the University of South Africa, she lectured for many years at the North-West University, Mafikeng campus. Lulu has authored numerous books and articles and also worked as a social worker for a number of years at the Odi Magistrates Offices in Ga-Rankuwa.

Rinie Schenck

Rinie is a Professor and Head of the Department of Social Work at the University of the Western Cape. Before joining the University of the Western Cape, she lectured for many years at the University of South Africa. Rinie has authored numerous books and articles, and contributed her expertise to considerable research in the field of social work.

Johannah Sekudu

Johannah is a Senior Lecturer in the Department of Social Work at the University of South Africa. She lectured for a number of years at the University of Pretoria and North-West University (Mafikeng campus), and worked as social worker at the Pretoria Child and Family Care Society and Ga-Rankuwa Hospital for a number of years.

Mimie Sesoko

Mimie is the Head of the Department of Social Work at the University of South Africa. Her research interests include social policy, community development, women and economic empowerment and rural development. She was involved in lecturing in social work at the University of South Africa for a number of years. She was also the program director of the W.K. Kellogg Foundation for the Africa program. Mimie worked as social worker at various government- and non-governmental organisations.

Peter Schultz

Peter is a lecturer in the Department of Social Work at the University of South Africa. He qualified at the University of Stellenbosch in 1976 and obtained a Master degree from the University of Pretoria in 1987. He worked as a social worker, social work supervisor and manager at different organisations – in the government sector, non-governmental organisations, community-based organisations, industry and private practice. He is also involved in topical research on substance abuse and treatment and compiles manuals on the management of children living on the street as well as on substance abuse.

Preface

This is truly a South African book. It was born out of a need to make a difference in the social work field. The authors are academics with teaching and learning, and practical and theoretical experience in case work, group work and community work. They have exposure to different fields of practice and knowledge in social auxiliary work. Together they were able to brainstorm and reflect on the gaps in the social work field, and on the number of books that lack practical and South African examples or case studies that students can relate to.

The book is structured to make it easy for the learner, practitioner and even the academic to engage in and to learn from practical examples and story lines provided in most chapters. The reader can relate and reflect on the examples as they apply to his or her own setting. These examples are exciting and relate to South African settings and situations that are outlined in the boxes.

The book addresses many components of social work in today's ever-changing environment and provides the new student with the basic understanding of different topics in social work from a developmental perspective. Included in the text are: definitions of social work and its historical development, ethics which cut across all chapters, specialised fields of practice, and the introduction to selected theories, models and approaches. It is assumed that once a student grasped the basic concepts of any discipline, they can continue to add and build up to more advanced knowledge. A good foundation tends to be more sustainable and affords the student the opportunity to link the theory they are studying to actual practical situations.

To be able to apply one's mind around themes addressed in the different chapters, the authors used the talking heads, case studies, and group activities. The content of this book is presented clearly in simple easy-to-read English using reality-based case studies to create an understanding of the profession in real South African social work settings. The learning outcomes for each chapter are easy to follow and to apply. Self-reflection at the end of the chapter helps the learner to remind him- or herself on what he or she was reading or studying.

This book is therefore meant for levels 1 (NQF 5) and 2 (NQF 6) social work students who come to the social work programme with no knowledge of social work. They walk away with an immense knowledge that is simply packaged for these two levels where learning is participatory.

This is therefore a must-read book. It will give students the confidence and right attitude towards the profession. Students will find some of the concepts easy to apply in their studies. For the first- and second-year level, they will use it effectively as it relates to the practical situation in which they live. The book allows students to do self-study and helps them to be prepared for class, and therefore they will not find the classroom situation threatening. The book is not written in an abstract manner and the lecturer will find the different concepts easy to explain. Students will be able to apply the social work principles and values, including learning how to practice counselling skills and technique, as the book is easy to use and to apply.

Dr Mimie Sesoko
October 2015

PART
1

Chapter 1
The scope of social work

Chapter 2
Social auxiliary work

Chapter 3
The history of social welfare
and social work

Chapter 4
Social work: Values, principles
and ethics

The scope of social work

Prof. L. Qalinge

CHAPTER OUTCOMES

By the end of this chapter, you should be able to:

✓ have a clear understanding of social work as a profession

✓ define social work

✓ define the term social worker and understand what is required of you as a professional social worker

✓ understand the functions and roles of a social worker

✓ distinguish what makes the social work profession different from other professions

✓ understand basic skills and techniques used by a social worker during the intervention process

✓ distinguish between social work and social welfare

✓ understand common health and social pathologies that social workers deal with.

 Case Study 1.1   **Fikile's family**

Fikile is a 28-year-old single mother. She lives with her parents and two of her own children, Kagiso, a little girl aged three, and a 14-year-old boy named Tebogo. Tebogo has behaviour challenges as he is deeply involved in drugs and keeps bad company. Fikile's parents are unemployed and live on their pension. Fikile receives a child support grant for the two children, but struggles to make ends meet.

Fikile is in denial that her son abuses drugs and this infuriates her parents who try their best to make Fikile accept that the boy is on drugs. This creates a rift in a relationship between Fikile and her parents.

Tebogo continues to steal from his grandparents, and sleeps out on several occasions with no permission from the family. Most of the time Tebogo is not home with his family, and his family does not know his whereabouts. His academic performance at school has deteriorated because he does not attend school regularly or do his homework. In addition to this, Fikile faces further challenges with the father of her children who visits the family house as and when he pleases and upsets the family by demanding attention from Fikile and speaking badly of Fikile to Tebogo. This confuses Tebogo even more.

The grandparents do not like the father of the children because of his disruptive behaviour. For example, he comes to the family house drunk, encourages Tebogo to indulge in alcoholic drinks and subsequently causes a lot of commotion in the family. Fikile is thus depressed, frustrated, anxious and feels she cannot cope with the situation. She finally makes a decision to seek professional help, and finds herself in a social worker's office.

1.1 Introduction

1.1.1 Chapter 1: The scope of social work

Over the years, social work in South Africa has undergone different, fascinating changes influenced by the sociopolitical landscape. Among these changes is the shift from a residual welfare approach to a developmental approach, which emphasises economic development of communities, democratic participation, social justice and a human rights approach.

With poverty growing from year to year, the services of social workers have become more and more sought after. The change in the social conditions coupled with urbanisation and the ever-changing technological demands expose the younger generation to many challenges, such as drugs, violence, child sexual abuse, family disorganisation, teenage pregnancy, to mention just a few. These, never ending challenges impact on the normal development of young people compelling the welfare system to place more emphasis on improving service delivery to all vulnerable groups and to build strong partnerships with non-governmental organisations on the ground. To achieve this, South Africa requires a large number of social service professionals to provide quality care to the vulnerable and needy populations. Since most of the emerging social problems require social work intervention at community level to promote an environment conducive to the development of communities, more and more social workers are needed. Prevention and rehabilitation programmes therefore become more and more prominent in the role played by social workers.

South Africa is currently in dire need of social workers. According to the Democratic Alliance (2014), as of 2013 the country was in need of 68 498 social workers, but there were only 16 164 registered with the South African Council for Social Service Professions. This represents a 77 per cent shortfall and could affect the implementation of social welfare service.

There has been, over the years, a prominent skills transfer or brain drain of social workers from South Africa to First World countries, such as Australia, the United Kingdom, and the United States of America, in search of greener pastures. This has created a huge decline in the number of social workers left to service the country.

This book is designed to introduce beginner students to the world of social work. It is an inclusive book, looking at different aspects imperative in the education and training of social workers. It is mostly designed to expose students to indigenous South African conditions, and to prepare them to be creative and proactive in dealing with such conditions.

The book is divided into ten chapters with each chapter focusing on a different aspect of training as indicated below.

1.1.2   Chapter 2: Social auxiliary work

This chapter addresses social auxiliary work as a new service aimed at complementing the services of professional social workers, and emphasises the collaboration of the two in working towards enhancing the wellbeing of individuals and communities. As para-professionals, social auxiliary workers work strictly under the supervision of professional social workers. They are therefore a very important arm of the social work profession.

Like professional social workers, they are registered with the Council for Social Service Professions.

1.1.3   Chapter 3: The history of social welfare and social work

Chapter 3 covers the history of social welfare from an international perspective, and then explores in it in a South African context. The South African history covers social welfare through the apartheid residual era to our current developmental social welfare. This is discussed in terms of three different phases, namely social welfare prior the apartheid era when families and family members relied on each other for survival and meeting social needs; the social welfare of the apartheid years (between 1948 and 1994), when the National Party came into power and introduced different apartheid policies that clearly stipulated different access to benefits for social welfare recipients; and the final phase considers social welfare in the post-apartheid years, when the first democratic government came into power in 1994 and advocated for developmental social welfare. The chapter ends with a discussion on the development of the social work profession globally and in South Africa.

1.1.4 Chapter 4: Social work: Values, principles and ethics

Discussed in this chapter are the social work principles, values, ethics, norms and standards that are relevant to the profession. As a practice-based profession, these guide social workers, social auxiliary workers and students in the intervention process.

The role of the South African Social Service Professions (SACSSP) as a statutory body is discussed in detail. Case studies are used to illustrate ethical behaviour expected from social service professionals in the helping process.

1.1.5 Chapter 5: The helping process in social work

Chapter 5 addresses the helping process in social work from the generalist perspective; the different steps involved in the helping process; assessment; cultural sensitivity; the skills and techniques used during the helping process, as well as common theories, models, approaches and perspectives used in social work practice.

1.1.6 Chapter 6: Case work: Social work with individuals

Chapter 6 addresses case work as one of the primary methods of social work. The focus is on working with individuals, families and children. Basic skills needed by social workers to intervene in clients' troubled lives at the individual level (micro-level), as well as the intervention strategies used in social work with individuals, are explained.

1.1.7 Chapter 7: Group work

This chapter looks at group work as a method of intervention and aims to introduce students to the concept of group work, and the value and benefits of the use of groups in social work. Students will also be introduced to the different types of groups, the stages of group development as well as group processes.

1.1.8 Chapter 8: Community work: A social work method

Chapter 8 introduces community work as one of the methods in social work. The focus is on defining and examining the concepts of community work, development phases, development, and community development. Emphasis is placed on the history of community work to facilitate an understanding of how the method has evolved over the years, and community work processes are explained. Different case studies are featured to help learners apply their knowledge acquired from the chapter and to reflect on their learning process.

1.1.9 Chapter 9: Fields of social practice

This chapter covers various social issues that social workers deal with on a daily basis in social work practice. It includes a discussion of issues such as HIV and AIDS, child abuse, substance abuse, domestic violence, disabilities and more.

1.1.10 Chapter 10: Employment settings for social workers

This chapter gives an overview of the various settings, internationally and locally, in which a social worker is employed. It touches on both government and non-governmental organisations; describes the role of the social worker in Employee Assistance Programmes and the understanding of social work in private practice. Further explained in this chapter, is the role of social work within the South African legal system.

This introductory chapter (Chapter 1) is aimed at providing the beginner learner with basic information on social work and laying a sound professional foundation that will cultivate an interest and understanding of the profession which is explored in the remaining chapters of this book. You will notice that some of the concepts overlap, or talk to each other, thus assisting you in understanding social work in perspective.

The case study at the opening of the chapter is a practical example of a typical social work case within a South African context. It also gives you an example of a reason why people may seek the intervention of a social worker and how a social worker can assist using his or her knowledge, skills and techniques. The use of theory, values, skills and techniques is what distinguishes a social worker from any other lay helper.

This chapter addresses the following questions:
- What is social work?
- What is a social worker?
- What are the functions and roles of a social worker?
- What characterises social work as a profession?
- What are the values underpinning social work?
- What is the difference between social work and social welfare?

An understanding of the above concepts will assist you in critically reflecting on the case study of Fikile's family, and responding to the following questions:
- Why consult a social worker?
- What is the role of a social worker in Filkile's case?
- What will the social worker do for Fikile?
- What will she or he do to save the relationship between Fikile and her parents?
- What will he or she do to help Tebogo overcome his struggle with drugs?
- How does the whole family situation impact on young Kagiso?
- What welfare services can be offered to the family to assist in improving their standard of living?

To help you answer the above questions and create a better understanding of what we mean by social work and social worker, we will examine a number of concepts and terms.

1.2 What is social work?

As a first year Social Work student, you may have questions about what exactly social work is, or you may have your own idea of what social work is. You may also have had an opportunity to read about social work to help you choose the profession of social worker. From your reading, you may have questions that remain unanswered. In this section we will attempt to answer your questions by taking a closer look at what social work is all about.

Social work is generally referred to as a helping profession. The simple underlying principle of the profession is to help people face daily challenges and enhance their wellbeing. People approach a social worker because they are unable to cope with the daily challenges they face (see the case study on Fikile's family). This therefore confirms that a social worker is an individual trained in social work to help clients improve their social functioning. A broader view of social work goes further than helping people deal with daily challenges. As a profession, it facilitates social change and development, social cohesion, and empowerment and liberation of people. Principles of social justice, human rights, collective responsibility and respect for diversities are central to social work (Australian Association of Social Workers, 2013). Further, social work is viewed as the professional activity of assisting individuals, groups and communities in enhancing or restoring their ability to improve their social functioning and of creating environmental conditions conducive to growth and development. This is achieved through the application of social work theories, values, principles and techniques, which makes social work different to any other lay helping process. To create a better understanding of the above, it is important to explain that social work is divided into the following three basic methods of intervention.

- Case work, which focuses on one-on-one intervention, deals with individuals and families in an endeavor to bring about social change and psychosocial competence. (See Chapter 6 for detailed information on case work.)

Figure 1.1: Case work

- Social group work focuses on working with groups and using the power of group dynamics to bring about change.

Figure 1.2: Group work

- Community work focuses on facilitating change on a larger scale, for example, at community or organisational level. (Community work is discussed in detail in Chapter 8.)

As stated above, social workers in their professional capacity require specialised skills and techniques to understand human behaviour and to engage people and community structures to help people to function independently. It is very important for you to understand that social workers are not there to solve problems for people; they use their professional knowledge and skills to unearth people's capacities and potentials to deal with their own problems.

The above information is intended for you to understand the general view of social work, whilst the following section provides definitions of the professional concepts in social work.

Figure 1.3: Community work

1.2.1   Defining the concept of social work

Authors have come up with different definitions of social work, which all, in the end, amount to a broad description of what professional social work is. The following paragraphs include a few different definitions of social work.

Social work is a profession aimed at helping individuals, groups, or communities to enhance or restore their social functioning and to create societal conditions conducive to personal development. It is based on professional theories, values, principles, and techniques aimed at:
- helping people to access tangible services
- providing counselling and therapy to individuals, families, and groups
- helping communities or groups provide or improve social-economic and health services
- participating in relevant policy and legislative processes (National Association of Social Workers, 1983:4–5).

Farley, Smith and Boyle (2010:7) define social work as "an art, a science, a profession that helps people solve personal, group, and community problems and attain satisfying personal, group, and community relationships through social work practice."

It goes without saying that social workers, as professionals, require specialised skills to understand human behaviour in order to promote social change and empower communities to take control of their own lives.

Potgieter (1998:5) defines social work as "an important service which helps to ensure the smooth functioning of society by trying to break the patters in recursive cycles that affect the lives of people. When social work services collapse, or when they are not available, human beings suffer".

Because social work is not a profession in isolation, but one that operates on a global level, the International Federation of Social Workers (IFSW) and the International Association of Schools of Social Work (IASSW) have agreed on the following global definition of social work:

"Social work is a practice-based profession and an academic discipline that promotes social change and development, social cohesion, and the empowerment and liberation of people. Principles of social justice, human rights, collective responsibility and respect for diversities are central to social work. Underpinned by theories of social work, social sciences, humanities and indigenous knowledge, social work engages people and structures to address life challenges and enhance wellbeing." (International Federation of Social Workers, 2014)

From the above definition, it becomes evident that social work:

- is a profession
- aims to promote social change among individuals, groups and communities
- is an element of working towards growth and development
- is aimed at empowering people
- emphasises social justice, human rights, and respect for diversity
- uses theories, models and approaches to intervene within the indigenous context of clients.

1.2.2 Values

Social work is based and guided by a set of professional ethics and values, such as:

- **respect** for human beings, that is, respecting the inherent dignity and worth of people
- **accepting** people as they are (meaning people should not be discriminated against on the basis of colour, age, religion, sexual preferences, race and disability)
- treating each person as an **individual**, taking into consideration that each individual is as unique as his or her thumb print, thus understanding the experiential world of every person as central, unique and personal becomes very paramount
- keeping clients' tribulations as **confidential** as possible based on the rationale that all people have a right to privacy
- allowing each individual **self-determination** and purposeful expression of feelings.

It is these ethics and values that direct social workers towards helping the clients who land up in their social work offices.

You will find a detailed explanation and discussion of ethics and values in Chapter 4.

1.2.3 Person in the environment

In its course of helping clients, social work is guided by the paradigm of person in the environment. This means that in dealing with people who seek help, social work needs to take into consideration the environment in which people come from, including the social, economic, cultural and reciprocal interactions of all these factors. This is important because, in most instances, it is the failure of the environment to respond to the needs of people that creates challenges and problems.

EXAMPLE 1.1

In South Africa poverty is very rife, exposing people to situations which are not conducive to normal human habitation. For example, settlement areas commonly known as *mekhukhu* are areas characterised by lack of infrastructure, hygiene, sanitation and general lack of essential services. These areas present an unhealthy environment that negatively impacts on the lives of the people and therefore breeds social problems that impinge on the day-to-day living of people. In dealing with clients from such areas, it is imperative that the environment be taken into consideration.

STOP AND REFLECT

1 Reflect on your own environment in which you live or where you grew up, and indicate how it affected or still affects you as an individual and the larger community.
2 What do you think needs to change?
3 What can you do to bring about change?
4 How can the social worker assist in improving the environment?

The opening case study about Fikile relates to a family living in an underdeveloped area where the daughter lives with her parents in a two-roomed *mokhukhu* (informal structure made of wood, corrugated iron sheets or sticks). The parents occupy one room and the daughter with her two children occupy the other one room which serves as a living room, kitchen and bedroom. The first challenge here is lack of privacy for the daughter and her teenage son, who eventually runs to the streets and abuses of drugs. The role of social work in this case is to help the family to cope better in their environment. This is typically referred to as micro-practice or case work. The social work office may also assist in improving the environment by coordinating with other stakeholders, such as the municipality, churches and NGOs, to form a social action group (a group of people from the same geographic area coming together to advocate for their own needs) to improve the environment and thereby bring about change. This is typically referred to as macro-practice or community work. This means social work looks at the client in totality, as an individual, as part of a group, and the larger community within the context of their environment. It is therefore imperative that social workers pay attention to the environment in which people live, and it is the role of social work to help people change the environment so that it functions more effectively for individuals, families, and communities.

 STOP AND REFLECT

Analyse Fikile's environment and indicate how it impacts on the family as a system.

1.2.4 Social work is empowering

Social work as a profession is not focused on doing things for the people, but doing things with the people. This is an empowerment mode where social work deals with empowering clients to help them help themselves. (Empowerment refers to making people aware of obstacles that negatively impact on their lives. The aim is for them to take power and not to wait to be given power.) The old Chinese saying "give a man fish, and he will be hungry tomorrow, but teach a man to fish, and he will be able to feed himself for the rest of his life" still holds in the social work profession. Social work as a profession goes further than just teaching a man to fish, it also helps with identifying the pond and ascertaining if there are fish in the pond.

Social work practice uses a number of **theories**, **approaches** and **models** to empower clients, to understand their problems and to intervene at different levels. Most of these are borrowed from Psychology, Sociology and Anthropology, and assist social workers in understanding why things happen the way they do, giving direction as to how to intervene. Segal, Gerdes and Steiner (2013:7) confirm that theories have the capacity to explain social relationships; can help with understanding of human behaviour; may explain why people stigmatise others; and can make predictions about the likely outcome of people's efforts. This may explain the reason why you, as a Social Work student, are required to register for and study, amongst other subjects, Sociology, Psychology, Economics, Development Studies and Anthropology. Some theories, models and approaches commonly used in social work are the constructivism approach, ecological perspective, person-centred approach, behaviour modification, empowerment approach, developmental approach, and strength based approach. Because social work deals with urgent and sometimes crisis situations, crises intervention becomes very critical in social work practice.

Theoretically, social workers believe that all human beings have the potential and capacity to deal with their problems given the environment and resources they need. Theirs is to create a conducive climate and awareness of their strengths, potential and capabilities to deal with their daily challenges. This is based on Rogers' person-centred approach; strength based perspective, and developmental welfare approach. (These theories, models and approaches will be discussed in detail in Chapter 5.)

Following 1994, when the democratic government was born in South Africa, social work changed its paradigm towards social developmental social work, which emphasises empowering people through economic development, democratic participation in all issues relating to communities, taking ownership and social justice. (The developmental approach will be discussed in detail later in this chapter and in Chapter 3.)

It must be explained that social work has previously been heavily controlled by the political structures of the country, such as the policy of apartheid and separate development. These policies discriminated against the majority of people. As such, welfare services were distributed unequally between the two races with the white population receiving the best of all welfare services. Social workers were affected by these policies because they could not offer help to clients due to lack of resources. The welfare paradigm was paternalistic and thus did not contribute to the empowerment of communities. Lack of infrastructure and services contributed to multiple social problems among black communities, thus posing challenges to practising social workers in that they found themselves trying to solve unsolvable problems created by the apartheid government. Emphasis was placed on case work to the detriment of other creative methods of intervention. Social development therefore came into being as a means to deal with the injustices of the past, and as such it can be termed 'a rights based approach'.

Based on the developmental paradigm shift, Patel (2007:206) attempted to define developmental social work as "the practical and appropriate application of knowledge, skills and values to enhance the well-being of individuals, families, groups, organisations and communities in their social context. It also involves the implementation of research and the development and implementation of social policies that contribute to social justice and human development in a changing national and global context." (Social development is discussed in detail in Chapter 3.)

With the change to social development, social work found itself having to adapt to local conditions by taking a lead in developing appropriate developmental intervention strategies. This meant that educational institutions had to transform the curriculum to prepare students to work in vast, poverty-stricken communities so typical of South Africa. This process is ongoing.

It can be concluded that social work is the profession directed at helping individuals, groups, or communities to enhance their capacity for social functioning, and create a conducive environment for change, development and social justice.

With the above understanding of social work you may be able to understand why Fikile, in the opening case study, had to utilise social work services. The section that follows will look at what a social worker is.

1.3   What is a social worker?

It is imperative that you understand what a social worker is since you are aspiring to be one.

From the above definitions of social work, it is evident that a social worker is a social service professional involved in social work. In ordinary layman's terms, a social worker is normally referred to as someone, or a professional, who works with people who are experiencing challenges in their lives. This means that a social worker is someone that communities consider has the ability to deal with the health and social wellbeing of people who are unable to cope with daily challenges. This is why Fikile, in the opening case study, wanted to seek help from a social worker when she could not cope with all the challenges she faced.

On a professional level, there are different definitions of a social worker. They are as follows:

A social worker is a social service professional who focuses on a person in relation to his or her environment. The social worker acknowledges that an individual exists within a particular environment, and that it is this environment that sometimes impacts negatively or positively on the development of the individual. Based on this, a social worker helps to improve people's lives in their own environment by creating a fertile soil for self-understanding and development; and helps to improve their abilities to interact and relate to others in the environment they live in (Farley *et al.*, 2010:7). (The relevance of the environment has been explained in this chapter.)

The National Association of Social Workers (1983:4–5) defines a social worker as "a graduate of school of social work (with either a bachelor's, master's or doctoral degree), who uses her or his knowledge and skills to provide social work services for clients (who may be individuals, families, groups, communities, organisations, or society in general)."

Looking at another definition, Miley, O'Melia and Dubois (2009:59) explain the social worker as a social service professional who continuously strives to strengthen human functioning and promote the effectiveness of societal structures to positively respond to their needs.

Fikile's environement is made up of the family and the geographic location she lives in. It is responsible for the challenges she faces. This may be due to poverty, which indirectly contributed to Tebogo's abuse of drugs. A social worker can therefore help Fikile to restore her social functioning by intervening in Tebogo's behaviour of abusing drugs. He or she can help Fikile and the parents to relate or interact on a personal level to improve relationships, and help to empower the whole family to work together towards improving their wellbeing.

Looking at the global definition of social work, it can be deduced that a social worker is a practice-based social service professional who promotes social change and development of communities, focusing on social cohesion, empowerment, social justice, human rights and the liberation of people.

1.3.1   Social work qualification

You are reading this book because you are aspiring to become a professional social worker. This section provides information on how to proceed to become a social worker and on what is expected of you to become one.

1.3.1.1   Training and qualifications

To perform as a social worker, you need education and training in a wide range of areas and disciplines, such as values, ethics, diversity, human behaviour, health, social pathologies, Sociology, Psychology, Anthropology, Economics and Developmental Studies, to effectively deal with the developmental challenges faced by individuals, groups, families, and the larger community.

To qualify as a social worker in South Africa, one must have a four-year bachelor's degree in social work (BSW) from an accredited South African institution of higher learning. Within the South African context, a prospective social work practitioner is required to apply for registration with the Council for Social Service Professions (SACSSP) who evaluates the academic record to assess if the candidate has complied with all the requirements for registration. Based on the evaluation of the curriculum, the candidate will be registered as a fully qualified social work practitioner. The Council is the statutory body regulating the education and training of social workers. (The Council for Social Service Professions will be discussed in Chapter 4.)

So far we have explained what social work is, and what social workers do. This information may have given you a clearer picture of the profession, which may help you to decide whether social work is a suitable profession for you. This knowledge should also help you understand why Fikile chose to see a social worker to assist her with the challenges she was facing.

 STOP AND REFLECT

Test your knowledge by answering the following questions:
1   Why do you think Fikile, in the opening case study, deemed it necessary to see a social worker?
2   What do you think a social worker will do for her, and why?
3   What does an individual need to do to qualify as a social worker?

1.4   Characteristics of professional social work

Having discussed and defined what social work and the social worker are all about, it is now necessary to look at what characterises social work as a profession, and to examine the roles and functions of a social worker.

The following characteristics are adapted from the book by Farley *et al.* (2010:7–11).

1.4.1   Individual as a holistic being

"Social work looks at the individual as a **holistic being** in continuous interaction with the environment. Emphasis is placed on how the individual interacts with the family as a system responsible for socialisation of its subsystems. The systemic view of the family indicates that all subsystems within the larger system are in continuous interaction with one another to create a state of equilibrium. Any imbalance within a particular subsystem disturbs the equilibrium and social functioning of the entire system. The family is therefore often regarded as the case and a focal factor in social work."

1.4.2   Knowledge of community resources

"Identification and knowledge of community resources remain a cornerstone in helping people deal with daily challenges. This allows social workers to refer clients to appropriate services if the need arises. In the case study at the beginning of this chapter, social workers may refer Tebogo to a rehabilitation centre to deal with his addiction. They can also assist the larger community by planning and organising activities directed at improving conditions within the entire community. For example, a social worker may plan and organise with the community an awareness campaign against the use of drugs by young people."

1.4.3   Integration of theory and practice

"As indicated earlier in the chapter, social work practice uses a number of theories, approaches and models to understand a client's problems and to intervene at different levels. Social workers are therefore expected to understand theory in order to be able to integrate theory into practice. Social work practice is not merely thumb sucking, but is directed by theory, thus making intervention systematic and methodical.

Social work education emphasises integration of theory and practice to direct the helping process."

1.4.4   Primary methods of intervention

"Social work is based on three primary methods of intervention, which are case work, group work and community work.

- Case work involves the use of one-on-one or face-to-face relationships with individuals experiencing problems. It is also referred to as individual intervention.
- Group work utilises the group as a medium of support in which individuals in a group depend on one another to bring about desired changes. Collectivity and mutual aid are prominent in groups.
- Community work involves the social worker working with the community to facilitate change. This can also be referred to as macro-level intervention which focuses on working with neighbourhoods, organisations and the larger society to improve the quality of life."

In addition to the three primary methods, there are secondary methods that form the back bone of all the methods. These are called research and administration/management (which are not discussed in this book).

1.4.5   Statutory body

Social work is regulated by the statutory body called the Council for Social Service Professions as promulgated by the Act of parliament. (See Chapter 4 for more information on the Council for Social Service Professions.) The Council, amongst other functions, regulates the training of social workers and keeps the registration of all practising social workers.

1.4.6   Worker-client relationship

Building of a positive worker-client relationship is paramount in the helping process. This is achieved through respecting and accepting clients, being non-judgmental, allowing clients to determine their own course (self-determination), and making clients feel that their affairs will be kept as confidential as possible. A positive worker-client relationship facilitates the development of a warm and conducive climate, which is important to all therapeutic endeavors.

1.4.7   Multi-disciplinary profession

Social work is a multi-disciplinary profession borrowing from other disciplines, such as Sociology, Psychology, Anthropology and Development Studies, to understand health and social pathologies, human behaviour and interactions between and among people and their environments.

1.4.8   Problem solving

Social work recognises that social problems are the results of the environment not responding to the needs of the people, and that human behaviour is greatly influenced by the social institutions of humanity. To facilitate problem-solving, it is necessary for social workers to understand the environments people live in and how their environments impact on their daily lives. For example, Fikile, in our case study, lives in a settlement area. The parents' house is made of corrugated iron, and divided into two rooms. The parents occupy one room and Fikile and her two children share the other room. Privacy is violated, and the teenage boy feels more comfortable being on the street where he shares drugs with other children. Since Fikile is unemployed, she cannot cater for the needs of her children. The environment Fikile finds herself in is not conducive to the wellbeing of the whole family. Thus, in dealing with Fikile's problems, the social worker will need to understand the impact of growing up in settlement areas with no infrastructure, no sanitation, poor housing, no recreation facilities, and where the use of drugs and alcohol by children have become the norm. As such, Fikile's problem cannot be dealt with in isolation. It will include the entire family and the community in which they live.

1.4.9   Social work operates under the auspices of a welfare agency

Most social workers are employed in welfare agencies or institutions and as such operate within the framework and policies of the organisation they work for. The welfare agency or organisation provides resources for social workers to perform their services. Within the South African context, the majority of social workers are employed in public welfare agencies controlled by the government of the day. Some work for non-governmental organisations, community based organisations, and a small number operate within the private sector.

1.4.10   Belief in the strengths of the client

The basic aim of social work is to help clients help themselves or to help communities develop to a stage of sustainability. In their daily encounters with clients, social workers are not prescriptive, but work with the client step by step to reach a desired goal. Through their involvement in communities, they assist clients in identifying and utilising community resources at their disposal. Social workers strongly believe that all human beings have the innate potential to care for themselves, and what they need is an opportunity to realise their potential and to use it to manage their daily lives.

1.4.11   Rehabilitation, prevention and developmental social welfare

Social workers emphasise rehabilitation (which is restoring individuals, groups, and communities to a balanced state of equilibrium) and prevention (being proactive by introducing preventative programmes) in alleviating health and social pathologies. It is important to understand that rehabilitation is reactive as it focuses on restoring what has already happened, whilst prevention is pro-active because its aim is to prevent what might happen.

Recently, added to the list, is a focus on developmental social welfare, which emphasises economic empowerment, democratic participation and equality.

1.4.12 Team approach

A team approach and use of community stakeholders is encouraged throughout the problem-solving process. Social workers play the role of a broker and coordinator to create a synergy amongst teams and related services. It may not always be possible for a social worker to solve problems singlehandedly, thus the need for a team approach.

The above characteristics are outlined to help you understand why social work is deemed to be a profession. The sections that follow endeavour to introduce you to the professional roles and functions of a social worker.

 STOP AND REFLECT

1 In your own words, explain what makes social work a professional discipline.
2 What distinguishes a social worker from any other person prepared to help people, for example a volunteer?

1.5 Functions of a social worker

Social workers, by virtue of their qualification, have professional functions and roles that they are expected to play during the helping process as indicated below:.

1.5.1 Facilitate change and development

This function focuses on developing opportunities for linking individuals, groups and communities with resources, services, and opportunities to develop and change. In the case of Fikile, the function of a social worker may be to link her with a rehabilitation centre to help her son who is abusing drugs. She can be linked further with support groups for mothers with children abusing drugs.

1.5.2 Enhance problem solving

The fundamental function of a social worker is to enhance the problem-solving, coping and developmental capacities of individuals, groups, and communities. To enhance problem solving, the social worker uses skills and theoretical knowledge to help the client to tell her story, identify the problem, look at alternative ways of dealing with the problem and subsequently develop a plan of action to deal with the identified problem, while all the time actively involving the client in the decision-making process. Problems are in most cases multi-faceted. It is the role of the social worker to assist the client in breaking down the problem and prioritising urgent matters.

1.5.3 Coordination

Coordination aims at promoting the effective coordination of systems that provide individuals, groups and communities with resources and services. In this case, the social worker can work with the family as a system to improve interpersonal relationships and facilitate involvement of other systems in the environment to provide resources and support to the whole family.

1.6   Professional roles of a social worker

In addition to functions they perform, social workers have professional roles to play in the process of intervention. Kirst-Ashman and Hull (2010:28) define a role as a "culturally expected behaviour pattern for a person having a specified status or being involved in a designated social relationship." Roles can be used in working with individuals, groups or communities.

The following roles are adapted from Kirst-Ashman and Hull (2010:28):

1.6.1   Counsellor

As a counsellor, the social worker provides guidance to individuals, groups and communities and assists them in reaching a stage of psychosocial competence. For example, a social worker might have a one-on-one counselling session with Fikile to address her problems and help her decide which rehabilitation centre is best suited for Tebogo's condition.

1.6.2   Educator

As an educator, a social worker provides knowledge and information to clients for better social functioning. Consultation and education is paramount to the social work process. For example, a social worker may teach Fikile child management skills and also teach Tebogo about the effects and impacts of drugs on one's body.

1.6.3   Broker

The social worker links clients to needed systems, programmes, and resources to facilitate personal development. For example, the social worker may link Fikile to a substance abuse treatment centre to help Tebogo. A worker may also link Fikile to Tebogo's school to monitor his academic performance.

1.6.4   Mobiliser

A social worker may mobilise a community to create awareness about the use of drugs in the community and how drugs affect the lives of young people. In fulfilling this role, a social worker may also mobilise different stakeholders to provide financial and human resources to the awareness campaign.

1.6.5   Mediator

As a mediator, a social worker resolves arguments or disagreements amongst client systems. For example, a social worker may mediate between Fikile and her parents in order for the parents to understand Fikile's situation and give her all the support. The reason for mediating in this case is to improve interpersonal relationships between Fikile and her parents. A social worker may also mediate between Fikile and her boyfriend to end the dispute over the children.

1.6.6   Facilitator

In most of their functions, social workers are involved in some form of facilitation. For example, a social worker may facilitate a group for parents (including Fikile) with children abusing drugs. She may also facilitate community projects for income generation, or facilitate client's self-understanding.

1.6.7   Coordinator

As a coordinator, a social worker may coordinate resources and people in the community to fight the abuse of drugs by young people. Coordination involves pulling together resources and systems in an organised manner.

1.6.8   Negotiator

A social worker may negotiate between different client systems to reach a workable consensus. For example, a social worker may negotiate between Fikile and her parents to reach an under-standing of Tebogo's behaviour and abuse of drugs. Negotiating happens when there is a conflict between two or more systems.

1.6.9   Advocate

As an advocate, social workers speak on behalf of individuals, groups and communities. For example, a social worker may advocate on behalf of Tebogo to avert expulsion from school because of truancy and coming to school under the influence of drugs and alcohol. In this case, a social worker steps forward and speaks out on behalf of Tebogo explaining the family situation in order to promote fair and equitable treatment or to gain needed resources.

In fulfilling their professional roles, the social worker equally uses different skills to facilitate the helping process. These skills are learned and eventually develop into competencies used to help clients to help themselves. The next section will assist you in understanding common skills used by social workers during the intervention process.

Before discussing the skills, you are required to stop, look back at what you have learned thus far, and engage in the following activity.

 STOP AND REFLECT

Go back to the opening case study and idenitify the different roles that a social worker can play to assist the family as a system. If, for example, you mention broker, explain why and how.

1.7   Social work skills

This section is formulated to sensitise you to different skills used by social workers in the process of engaging with individuals, groups and communities. Only a few skills will be discussed in this chapter, as a detailed outline of skills is explained in Chapter 5.

A skill in social work is a competency that one acquires over a period of time as dictated by social work knowledge, values, ethics and standards to promote professional integrity during different phases of the helping process. There are a variety of skills that social workers use at different stages of the problem-solving process. Depending on the situation at hand, the social worker may select a particular skill or combine different skills to enhance the helping process.

The following skills are introduced to give you a basic knowledge of the different skills commonly used by social workers.

1.7.1 Listening

In order to understand a client's experiential world, his or her perceptions and realities, the social worker first needs to listen vigilantly to what the client is experiencing and how he or she is experiencing it. Listening can take the form of using body language, such as nodding the head, keeping eye contact, and sitting in a manner that convinces the client that you are interested in his or her story. (Grobler & Schenck, 2009:49) For example, if the social worker interacts with a client while working on his or her computer, or if the social worker's body is turned away from the client, it may send the message that the social worker is not interested in what the client is saying. This is bound to make the client feel rejected and lose confidence in the helping process.

1.7.2 Information gathering

The ability to help clients depends on how much accurate information the social worker is able to gather to develop the 'prognosis'. For the social worker to effectively help the client, a conducive environment needs to be created to encourage the client to open up for the worker to gather as much information as possible. The more information the social worker gathers, the more accurate the assessment will be. This will allow the social worker to address the relevant challenges faced by the client.

1.7.3 Relationship building

Relationship building is the cornerstone of any helping process. In meeting the social worker for the first time, the client may not feel comfortable to confide in the stranger who happens to be a social worker. It is therefore imperative for the social worker to build a professional worker relationship with the client. The building of a professional relationship is facilitated by the way a social worker addresses the client; how he or she looks at the client, the respect he or she shows the client, and the acceptance of the client as he or she is. The social worker needs to create and maintain a professional helping relationship at all times to create a conducive climate for the client to express his or her feelings and emotions.

1.7.4 Observation

Observation is very important in social work. Because of the conditions clients may find themselves in, it may not be easy for them to express their true feelings to a stranger. What they sometimes say may not be congruent with their facial or bodily expressions. This is where observation comes in. The social worker needs to be cautious to observe a client's feelings and emotions. This entails reading between the lines, and being able to reflect back to the clients any inconsistencies in order to assess the client's needs. The social worker must at all times be able to observe and interpret verbal and non-verbal behaviour or cues from the client.

1.7.5 Questioning

For the social worker to help the client there is a need to collect as much information from the client as possible. This information will help to form an assessment of the client's problems. This therefore means that the social worker has to engage individuals, families, groups and communities by asking relevant questions and probing whenever possible. In the process of questioning, the social worker has to observe values and professional ethics by asking questions relevant to the case and asking questions in a way that will make it easy for the client to respond. Sensitive questions that may evoke deep seated emotions need to be avoided depending on the stage of the intervention process. Value laden questions and any form of judgment, including blaming and interrogation, must be avoided at all cost.

1.7.6 Empathy

Empathy refers to a social worker being able to see the problem from the client's own frame of reference and being able to feel what the client feels – or a social worker being able to immerse herself in the shoes of the client. Grobler and Schenck (2009:55) refer to this as "stepping out of our own comfort zones or frame of reference and into the experiential world of the client, no matter what it may be."

1.7.7 Reflect

This is the ability to reflect back on the client's feelings, emotions and content.

1.7.8 Communication

Communicate openly using language that is acceptable and understandable to the client, attend to verbal (spoken words) and non-verbal communication (use of gestures, body language, and facial expression), tone down aggressive communication and amplify suppressed communication. To facilitate communication, the social worker needs to create a warm climate to make the client feel accepted and understood.

1.7.9 Facilitate

Facilitate the problem solving process without imposing your values on the client. Facilitate communication by using different techniques that will help the client to open up.

Having introduced you to the skills commonly used in social work practice, it is important to take you through to the social welfare system since the majority of social workers work within this system.

1.8 Social work and social welfare

Social work and social welfare exist alongside each other to an extent that they are sometimes considered to be one and the same thing. The two are normally confused and there is a tendency to use them interchangeably or synonymously. This section is therefore devoted to assisting beginner students in understanding the difference between the two concepts. The emphasis will be on social welfare since social work has already been defined and explained.

Social welfare is a system of organised social services and programmes that help to alleviate human suffering. It is aimed at improving the lives of a large number of people who need support and help to sustain their wellbeing. As an organised system, it comprises diverse activities aimed at helping individuals, families, groups and communities to cope with daily challenges affecting their lives. It focuses on the social development of communities to improve their standard of living and to create opportunities for better living. Social welfare focuses on prevention, rehabilitation, alleviation of stressful conditions, and contributes to the solution of health and social pathologies impacting on the growth and development of individuals, families, groups and communities. It is thus reactive as well as proactive in its services of nation building.

Social welfare in South Africa provides comprehensive support to individuals and families through programmes such as primary health care, social relief in the form of different grants to vulnerable populations (such as a child support grant, foster care grant, disability grant, and old age pension), and low cost housing. Social workers as professionals are involved in most of the activities within the social welfare system. It must be understood that they do not work in isolation, but in collaboration with other professionals and disciplines. Social welfare and social work are therefore both terms that refer to the development and provision of public or private social services to promote social justice amongst individuals, families, groups and communities. As indicated above, while the term social welfare refers more generally to the wellbeing of individuals, groups and communities, as well as the system of social service delivery, the term social work refers more distinctively to the professional practice of delivering these social services. The change in the government structures which impacted on the holistic social welfare system in South Africa is explained hereunder.

1.8.1 Change in the welfare system

With the dawn of the new democratic government, South Africa saw the need to move from the old residual social welfare system, which was highly paternalistic, to developmental social welfare based on the Constitution which indicates that everyone has the right to:
• an environment that is not harmful to health or wellbeing
• access adequate housing
• health care services, including reproductive health care;
• food and water
• social security.

This culminated in the White Paper for Social Welfare which was subsequently adopted by Parliament in 1997. The policy framework espoused in the White Paper focuses on changing the welfare system that favoured a minority group over the majority of the population. Because of this policy, the black population, though in the majority, did not have equal share to the welfare cake. Almost all social services served the needs of the white population to the detriment of the black people of South Africa. This policy change required a total transformation of the welfare system, which had far reaching implications for the human and financial resources of the country. From the White Paper, developmental social welfare was born. It gave rise to an integrated system of social development services that facilitate human development and improve the quality of life of communities. This was based on the government's realisation that poverty, so rife in South Africa, required social development rather than a social work response (Gray and Mazibuko, 2002:192). This, however, did not mean social work was to be relegated to the dustbins of history, but as Gray explains, there is always place for social work within developmental social welfare for provision of micro- and macro-intervention strategies, including issues such as social policy, administration, and research. Because of this change, social work needed to generate intervention models that go beyond case work, which was almost synonymous with social work, to respond to the peculiar problems of the country.

Developmental social welfare is based on the following four principles.

1.8.1.1   Social justice
Social justice refers to a just and equal society where there is fairness, acknowledgement of diversity, and mutual obligation amongst all people in a society.

1.8.1.2   Equality
Equality refers to a situation in which people have equal access to social services, resources and opportunities to develop and grow. It can also mean access or provision of equal opportunities, whereby individuals are protected from being discriminated against. Discrimination in equality can occur in race, sex, health, religion, family structure, age, politics, disability, culture, sexual orientation or beliefs.

1.8.1.3   Participation and democracy
This refers to people having a right to participate freely, directly or indirectly, in matters that affect them and to make choices that they deem to be constructive in developing their wellbeing. A democratic society is one in which beneficiaries are consulted, included, and encouraged to take part in all matters of the society or organisation that they belong to. Participation and true democracy must be people-centred, because they are about people, for people and with people and of the understanding that power is vested in people.

1.8.1.4   Social change
Social change refers to the notion of social progress or sociocultural evolution. Social change gives the philosophical notion that society is moving forward by dialectical or evolutionary means. Social change refers to changes in attitudes, behaviours, laws, policies, and institutions to better mirror the values of inclusivity, fairness, diversity, and opportunity. It may also refer to a paradigm shift from one state of mind to another.

Social services are offered within the structure of the social welfare system. Ideally, the delivery system is constructed to respond to social needs and social problems at all levels. The following section is designed to expose you to the common social problems that social workers work with within the welfare system.

1.9   Health and social problems

Social workers as professionals deal with a wide range of health and social problems. To be able to help clients, social workers need to have a good understanding of common social ills prevalent in the communities they work in. These are not exhaustive because societies change, grow and develop over a period of time.

Common health and social pathology challenges that social workers repeatedly battle with are:

- HIV and AIDS
- domestic violence
- substance abuse
- poverty
- sexual abuse
- physical and emotional abuse
- child abuse.

These challenges are discussed in detail in Chapter 8 in order to deepen your understanding of the roles and functions of social workers in dealing with these pathologies.

1.10 Conclusion

This chapter introduced you to a number of concepts and terms pertaining to the social work profession. By now you should be able to form a clear picture of the profession you are study-ing towards and assess your passion in working with people. The opening case study is designed to give you a common practical example of the cases social workers are confronted with. Social work, in its various forms, addresses the multiple, complex transactions between people and their environments. As a profession, it intervenes at the individual, group and community levels. Its function is to enable all people to develop to their full potential, improve their lives, and prevent health and social pathologies. Focus is always on problem solving and changes through playing certain professional roles and applying skills and techniques. As such, social workers are change agents in society and in the lives of the individuals, groups, families and communities they serve. Social work is an interrelated system of values, theory and practice.

End of chapter questions

Now that you have a clear understanding of social work, go back to the opening case study and answer the following questions.

1. What is your understanding of the concepts social work and social worker?
2. What is your understanding of social work as a profession?
3. Why do you think Fikile had to see a social worker?
4. What is it that you think the social worker can do for Fikile that cannot be done by an ordi-nary person on the street?
5. Looking at the functions of social work, how do you see them fitting into Fikile's situation?
6. What are the roles that a social worker can play to help: Fikile, Tebogo, Fikile's parents, and Tebogo's father?
7. What about Kagiso? What can the social worker do for her as a member of the family?
8. Look at each of the skills and decide where and when the social worker can apply some of the skills in helping Fikile's family.

End of chapter activity

1. Visit the welfare agency closest to you and observe:
    a.   the type of organisation
    b.   the services offered
    c.   the common social problems social workers deal with
    d.   the manner in which the social problems are dealt with
    e.   the professional roles that social workers play (the more you can identify, the better).
2. In your tutorial group, share your observations with one another.

Key concepts

- **Social work** is "a practice-based profession and an academic discipline that promotes social change and development, social cohesion, and the empowerment and liberation of people. Principles of social justice, human rights, collective responsibility and respect for diversities are central to social work. Underpinned by theories of social work, social sciences, humanities and indigenous knowledge, social work engages people and structures to address life chal-lenges and enhance wellbeing." (International Federation of Social Workers, 2014).

- A **social worker** is a social service professional who focuses on a person in relation to his or her environment with the aim of improving people's lives by creating a fertile ground for self- understanding and development; and improving people's abilities to interact and relate to others within the environment they live in.
- A **skill** in social work is a competency that one acquires over a period of time as dictated by social work knowledge, values, ethics and standards to promote professional integrity during different phases of the helping process.
- A **role** is a "culturally expected behaviour pattern for a person having a specified status or being involved in a designated social relationship." (Kirst-Ashman & Hull, 2010:28)
- **Social change** refers to the notion of social progress or sociocultural evolution as indicated by change in attitudes, behaviours, laws, policies, and institutions to better mirror the values of inclusivity, fairness, diversity, and opportunity. It may also refer to a paradigm shift from one state of mind to another.
- **Social welfare** is a system of organised social services and programmes to help alleviate human affliction and improve the lives of a large number of vulnerable people who need support and help to sustain their wellbeing.
- **Developmental social work** is people-centred and focuses on economic development, democratic participation of communities, and ensuring human justice and equitable distribution of resources.

References

1. AUSTRALIAN ASSOCIATION OF SOCIAL WORKERS. 2013. What is social work. [Online]. Available: https://www.aasw.asn.au/information-for-the-community/what-is-social-work [17 April 2015]
2. DEMOCRATIC ALLIANCE. 2014. *South Africa has a 77 % social worker shortage.* [Online]. Available: http://www.da.org.za/2013/08/south-africa-has-a-77-social-worker-shortage/ [18 March 2015]
3. FARLEY, O.W., SMITH, L.L. & BOYLE, S.W. 2010. *Introduction to social work.* 11th ed. Boston: Pearson Education Inc.
4. GRAY, M. & MAZIBUKO, F. 2002. Social work in South Africa at the dawn of the new millennium. *International journal of social welfare,* 11(3):191–200.
5. GROBLER, H. & SCHENCK, R. 2009. *Person-centred facilitation.* 3rd ed. Cape Town: Oxford University Press.
6. INTERNATIONAL FEDERATION OF SOCIAL WORKERS. 2014. *Global definition of social work.* [Online]. Available: http://ifsw.org/policies/definition-of-social-work/ [19 March 2015]
7. KIRST-ASHMAN, K.K. & HULL, G.H. 2010. *Understanding generalist practice.* Brooks Cole Cengage Learning.
8. MILEY, K.K., O'MELIA, M. & DUBOIS, B. 2009. *Generalist social work practice: an empowering approach.* Boston: Pearson/Allyn and Beacon.
9. NATIONAL ASSOCIATION OF SOCIAL WORKERS. 1981. *NASW standards for the classification of social work practice.* Silver Spring, MD: National Association of Social Workers.
10. NATIONAL ASSOCIATION OF SOCIAL WORKERS. 1983. *Standards for social service manpower.* New York: National Association of Social Workers.
11. PATEL, L. 2007. *Social welfare and social development in South Africa.* Cape Town: Oxford University Press.
12. POTGIETER, M.C. 1998. *The social work process.* Cape Town: Prentice Hall.
13. SEGAL, E.A. GERDES, K.E. & STEINER, S. 2013. *An introduction to the profession of social work: becoming a change agent.* Brooks Cole Cengage Learning.

Social auxiliary work

Peter Schultz

CHAPTER OUTCOMES

By the end of this chapter, you should be able to:

✓ give a brief overview of the history of social auxiliary work

✓ identify and describe the fields in which social auxiliary work is involved

✓ identify different role-players involved in the field of social work

✓ explain the role of the social auxiliary worker in the field of social work

✓ refer to the relevant Acts in the field of social work.

 Case Study 2.1 **Agmed and his family**

Agmed moved to South Africa from Somalia five years ago. He is 35 years old and opened a shop in KwaMashu in KwaZulu-Natal. At first he lived in the back of his shop until his wife and two children, aged six and nine years old, arrived and found a house on the outskirts of the township. Since then he opened two more shops and was well-liked by most of the surrounding residents who came to buy goods from his shop.

A few months ago, one of his shops was burnt down together with a few other shops that were first looted. The media referred to these acts as xenophobic attacks by the locals and the South African Police Service was called in to protect them and what was left of their shops. The looters soon increased in number and started stoning cars and shop fronts, and set a car alight.

In the media and on the political front many reasons were given for this outbreak. The reasons included xenophobia, afrophobia and lawlessness by criminal elements. Scores of people were arrested, and the so-called foreigners were moved into temporary shelters for protection.

Before the outbreak of violence, Agmed and his family settled in well with both children attending school. Now they are afraid for their lives and afraid of the violence, but do not want to go back to Somalia as they stay in South Africa legally. However, they have lost everything and they do not know what to do.

 STOP AND REFLECT

1 Do you think that social workers and social auxiliary workers should become involved in situations like this?

 a If you believe they should not, who do you think must assist them?

 b If you believe they should, how do you think they can be assisted?

2.1 Introduction

Social auxiliary work, according to the Department of Social Development (2015), means an act or activity practised by a social auxiliary worker under the guidance and control of a social worker and as a supporting service to a social worker to achieve the aims of social work. This description implies that the functions of social auxiliary workers are planned, directed and supervised by social workers in their service rendering. It furthermore implies that these functions are supportive to the social worker in executing their tasks in their field of practice, thus in essence their functions become that of team members.

Throughout history there have always been people who assisted the so-called needy. Whether it was due to a religious conviction or a sense of altruism, or whether it was as a paid employee or a volunteer, many people have wanted to assist others in trouble. Long before social work existed, religion and altruism contributed to what is known today as welfare. As welfare developed over time, it required more distinct roles and knowledge and this led to the modern phenomenon of social work.

Social work in the United States of America and the United Kingdom became a regulated and specialised profession at around the turn of the twentieth century (Ambrosino, Ambrosino, Heffernan & Shuttlesworth, 2012:23; Kirst-Ashman, 2013:13). However, as the profession grew, so did the demands on social workers. Volunteers and indigenous helpers were very supportive as they bridged the gaps between social workers and communities, and social workers and families or clients. Both these groups brought with them their personal skills obtained from their communities and life experiences from their involvement with people in general. None of these two groups of people was trained or paid for their contributions to welfare and social work agencies.

Kadushin (1986:498) points out that "Family service and child welfare agencies have always employed a small number of 'case-aides' or 'social work assistants'." He also points out that the purpose of employing them is "... to remove the 'low-level functions' from the 'high-level' professional to increase productivity". With the development of social work as a profession, the needs of people required specialisation, created greater expectations of social workers and placed higher demands on them. Nel (as cited in Lombard & Pruis, 1994:258) states that the term 'auxiliary worker' was accepted by the United Nations as far back as 1958 when it was described as someone who has been trained in a particular field "... with less than professional qualifications and who assists and is supervised by a professional worker".

Although it is generally recognised that social auxiliary work was identified more than 20 years ago when the first regulations for the registration of social workers was tabled in parliament in 1991, its development in South Africa already started almost 40 years earlier. In 1976 the Auret Commission was established to look into separate legislation for the social work profession (Lombard & Pruis, 1994:257). It was also required to identify, amongst other things, the need for people to compliment the work of social workers. In 1978, with the promulgation of the Social and Associated Workers Act (Act 110 of 1978) and the following meeting of Council in 1980, social auxiliary workers, who were previously called 'associated workers', were recognised.

2.2 Training for social auxiliary workers

As far back as 1976, the Committee of Inquiry into Separate Legislation for the Social Work Profession made reference to what was then referred to as 'associated workers' (Lombard & Pruis, 1994:257). This was based on the need for people to assist social workers. With the amendment of the Social and Associated Workers Act (1978) to the Social Work Act, the term 'associated worker' was replaced with 'auxiliary worker' and has remained so ever since. Social auxiliary workers have been successfully involved in especially the non-governmental organisation (NGO) sector. Although the involvement of social auxiliary workers is a historical fact, the need for their services has grown significantly over the past few years, especially after the new Children's Act came into being. It is especially within the public sector that this need has escalated, and especially so from within the Department of Social Development.

But as the need for these services grew, so did the need for appropriate training, especially as social auxiliary workers had to comply with Section 18 of the Social Service Professions Act (Act 110 of 1979, as amended). This section requires the registration of social auxiliary workers who hold a qualification obtained in South Africa and who are deemed to be fit and proper persons by the Council.

Persons who want to register as social auxiliary workers have to indicate completion of learning and practice obtained in one of the following ways, according to Section 2(1) of the regulations relating to the registration of social auxiliary workers and the holding of disciplinary inquiries:

a) A Further Education and Training (FET) Certificate in Social Auxiliary Work equivalent to an NQF 4 level qualification registered with South African Qualifications Authority (SAQA).

b) A Certificate in Social Auxiliary Work offered by the South African Council for Social Service Professions (SACSSP) before 30 June 2006 or written approval by the Council for enrolment at a later date as determined by the Council.

c) A qualification obtained after completion of a learning programme at a training provider which the SACSSP regards as equal to or higher than the qualification referred to in sub regulation a).

d) Theoretical and/or experiential learning approved by the SACSSP equivalent to the qualification referred to in sub regulation a) on condition that the applicant submits a portfolio of evidence meeting the requirements reflected in the FET Certificate in Social Auxiliary Work.

e) Proof from a recognised training provider that the candidate successfully completed both the theoretical and practical learning of two year courses in the subject Social Work, with a recognised provider.

If the person who wants to register as social auxiliary worker with a qualification obtained outside South Africa, Section 7(d) of the regulations apply. According to this section, an applicant for registration must provide the folllowing:

(i) An original document providing proof from the provider where the applicant received the education and training, of the content, nature and duration of the theoretical and experiential learning received.

(ii) A certified copy of documentary proof that the provider where the applicant received the education and training in Social Auxiliary Work is accredited, specifying the body of accreditation that the provider has, or if the provider was not accredited, proof of any other form of recognition.

(iii) In the case of an accredited provider, a certified copy of documentary proof from the accrediting body that the qualification is or was the accepted education and training for social auxiliary work in the country concerned.

(iv) In the case of a woman who is or was married, a certified copy of her marriage certificate.

(v) The registration fee referred to in section 6 of the regulations.

In addition to the above, the qualification may be obtained in part or as a whole through Recognition for Prior Learning (RPL), or by means of a short course recognised by the SACSSP for this purpose, the latter in a particular field of practice on certain conditions specified by the SACSSP.

The SACSSP document on RPL Policy for the Social Service Professions refers to the definition of 'Recognition of Prior Learning' in the National Standards Bodies Regulations (No. 18787 of 28 March 1998) to the SAQA Act, 1995 as follows: "RPL means the comparison of the previous learning and experience of a learner, howsoever obtained, against the learning outcomes required for a specific qualification, and the acceptance for purposes of qualification of that which meets the requirements." This means that irrespective of how and where a person achieved the learning, if this learning meets the requirements of a qualification (or part of it), it can be recognised for credits.

Although the SAQA policy indicates that it is possible to obtain a whole qualification through RPL, the SACSSP will consider this option in terms of social auxiliary work in cases where qualifications on NQF level 4 and below, where applicable, will be recognised for registration purposes where all the credits have been obtained through RPL.

According to the RPL Policy, RPL should not be perceived as an easy alternative to gain credits, a qualification or access to a learning programme, or to obtain registration with the SACSSP in order to practice. Only evidence which is both sufficient and current in terms of the required outcomes will be considered. The evidence considered to obtain credits for social auxiliary work include:
- attending appropriate short courses and/or in-house training programmes
- having worked and gained valuable learning through relevant life and work experience
- having not completed the relevant NQF level 7 qualifications.

In addition to these requirements for considering RPL, prospective students must be able to read, write, listen and speak English on a level equivalent to NQF 3 as most of the textbooks and documentation are in English

The training of social auxiliary workers was initially provided by the SACSSP in collaboration with employers in 1993. Two years later, in 1995, with the promulgation of the SAQA Act and the requirements provided by this Act, a Further Education and Training Certificate (FETC) in Social Auxiliary Work was developed on an NQF level 4 and it was officially registered on the SAQA database in 2003, after which it had been renewed every three years. In 2009, based on increasing demands from social work practice, the professional Board for Social Work and the SACSSP resolved that this qualification should be upgraded to an NQF level 5 qualification, becoming a higher education qualification. This was confirmed in 2011 and it contains subjects similar to social work training, including, amongst other things, an overview of welfare and welfare policy, social work, human behaviour, the methods of social work and areas portraying special needs such as poverty, mental illness, substance abuse, HIV and AIDS, and working with children.

The training, furthermore, makes provision for relevant supervised practical work. Social auxiliary workers are also clearly trained in terms of their role as a team member working together with and under the supervision of a social worker.

In order to achieve this role successfully, the following exit level outcomes, which have to be achieved, are reflected in the SAQA document:
1 Demonstrate basic understanding of the South African social welfare context, the policy and practice of developmental social welfare services and the role of the social auxiliary worker within this context.
2 Define and demonstrate understanding of the purpose of social auxiliary work and the role and functions of a social auxiliary worker in relation to a social worker within the South African context.
3 Consistently reflect the values and principles contained in the Bill of Rights and the social work profession`s Code of Ethics in service delivery as a social auxiliary worker.
4 Demonstrate a basic understanding of the South African judicial system and the legislation governing and impacting on social auxiliary work and social work. Legislation includes the Social Service Professions Act, Non Profit Organisations Act, the Basic Conditions of Employment Act, the Skills Development Act, and the Labour Relations Act.
5 Demonstrate a basic understanding of human behaviour, relationship systems and social issues. Social issues include poverty, unemployment, HIV and AIDS, crime, child abuse, domestic violence, drug abuse, housing, etc.
6 Implement appropriate social auxiliary work methods and techniques to address the social needs of Client Systems 1. Social Auxiliary Work methods and techniques include individual care, family care, group care, community care and introductory research.

7 Use appropriate resources in service delivery to client systems. Resources include human, financial, public and private sector organisations, multi-sectorial structures and bodies.

8 Work effectively with social workers and members of multi-sectoral teams in social service delivery. Teams include the social work team consisting of social worker, student social worker, social auxiliary worker and volunteers.

9 Work effectively as a social auxiliary worker to address the special needs and problems experienced by at least three of the priority focus groups in social welfare. Special needs include those experienced by people affected by mental, physical and sensory disabilities, chronic illnesses, drug abuse, crime, unemployment, poverty, family disintegration, child abuse and neglect and street children. Focus groups include children, older persons, the youth, women, people with disabilities, and the poor.

10 Keep precise records and compile accurate reports on social needs and social auxiliary work activities and file them appropriately. Records and reports include process notes, process reports, summary reports, evaluation and team reports linked to the various interventions; and minutes of meetings.

11 Provide an efficient research and administrative support service to the social worker.

12 Demonstrate basic knowledge of financial matters related to social auxiliary work.

13 Demonstrate self-awareness regarding personal capacities, attitudes and skills and a willingness to develop them further under the supervision of a social worker.

The following critical cross-field outcomes are embedded in the Exit Level Outcomes:

- Identify and solve problems using creative thinking. (Exit Level Outcomes 6 and 9)
- Work effectively with others as a member of a team, group, organisation and community. (Exit Level Outcomes 2, 7 and 8)
- Organise and manage oneself and one's activities responsibly and effectively. (Exit Level Outcomes 10 and 13)
- Collect, analyse, organise and evaluate information. (Exit Level Outcomes 6, 10 and 11)
- Communicate effectively using visual, mathematical and/or language skills in the modes of oral and/or written presentation. (Exit Level Outcomes 5, 6, 8, 9 and 10)
- Demonstrate cultural and aesthetic sensitivity in dealings with clients, colleagues and communities. (Exit Level Outcomes 3, 5, 6, 7, 8 and 9)
- Demonstrate an understanding of the world as a set of related systems by recognising that problem-solving contexts do not exist in isolation. (Exit Level Outcomes 5, 7, 8 and 9)
- Demonstrate ethical and professional behaviour. (Exit Level Outcomes 3, 6, 8 and 9)
- Lay the foundation for life-long learning and on-going competency. (Exit Level Outcome 13)

2.3 The functions of the social auxiliary worker

According to the regulations of the South African Council on Social Service Professionals Act (Act 110 of 1978 as amended), social auxiliary work refers to any activity or conduct which is practised by a social auxiliary worker under the guidance and supervision of a social worker in order to achieve the aims of social work. All persons practising as social auxiliary workers must be registered with SACSSP, as is the case with social workers. Registration with the SACSSP provides professional recognition, but also protects the interest of the profession.

In line with the purpose and rationale of the qualification described in the SAQA document, the SACSSP requires of social auxiliary workers, after completing their studies, to at least be equipped with the following:

- A basic understanding of the South African welfare context. This knowledge and understanding will help them form a framework of where they fit into the 'bigger picture' of social service delivery. They will obtain clarity in terms of their position as a team-player together with social workers and other professionals in order to address social issues.

- An understanding of the policies and practices in terms of developmental social services, and an understanding of their role within this context. This understanding is important as it gives insight into the role and inputs individuals, groups and communities have in determining towards their own wellbeing, particularly in the traditionally under-resourced areas.
- The ability to indicate a basic knowledge of human behaviour, relationship systems and social issues, as this will assist them in addressing the social needs they encounter, using appropriate social auxiliary work methods and techniques.
- The skills to work as a team member, primarily in supporting the social worker and social work team or organisation in which they work.
- Conduct that is ethical in all matters, reflecting the values and principles contained in the Bill of Rights and the social work professions' Code of Ethics.

Against this background, social auxiliary workers work with social workers and members of a multi-sectoral team under the guidance of a social worker utilising available resources in their service delivery to client systems. Although they may not do the work of the social worker, including any therapeutic and statutory work, they may assist with individuals, and the reunification services to families, groups or communities. In their provision of services they must keep accurate records of all their activities as well as assist social workers in their administration and research.

2.3.1 Case work

Case work (discussed in greater detail in Chapter 6), or more specifically social case work, refers to assisting individuals and families. Case work is a process which begins with the intake of the individual or family coming to the organisation for assistance and ends when the need is addressed and no further assistance from the social worker or the social auxiliary worker is required.

As far as assisting in service provision to individuals is concerned, examples of the involvement of social auxiliary workers includes "arrangements for social assistance; assisting the unemployed; prevention services such as giving information on a healthy lifestyle, AIDS and budgeting; making arrangements and supporting families during illness and after the death of a family member" (Lombard & Pruis, 1994:262). The work involved during the intake of clients, such as obtaining basic biographical information, the opening of files, and following up on interviews, are also instances where social workers can be assisted. The scope of practice of social auxiliary work is highlighted in the following case studies.

Figure 2.1: Example of a counselling set-up

Assisting with case work 1

A social auxiliary worker was requested to visit a family of six. The breadwinner of the family passed away on his way home when the taxi he took was involved in an accident three days before. As this family is a client of the agency, the social worker asked the social auxiliary worker to find out about the family's circumstances and how they are coping.

On arrival, the social auxiliary worker finds the family is still mourning and there are many visitors who have come to express their condolences. The spouse of the deceased is upset and resistant to talk. The one son says that the family is suddenly left without an income and they do not know who will pay for the funeral. Furthermore, there are three children who are still at school and the school fees are four months in arrears. They are also behind in paying their electricity as well as the rent for their house.

While the son informed the social auxiliary worker about their finances, the eight-year-old daughter is pushed forward by her twelve-year-old sister who demands the little one inform her of the fact that she is bullied at school and that the school does not want to help the family. At the same time, the sister of the deceased wants the social auxiliary worker to go with her to her late father's employer and demand money to assist with the funeral.

The social auxiliary worker may initially feel overwhelmed by the situation, but must remember that he or she was sent by the social worker to establish the circumstances, and this needs to be clear from the onset. It is suggested that she does not at all become involved in any discussion regarding the matters, but merely note them down and even ask if there are further issues. If any of the family members have a phone, it is wise for her to take a contact number. She will then prioritise the matters at hand and report back to the social worker as a matter of urgency.

The feedback from the social auxiliary worker, given to the social worker, may include the following:
- The family is mourning the loss of a loved one. There were many visitors from the community to support the family emotionally.
- The spouse of the deceased is battling emotionally to come to terms with the loss.
- The death leaves the family in financial difficulty as the late father was the only breadwinner. There is therefore no money for the funeral, the rent of the house and electricity, and school fees are in arrears. There is no immediate plan to address this situation.
- The youngest child is bullied at school and it seems as if the school is not addressing this issue.

The social worker and social auxiliary worker can then agree on the following:
- The funeral is the first priority.
- The social worker should sit down with the family to provide emotional support and to determine what arrangements can be made for the funeral
- The social auxiliary worker should contact the school and municipality to negotiate a temporary postponement in repaying the school fees, rent and electricity due to the family situation.
- After the funeral, the social worker should follow up on the issue of bullying with the family and at the school
- The social auxiliary worker should establish if there are groups or programmes in the area which attend to the family's needs.

 Assisting with case work 2

The social auxiliary worker is employed by a community-based organisation involved in treating substance abusers. He sees all new persons and their families who request assistance with their substance abuse problems. When they arrive he briefly explains to them the problem of chemical substance abuse and the assistance the organisation offers. He explains the organisation's expectations of each client and if the client agrees to continue, he gathers all their biographical information as well as the drug and treatment history of the substance abuser. When he has obtained all the information, he records it in a file opened for the client and brings it to the social worker for his or her attention.

Once the social worker receives the information from the social auxiliary worker, she studies the information and draws up an individual development plan with the client to use as a reference during the treatment. The social worker will explore, in greater depth, with the client the information collated by the social auxiliary worker.

During the course of the programme, the social worker will primarily be responsible for therapeutic group work as well as the counselling of the client and his or her family members, while the social auxiliary worker will assist with practical matters, such as the setting up of appointments and information sessions about addiction for both clients and family members.

It must be emphasised that case work done by the social auxiliary worker is always in support of the social worker while the social worker guides the process of assisting the individuals and families.

There are instances when the social auxiliary worker is unable deal with an issue and needs to refer an individual or family. Referral means to link a client to a resource that is better equipped to address the specific problem. The client is involved in this decision and needs to understand what the resources are and why the referral takes place. This is always done in cooperation with the social worker. Referrals are usually made to the social worker or specialist organisations.

Knowledge of these organisations is important to be able to make appropriate referrals for individuals or families. Examples of organisations that render specialised services to children and families include:

- Child Welfare South Africa
- the Council for Church Social Services
- the Apostolic Faith Mission Executive Welfare Council
- the Salvation Army
- the ACVV (Afrikaanse Christelike Vroue Vereniging)
- FAMSA (Families South Africa).

Organisations focusing on specialist services include:

- Autism South Africa assists those who have autistic challenges
- DEAFSA (Deaf Federation of South Africa) assists people with a hearing impairment
- CANSA (Cancer Association of South Africa) assists those suffering from cancer
- SANCA (South African National Council on Alcohol and Drug Dependency) supports the prevention and treatment of substance abuse
- NICRO (National Institute for Crime and the Rehabilitation of Offenders) attends to offenders and their families.

Social auxiliary workers will also come across clients who need financial assistance. After assessing whether they meet specific requirements and verification with the social worker, the following options are available.

- **Grant for older persons:** The applicant must be a SA Citizen. A male must be 63 years or older; a female must be 60 years or older. He or she must comply with a means test, must not be cared for in a state institution, and may not receive another grant.
- **Disability grant:** The applicant must be SA Citizen. A male must be between 18 and 59 years of age; and female between 18 and 62 years of age. He or she must submit a medical/assessment report confirming a disability, and the medical report must not be older than three months. He or she must comply with a means test, must not be cared for in a state institution, and may not receive another grant.
- **Foster child grant:** The applicant and child must be residents in South Africa, and have a court order indicating foster care status. The foster parent must be a South African citizen, permanent resident or refugee, and the child must remain in the care of the foster parent.
- **Child support grant:** The primary caregiver must be a SA Citizen. Both the child and the applicant must reside in South Africa. The applicant must be the primary caregiver of the child concerned, and the child must be under the age of 15 years. He or she must comply with a means test. He or she cannot apply for more than six non-biological children, and the child cannot be cared for in a state institution.

- **Care dependency grant:** The applicant must be a SA Citizen. The applicant and child must be residents of South Africa, and the age of the child must be under 18 years. He or she must submit a medical/assessment report confirming permanent or severe disability, and comply with a means test (except for foster parents). The care dependent child must not be cared for in a state institution.
- **War veteran's grant:** The applicant must be SA Citizen, must be 60 years or older or must be disabled. He must have fought in the Second World War or the Korean War, and must comply with a means test. He must not be cared for in state institution, and may not receive another grant.
- **Grant-in-aid:** The applicant must be in receipt of a grant for older persons, disability grant or war veteran's grant and require full-time attendance by another person, owing to his or her physical or mental disabilities. He or she must not be cared for in an institution that receives a subsidy from the state for the care/housing of such a beneficiary.
- **Social relief or distress:** The applicant must be awaiting permanent aid and be found medically unfit to undertake remunerative work for a period of less than six months. The breadwinner must be deceased and there must be insufficient means available. The applicant must be affected by a disaster while the specific areas must not have been declared disaster areas yet and the applicant must have appealed against the suspension of his or her grant. The grant is issued monthly for a maximum period of three months.

2.3.2   Group work

Social auxiliary workers can assist in social group work. Group work is discussed in greater detail in Chapter 7. There are different types of groups that can be identified in social work of which awareness groups, educational groups and support groups as well as growth groups and therapy groups are examples of groups where social workers or social auxiliary workers can play a facilitating role. In these groups, their role is to assist group members in learning more about themselves and their understanding and interaction with their circumstances. Recreation, activity and task groups are further examples of groups which could be facilitated by social auxiliary workers.

Although treatment groups are normally the task of the social worker, as their main focus is to bring about change, empowerment and development of group members, not all of the different treatment groups necessarily require in-depth intervention or the advanced skills of social workers. However, social auxiliary workers need to understand the difference between the different treatment groups to determine where they can become involved and where they cannot. Due to the remedial nature of the therapeutic group, these groups are entirely the task of the social worker.

The following groups are groups where social auxiliary workers can become involved.

- **Support groups:** These groups are established to help group members cope with circumstances by allowing them the opportunity to share their negative life events and improve their coping skills so that they can function effectively for the rest of their lives (Strydom & Strydom, 2010:124). Examples of such groups include aftercare groups for people who have received treatment for substance abuse or who have to adjust to the community after a period of hospitalisation or imprisonment.
  Social auxiliary workers merely provide assistance on a basic level. When group members, during support group sessions, become very emotional or start disclosing more deep-seated and sensitive information, they have to be referred to the social worker. Social auxiliary workers must always work closely with the social worker to make these referrals effectively without serious interruption, which may negatively affect the group members. Supervision and guidance from the social worker is vital in this regard.

- **Educational groups:** Educational groups focus on helping members to acquire knowledge and learn different or more complex coping behaviours. Examples of these groups include groups acquiring parenting skills, family members needing assistance in helping partners, parents or children adapting to impairment, or assisting immigrants in settling into their new community. According to Zastrow (2007:140) the group leader is usually a professional person with considerable training and expertise in the subject area. It is important that the social auxiliary worker, who facilitates these educational groups, must do an in-depth study of the subject matter and, as is the case with support groups, ask the social worker for guidance in this regard. When the group demands require more in-depth knowledge or skills, the social worker should take over these groups.
- **Growth groups:** Toseland and Rivas state that these groups are also referred to as self-improvement groups in which group members strive and work towards living a more satisfying life through their relationships with other people (as, cited in Mohapi, 2010:8). Examples of such groups are largely a variety of marriage counselling groups, including those improving communication skills, understanding and coping with differences in marriage, as well as groups undergoing assertiveness and anger management training. As is the case with any group facilitated by social auxiliary workers, their involvement is on a basic level. In these groups, when group members require obtaining more advanced skills and the changing of the person's thoughts, feelings and behaviours, the group has to be referred to the social worker.
- **Socialisation groups:** These groups are also referred to as recreation groups and focus on group members becoming more socially acceptable (Zastrow, 2010:152). The social auxiliary worker will generally facilitate basic socialisation groups, which are of a more recreational nature, for example the elderly groups doing activities, such as knitting and reading, or adolescent groups planning their careers.

 Group work

Case Study 2.4

Chanene, a social auxiliary worker, is requested to facilitate a support group for parents of school-going addicts. She has regular contact with the school where SANCA is providing education and consultation services. The support group also has elements of education and growth groups.

Chanene has contacted 12 parents of whom nine have agreed to attend the support groups. They come together at a nearby church hall once a week and share their experiences and learn different ways of coping from each other. The purpose of the group is not therapeutic and the members know that they are not there to 'fix' one another. They have agreed on certain group rules of which respect and confidentiality are the most important.

Group members share the positive and negative experiences that they have had relating to the learner struggling with chemical substance abuse. Each member shares the event, how it made them feel and how they addressed the situation. Chanene avoids the process of going into in-depth sharing of feelings by requesting members to respond factually in terms of how they have dealt with the situation. Members are aware that the social worker can be called in at a next session if more in-depth knowledge, skills or feelings need to be discussed. Once each member has had an opportunity to share during the sessions, Chanene sums up the key factors most group members agreed on about the different situations.

Chanene follows up on parents who miss sessions and reports back to the school social worker on their progress. She also has sporadic meetings with SANCA to obtain further knowledge and skills to assist the parents. The social worker from SANCA will occasionally visit the group to provide further knowledge and insight into the problem of addiction.

2.3.3 Community work

Community work (discussed in greater detail in Chapter 8) is most likely the primary area in which social auxiliary workers can make a meaningful contribution in assisting social workers. They can become involved in networking, setting up committee meetings, social awareness, linking community members to resources, etc. They will not only work closely with social workers, but involve, or become involved with, volunteers, auxiliary community development officers and liaison officers who also work towards the same goal of prevention and empowering the community.

A community, according to Maistry (2010:157), generally refers to people in a specific geographical location or physical space that is demarcated by real or imagined boundaries. Communities, in a broader context, are made up of people with different cultural and life experiences, and different perceptions. These include individuals, families and different groupings of people who stay together. In its narrower sense, community refers to people obtaining a sense of belonging based on similar values and interests, such as religion, culture, gender or class, or a social action group believing in a specific course.

The concepts 'community work' and 'community development' are often used interchangeably. Community work, as is the case with group work and case work, is an integral method of social work. The tasks of the social worker and the social auxiliary worker are to ensure that their work with the community and its members build on their strengths to bring about change in the community while making sure social justice takes place. During these interventions, the needs of the community and individual members of the community are addressed by linking them to existing resources or alternatively developing new resources in which the community can actively participate.

 Case Study 2.5 **Assisting in community work**

Alice, a social auxiliary worker, was employed by a faith-based organisation working with elderly people. The pastor of the congregation, who oversaw various community projects initiated by the church, wanted to start a handcraft group for the elderly in their community. He was of the opinion that it would keep them occupied and socially active as well as bring in some extra money. It was the task of the auxiliary worker to get the project started.

Alice started off with a simplistic research project by obtaining a list of all the persons in their church. She determined how many elderly people there were and how many would be interested in joining a group. She then, through the pastor, got lists of elderly people from the other churches in the area as well as asked family organisations in the area, and the day hospital/clinic if they knew of any elderly people. Once the social auxiliary worker had obtained all the information, she identified 24 people who indicated interest in the group. This group gathered for the first time at the church and convinced Alice that they wanted to start a sewing and knitting group. They wanted to make clothing to sell to other community members.

Alice found a venue, which was situated close to the station and taxi rank, making it very accessible for everybody, and arranged for them to meet every morning. She also approached the pastor to arrange for materials and wool to be utilised during the group sessions. The group started as planned.

After three months, four more members joined and the activities started to generate money slowly. Alice initiated a sub-group that received basic business skills to help the group grow further. Based on their success, two other groups started in other parts of the community to deliver their handcrafts to the original group to market and sell. Some of the members arranged a meeting with the pastor and social worker to register a small business and obtain a bank account.

The group is currently running successfully in that it provides the elderly people involved with new meaning and purpose, it provides a small additional income to the group members as well as creates sufficient additional income to support a number of other smaller projects.

2.3.4 Administration

There are many administrative tasks that must be done within an organisation and these tasks will differ between organisations in terms of volume, context and office systems. However, administrative functions are not negotiable and form an integral part of the service delivery of an organisation.

Although the overall overseeing of administrative activities remains the responsibility of the social worker, the administrative duties expected from social auxiliary workers include the following.

- **Organising activities:** The social auxiliary worker plans and organises his or her daily activities agreed on with the social worker in order to provide timeous and effective interventions. The social worker organises and supervises the overall functions of the social auxiliary worker.
- **Time management:** Although the social worker sets timeframes for services on an organisational level, the social auxiliary worker must ensure that these deadlines are met. If he or she is not able to meet the deadlines, the social worker has to be informed as soon as possible.
- **Opening and closing of files:** The social auxiliary worker is responsible for the opening and closing of case work, group work and community project files, as there are professional responsibilities linked to the opening and closing of social work files, including confidentiality issues as well as drafting a summary report before closing a file. This is done under the supervision of the social worker who does the final assessment to determine whether the file can be closed or not.
- **Record keeping and report writing:** Report writing is an integral part of keeping records within an organisation. The social auxiliary worker is responsible for writing process reports and notes, and progress reports as well as summary reports of all the individuals, families and groups he or she deals with. These reports and notes must be filed and stored in a safe place to ensure client confidentiality.
- **Controlling the use of vehicles:** Control of the utilisation of organisation vehicles used for official purposes is done by means of recording the trips and purposes thereof in logbooks after each visit.
- **Compilation of reports for assessment and referrals:** Social workers are primarily responsible for drawing up assessment and referral reports with the social auxiliary worker only contributing to matters he or she was directly involved with. All referrals need to be verified with the social worker.
- **Signing of attendance registers:** The social auxiliary worker is expected to sign attendance registers.
- **Compilation of statistics and compilation of daily diaries:** The social auxiliary worker can assist the social worker with compiling monthly and annual statistics as required by the organisation. Completing daily activities in a diary is a function that the social auxiliary worker is responsible for. It serves as a guideline for planning activities together with the social worker and is a way of indicating accountability.
- **Recording of minutes:** In most cases, meetings have agendas and minutes as a record of the meeting and decisions made during the meeting. This is a function that the social auxiliary worker can be involved in and must master competencies for to do so.

2.3.5 Research

Research is generally perceived as a complex task in social work and is usually the responsibility of the social worker with the social auxiliary worker being involved in a practical and supportive capacity.

In social work practice, two broad research approaches are identified, namely quantitative research and qualitative research. Quantitative research is primarily numerical and statistical in nature, while qualitative research involves itself with life experiences, behaviour and interactions between people.

The latter form of research is more generally used in the field of social work.

Research is generally done in phases or steps. Firstly, there must be a clear topic or problem for the research, with clear goals and objectives, indicating that a qualitative approach is applied. This is followed by a description of how the research is conducted, including how the information is collected, who the target population of the study is, and how the information will be analysed. Finally a research report is written including the conclusions that were made with further recommendations. This becomes a research document and falls within the scope of the social worker's responsibility.

2.4 Supervision of social auxiliary workers

Supervision of social auxiliary workers can be regarded as an additional function of a social worker. Although the social auxiliary worker assists the social worker with guided interventions and administrative tasks, they function as a team in their service rendering programmes. However, because the social worker oversees and manages the interventions, he or she is primarily responsible for their implementation. This requires good planning of the programme, and guidance of the social auxiliary worker within the application of the programme.

It is a requirement of the Act that social auxiliary workers may only practice under supervision of a social worker and cannot function independently. Supervision, in this sense, refers to the responsible social worker guiding and training the social auxiliary worker in the execution of his or her supporting functions, including following up on the activities of the social auxiliary worker. Suraj-Narayan (2010:191–193) points out a number of functions implied in the relationship of supervision. These functions include administrative, educational and supportive functions embedded in the professional relationship between social worker and social auxiliary worker.

- **Administrative function:** The administrative tasks of the social auxiliary worker have been described in this chapter. These need to be managed to ensure effective service delivery, as administration is foundational in all social work interventions as it forms an integrated part of them. Supervision guides and assists the social auxiliary worker in complying with the set standards of administrative duties required by the organisation they work for. The overseeing of these duties may be experienced as 'checking up' on the social auxiliary worker's activities, but in essence it aims to enable him or her to set priorities and streamline his or her work.
- **Educational function:** This function of supervision highlights the professional development and accompanying personal awareness and growth of the social auxiliary worker in the one-on-one relationship with the supervising social worker. This development is further enhanced by additional opportunities for learning, such as staff development, attending selected training programmes and regular performance appraisals. The relevance of this function is to provide for improved knowledge and skills whereby competencies are enhanced in working with clients or activities the social auxiliary worker is responsible for.

- **Supportive function:** Although social auxiliary workers are primarily involved with so-called 'basic' tasks, these tasks are often demanding and at times emotionally laden. The social worker fulfils a supportive function in assisting the social auxiliary worker in various applicable ways, including debriefing, facilitating stress management, re-distributing tasks, and/or referral for more appropriate assistance if applicable.

According to Kadushin (1992:22) supervision is an interactional process, in which the supervisor usually engages in a sequential series of deliberately and consciously selected activities. However, apart from these planned and structured supervision sessions, social auxiliary workers may have frequent unplanned sessions that are primarily related to the tasks that are performed as part of the workload of the social worker.

I don't understand why husbands are so rude, disrespectful and intimidating towards their wives. It really upsets me. I become angry towards men, even if they have not done anything.

Your involvement in family work exposes you to difficult marriages in which wives often seem to be the victim. This is something that disturbs you.

Yes it does. I mean, don't the men see that it really hurts their wives ... It is insulting and robs them of their dignity. Is there anything we can do to help them?

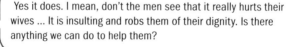

What do you think can be done? Is there anything you would like to suggest?

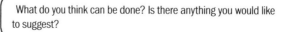

Maybe we can report these husbands to the police? Or maybe we can empower the women to go to the police themselves? It is also possible for us to train the women to stand up for themselves against their husbands.

I can see that you are putting much thought into this matter. There are two things I would like you to consider doing. Firstly, speak to these women in order to try and understand their circumstances and then find out from them what they see as a solution. I would also like you to spend some time thinking about why this in particular upsets you so much. Once you have done this, please come back to me so we can discuss it.

Figure 2.2: Supervision as an interactional process

In the conversation between social worker and social auxiliary worker, the function of the social worker is both one of supporter and educator. The social auxiliary worker is affected by experiences and perceptions encountered in her line of work. By referring the social auxiliary worker back to the situation, he or she can obtain more information on the matter and gain an understanding of the client's own frame of reference. By requesting the social auxiliary worker to do some introspection, he or she can achieve greater self-awareness.

2.4.1 Social auxiliary work and the Code of Ethics in social work

Both the social worker and the social auxiliary worker are bound by the regulations of the Council in terms of their registration and upholding of the Code of Ethics of Social Work. It is therefore vital that they both familiarise themselves with the content of the Code of Ethics to avoid legal complications. Even though the social auxiliary worker works with, and under the supervision of, the social worker, it does not detract from his or her responsibility to regularly refer to the Code of Ethics, especially the general ethical standards of the Code of ethics. These aspects are described in greater detail in Chapter 4.

2.5 Volunteers

The role of volunteers in general as well as in the welfare field, more specifically, has a long history and it often seems as if the role of volunteers in developing welfare and social work is often taken for granted and not appreciated. Volunteerism is known as an altruistic activity with the intention of assisting others in improving their circumstances and quality of life. Volunteering is done without receiving payment.

Two types of volunteering is distinguished, namely managed and unmanaged, with the latter referring to people who sporadically and spontaneously respond to situations in terms of support and practical help over a short period of time, mostly humanitarian in nature.

Managed volunteering is generally organised over a longer period of time and usually takes place through organisations in the non-profit, private and public sectors. Examples are often found in community and faith-based organisations, government and NGO projects, such as home-based care programmes, Rotary and Lions Clubs and private organisations, such as the Volunteer Centre.

The *White Paper for Social Welfare* (1997:98) defines a volunteer as "a professional or non-professional person who provides a service to a welfare or developmental organisation, usually without reimbursement." This person is somebody who voluntarily offers of his or her time and skills in an area important to them without payment as the activities in themselves are fulfilling. Generally, volunteers become involved in activities from a sense of obligation or because they may make them feel needed and valued, leading to their personal growth.

With the implementation of the new welfare policy in 1997, social work underwent a fundamental change in the direction of social development, bringing with it a greater emphasis on assistance and intervention from within communities. Prevention, empowerment and development strategies were implemented to enable communities to become more independent and self-sufficient. In order to implement these strategies, more people were needed, and with less funding available it inadvertently became the plight of the volunteer.

Welfare organisations utilising the services of volunteers are those that are experiencing difficulty in man-power and/or financial resources. They are not able to pay salaries but would at least try and cover the expenses incurred by volunteers during their activities. In addition, they are able to provide training in terms of more specialised knowledge and skills, which is something that can create better employment opportunities for some volunteers.

Non-professional volunteers are limited in terms of what they may offer. This extends to practical caring and support of people and/or administrative or organisational tasks. It will partially overlap with the tasks of social auxiliary worker except that the latter is trained to deal with the more advanced needs of clients.

Examples of non-professional volunteers include people who become involved in the so-called HBC, home- and community-based care. The need for these volunteers arose from the impact of HIV and AIDS on our communities. This service is primarily linked to health services and secondly to the welfare of the people in the community. It supports the services offered by hospitals, clinics and other treatment institutions and is particularly valuable to vulnerable children in that its services make it possible for them to stay in familiar surroundings instead of being hospitalised.

However, many problems with home-based care are in need of attention, including: the selection of volunteers to do home-based care, the recognition of home-based care on the same level as institutional caregivers, and the provision of a fair stipend for the work they do. These caregivers also need to be recognised by other professions involved in community work, including the social work profession.

 Case Study 2.6 **Voluntary work**

John lost his hearing as a child due to a high fever. This interrupted his schooling and eventually he had to attend a special school for the hearing impaired where he completed Grade 12. He had to make new friends and felt excluded from the broader society, which he had difficulty coming to terms with. His unresolved alienation and subsequent anger led to his drug abuse, which eventually caused him to come into conflict with the law. He became a court diversion provided he attended a treatment programme for drug abuse. He tried to locate such a facility which could accommodate hearing-impaired people, but as there was none, he was forced to attend a support group in the hope that he may follow the programme.

Mbongiseni grew up in a home where his father was an alcoholic, but he has recovered and has been sober for more than eight years. Mbongiseni has much compassion for people encountering problems with drugs and decided to become involved in voluntary work at an organisation providing support for persons struggling with chemical substance abuse. This is where he met up with John and immediately committed to helping him. Mbongiseni made an enquiry at an association for the deaf and received training in sign language and lip-reading. He eventually became involved in interpreting for John at his group sessions. In return, he is learning and experiencing more about substance abuse, something he values strongly as this helps him to better understand his father.

Gerald, a social auxiliary worker, worked closely with Mbongiseni in assisting John. He, however, is more involved in support and education groups, assisting family members of those struggling with chemical substance abuse. Gerald has also established contact with an association for the deaf, but unlike Mbongiseni, his aim is to network with them and to facilitate information groups on substance at the organisation. Gerald works closely with the social worker, but Mbongiseni is not required to report back to the social worker on John's progress as his function as a volunteer in this instance does not require it.

2.6 Conclusion

Social work is, in essence, based on team work. Social work is about working with people, either as colleagues, clients, other professionals, volunteers or community members. Most likely, colleagues, social auxiliary workers and/or volunteers are the people a social worker will most often work with in his or her day-to-day activities.

With the move towards more community-based and developmental intervention, the role of social auxiliary workers and volunteers, including home-based caregivers, becomes increasingly relevant in the South African welfare environment. These people become key instruments in the work done by social workers and other professionals.

End of chapter questions

1. Identify and describe the social work methods in which social auxiliary work is involved.
2. Identify different roles of social workers, social auxiliary workers and volunteers involved in the field of social work.
3. Explain the functions and responsibilities of the social auxiliary worker in the field of social work.
4. Refer to the relevant Acts in the field of social work.
5. How important are the functions of supervision for social auxiliary work?

Key concepts

- **Casework**, **case work**, or more specifically **social case work**, refers to assisting individuals and families. Individuals or families may experience a number of problems, including relationship problems, stress and abuse, for which they need professional assistance. When a person with a marital problem wants to find help to restore the relationship, he or she can see a social worker individually who can assess him or her and schedule weekly sessions where he or she is seen alone, and at times with his or her spouse, to assist in restoring the relationship.
- **Community work**, as is the case with group work and case work, is an integral method of social work. The tasks of the social worker and the social auxiliary worker are to ensure that their work with the community and its members build on their strengths to bring about change in the community while they make sure that social justice takes place. A community may for example struggle with alcohol abuse. A social worker (and social auxiliary worker) can approach community leaders, families as well as schools, SAPS and clinics to make an assessment of the situation and schedule meetings to seek and implement solutions to address this problem.
- **Group work** is a social work method by which people are assisted with social-emotional problems in a group setting. For example: Teenagers who are struggling with their self-image and assertiveness issues can share these experiences with a group and learn new skills to change their behaviour and relationships in a constructive way.
- **Home-based care** is a service primarily linked to health services and secondly to the welfare of the people in the community. It supports the services offered by hospitals, clinics and other treatment institutions and is particularly valuable to vulnerable children in that its services make it possible for them to stay in familiar surroundings instead of being hospitalised.
- The international definition of **social work** captures the core of what the profession entails: "Social work is a practice-based profession and an academic discipline that promotes social change and development, social cohesion and the empowerment and liberation of people. Principles of social justice, human rights, collective responsibility and respect for the diversities are central to social work." (International Federation of Social Workers, 2014)
- **Social auxiliary work**, according to Social Auxiliary Work Learning Programme of the SACSSP, means an act or activity practised by a social auxiliary worker under the guidance and control of a social worker and as a supporting service to a social worker to achieve the aims of social work.
- **Supervision** is a working relationship between an experienced and inexperienced worker, during which the experienced person provides guidance to the inexperienced person in order to improve his or her knowledge and skills.

- The *White Paper for Social Welfare* (1997:98) defines a **volunteer** as "a professional or non-professional person who provides a service to a welfare or developmental organisation, usually without reimbursement." Volunteers are often involved in religious supportive activities, such as fundraising efforts and practical assistance.

References

1. AMBROSINO, R., AMBROSINO, R., HEFFERNAN, J. & SHUTTLESWORTH, G. 2012. *Social work and social welfare: an introduction.* 7th ed. Canada: Thomson Brooks.
2. DEPARTMENT OF SOCIAL DEVELOPMENT. 1997. *White paper for social welfare.* Pretoria: Government Printers.
3. DEPARTMENT OF SOCIAL DEVELOPMENT. 2015. *Social auxiliary work: a supportive service.* [Online]. Available: http://www.dsd.gov.za/index2.php?option=com_docman&task=doc_view&gid=82&Itemid=3 [22 April 2015]
4. INTERNATIONAL FEDERATION OF SOCIAL WORKERS. 2014. *Global definition of social work.* [Online]. Available: http://ifsw.org/policies/definition-of-social-work/ [19 March 2015]
5. KADUSHIN, A. 1992. *Supervision in social work.* 3rd ed. New York: Columbia University Press.
6. KADUSHIN, L. 1986. *Supervising para-professionals in social work.* Unpublished report.
7. KIRST-ASHMAN, K.K. 2013. *Introduction to social work and social welfare: critical thinking perspectives.* United Kingdom: Brooks/Cole.
8. LOMBARD, A. & PRUIS, S. 1994. Social auxiliary work. *Social work/Maatskaplike werk,* 30(3):257–267.
9. MAISTRY, M. 2010. Community development. (*In* Nicholas, L., Rautenbach, J. & Maistry, M. (eds.), *Introduction to social work.* Cape Town: Juta. p. 157)
10. MOHAPI, B.J. 2010. *Social group work: integrated theory and practice (only study guide for SCK 403C).* Pretoria: Unisa.
11. SOUTH AFRICAN QUALIFICATIONS AUTHORITY (SAQA). 2003. *Further education and training certificate: Social auxiliary work.* [Online]. Available: http://regqs.saqa.org.za/viewQualification.php?id=23993 [1 September 2014]
12. STRYDOM, H. & STRYDOM, C. 2010. Group work. (*In* Nicholas, L., Rautenbach, J., & Maistry, M. (eds.), *Introduction to social work.* Cape Town: Juta. p. 124)
13. SURAJ-NARAYAN, G. 2010. Management and administration. (*In* Nicholas, L., Rautenbach, J, and Maistry, M. (eds.), *Introduction to social work.* Cape Town: Juta. p. 191)
14. ZASTROW, C. 2007. *The practice of social work: a comprehensive work text.* 8th ed. Belmont, USA: Thomson Brooks/Cole.

The history of social welfare and social work

Paul Mbedzi

CHAPTER OUTCOMES

By the end of this chapter, you should be able to:

✓ understand the concepts social welfare and social work
✓ understand the development of social welfare globally
✓ understand the background of social welfare and social work in Africa
✓ Understand the development of social work education in Africa
✓ understand the history of social welfare in South Africa
✓ understand the development of social work internationally
✓ understand the history of social work in South Africa.

3.1   Introduction

There has been a significant change in the social welfare system and the social work profession in the past years. This chapter is therefore aimed at illustrating the development of social welfare and social work (both internationally and in South Africa) until today. We shall begin by elaborating on some of the most important concepts within the social welfare context, namely: social welfare, social welfare policy, and social work.

You have already been introduced to these important concepts in Chapter 1, but we shall briefly discuss them, for the purpose of highlighting the differences.

Each of these concepts is discussed in the sections that follow.

3.2   The meaning of the concept 'social welfare'

"Social welfare is defined as a nation's system of programs, benefits, and services that help people meet those social, economic, educational, and health needs that are fundamental to the maintenance of society" (Zastrow, 2014:3).

The definition above tells us that social welfare does not only focus on meeting the social needs of the people/society, ignoring the economic, educational, and health aspects of it. It is equally important to take note of the fact that social welfare is not only intended to meet the people's or society's needs, but also to address social problems through various welfare programmes. It is for this reason that the welfare system does not consist of professional social workers only, but other professionals such as educators, health practitioners, auxiliary social workers, community development workers, probation officers, child and youth care workers, social security personnel, and many others. Figure 3.1 illustrates the interdisciplinary team found within the social welfare context.

Figure 3.1: The interdisciplinary team found within the social welfare context

Social welfare focuses on, inter alia, income protection, attaining autonomous livelihoods and minimum living standards, and the meeting of needs of the populations at risk, such as children, youth, women, families, the elderly, and people with physical and mental disabilities and chronic illness, including HIV and AIDS (Patel, 2010:20).

Social welfare services and programmes are mainly aimed at the prevention and alleviation of social problems to improve the wellbeing of society, and these services are provided by volunteers, non-governmental and governmental organisations, also known as social welfare institutions. The social institutions are governed by the social policies and regulations of the country, which differ from one country to another.

3.3 Social welfare policies

Social welfare policies are regarded as the collective strategies that aim to address social problems and they are implemented through social welfare programmes and carried out by social service professionals, such as social workers. It is important to take note that social welfare policies are made to protect people and provide guidelines for care. For instance, an elderly person, who needs care, may be taken to an institution or an old age home, and the institution would be expected to provide its services as prescribed by the policy. So policies are made available to protect people and provide guidelines for care.

There are three main approaches to social welfare policy, namely, residual approach, institutional approach, and social development approach.

3.3.1 Residual approach

The residual approach takes into account the two natural systems through which people meet their needs. They are the capitalist market economy, and individuals and their families. The capitalist market economy is a system whereby prices are determined by the interaction of supply and demand, and there is free competition. When these two systems fail to meet people's needs, state welfare is introduced, only for a short period, as an emergency aid to assist people in crises. The family and individual take over the responsibility of meeting their needs as soon as the crisis is eradicated. Given the above example of an elderly woman who needs care, the residual approach can be applied for emergency purposes and only for a short time, with the belief that she should be able to take care of herself, if not, her family should be able to assist her as soon as the crisis is eradicated.

3.3.2 Institutional approach

The institutional approach argues that it is the state's responsibility to support its members who are unable to provide for themselves due to circumstances beyond their control. Given the above example of an elderly woman who needs care and assistance, since she cannot take care of herself anymore due to circumstances beyond her control (for example, old age and ill health), the government would take the responsibility to ensure that she receives the necessary care and support. For instance, she might be taken to an old age home where she would be taken care or be provided with free services as prescribed in the policy. The institutional approach makes social welfare available to every citizen of the country, regardless of his or her financial situation. This was broadly implemented by governments in Europe and the United State in the post Second World War period in order to reconstruct their societies. The institutional approach was challenged by conservatives who believed that it created dependency on the state.

3.3.3 Social development approach

Developmental social welfare emphasises the social and economic development of individuals, families and communities. It includes raising awareness of social concerns and, at the same time, developing methods to combat social challenges.

The social development approach to social welfare seeks to encourage people to participate and collaborate in their own development. Patel (2005) (as cited in Nicholas, Rautenbach & Maistry, 2010:52) identifies five features central to the idea of social development, namely:
1. the perspective is rooted in a rights-based approach to development
2. it is concerned with harmonising economic and social policies
3. it embodies the idea of promoting participation in development
4. it is based on the partnership model
5. It attempts to overcome the divisions that have existed historically between micro-macro intervention strategies.

The basis for this approach is the government's constitutional responsibility to address the inequality and discrimination in access to services and in meeting the basic needs of people. This approach differs from the welfare model during the apartheid era, which focused on the institutional policies for whites and residual system for blacks. With the developmental approach, there are elements of inclusion, fairness, participation, and equality for individuals, families and communities.

3.4 What is social work?

"Social work is internationally defined as a profession that promotes social change, problem solving in human relationships, empowerment and the liberation of people to enhance well-being" (Barsky, 2006:14).

Social work is the primary profession that works within the social welfare system and it seeks to implement planned social change activities prescribed by social welfare institutions. Planned social change refers to identifying a social problem and seeking ways to address it in order to bring social justice and equity.

The most fundamental obligation in social work is to promote social change, social development, social cohesion, and the empowerment and liberation of people. Social work intervention is required when people's (individuals, groups or communities) situations are believed to be in need of change and development.

The three concepts discussed above, namely social welfare, social welfare policies, and social work, are instrumental within the social welfare context and they are mostly intertwined. It would be difficult to discuss one without hinting at another.

In the next section, we discuss the development of social welfare globally and touch on the most important historical events that happened over a period of time.

 SELF-ASSESSMENT

1 Briefly describe the concepts social welfare, social welfare policy and social work and explain how they are connected.
2 Name and briefly discuss three examples of social welfare programmes that apply to the area where you live.
3 Briefly describe the three approaches to social welfare policy.
4 Briefly discuss the fundamental obligation in social work and provide examples.

3.5 The international development of social welfare

Social welfare systems across the globe have been shaped by the complex social, cultural, economic, and political histories of countries and regions (Patel, 2010:18). It is for this reason that the history or the development of social welfare systems in various countries differ, even though the main objective is to prevent and alleviate the social problems encountered with the aim of improving the wellbeing of the people and society.

Social welfare is believed to have originated in the early years when mutual aid was essential for survival and families were responsible for taking care of their members.

"Before the Industrial Revolution (which is believed to be a period from the 18th to the 19th Century), the responsibility of meeting the needs of those who were unable to be self-sufficient was largely taken by the family, the church, and even neighbours" (Zastrow, 2014:10). This was mainly done for humanitarian and self-gratification purposes. There was no formal or state assistance and people had to cope regardless.

In England, before mercantilism, the care of the poor was a function primarily of the church (Ambrosino, Ambrosino, Heffernan & Shuttlesworth, 2012:15). The church was the main source of assistance for the poor and the first government legislation was passed as a result of the Black Death – bubonic plague – which began in 1348 and killed at least two thirds of the English population. King Edward III mandated the Statute of Laborers Act in 1349, which required able-bodied individuals to accept any type of employment within their communities.

Later on, the feudal system and religious efforts could not cope with the increasing demands and needs of the poor. As a result, the poor were left to survive on their own. This eventually led to malnutrition, poor health, broken families and death. During the beginning of the Industrial Revolution, there was a major influx of people to the cities looking for employment in the manufacturing facilities. However, there were not enough jobs to cater for the increasing number of people in the city. The majority of the people were illiterate and not qualified for the jobs available. This led to a high level of unemployment, leaving large numbers of poor unemployed people lingering in the streets and begging for assistance.

The government responded by passing a law called the Elizabethan Poor Act (Elizabeth 43) in 1601 in an attempt to establish a national policy regarding the poor in the cities. The law was passed during the reign of Queen Elizabeth I.

The Elizabethan Poor Act established the following categories of relief recipients:

- The **able-bodied poor** were given lower grade employment and citizens were prohibited from offering them financial help.
- The **impotent poor** (people unable to work, for example the elderly and those living with a disability) were usually placed in an institution.
- **Dependent children**, whose parents or grandparents were unable to support them, were apprenticed out to other citizens (Zastrow, 2014:10).

The Elizabethan Poor Act provided a standard to which the poor were to be treated and managed. It was established in England until 1834 and in the United States until the Social Security Act was passed in 1935.

The most important components of the Elizabethan Poor Act, specifically in relation to US policies toward the poor, were the establishment of:

- clear government responsibility for those in need
- government authority to force people to work
- government enforcement of family responsibility
- the principle of local responsibility
- strict residence requirements (Ambrosino *et al.*, 2012:6).

The Poor Law of 1601 set the pattern of public relief in both great Britain and the United States for the next 300 years (Zastrow, 2014:11).

Most organisations that were charitable and humanitarian in nature were developed in Europe in the seventeenth and nineteenth Centuries due to the Industrial Revolution. These brought a lot of changes to social welfare. Prior to the Industrial Revolution, there were fewer citizens in Europe and America. The charitable organisations that assisted people in need had a different approach to government regarding the assistance of those in need.

The beginning of institutionalised public, non-governmental social welfare is usually thought of in terms of the creation of the Charity Organisation Society in England in 1869 (Macarov, 1995:5). The main idea of the Charity Organisation Society was to coordinate the many charities that operated individually, sometimes competing with each other. The charitable organisations dealt mostly with relieving poverty, settlement housing, recreation, employment and counselling.

Social welfare was formalised and professionalised in the early nineteenth Century. During this period, people with formal training were employed, unlike before when social welfare services were provided by untrained volunteers. There was a great need for the professional development in the field of social welfare, and this resulted in the establishment of the first schools of social work and social welfare in universities.

3.6 The background of social welfare and social work in Africa

Africa is a large continent that covers more than 30 million square kilometres (about 22.3 % of the total land surface of the world) (Shawsky, 1972:3). Most African countries are predominately rural and depend economically on primary products, such as agriculture and fishing. Historically, the family and the clan took the responsibility for the survival of their members. This means that the family and the clan used to take the responsibility for the sick, elderly and children.

The concept 'social welfare' was introduced for the first time on the continent during the colonial period, mainly by the two European countries (Britain and France) that were the major colonial powers on the continent. For instance, the British social welfare programmes focused on juvenile delinquency and correction, and French welfare focused on medico-social programmes (Shawsky, 1972:5). Most ministries and social welfare departments in Africa were established after independence, especially in rural areas, and they almost all started departments of social work. The American influence across the globe made it possible for the introduction of a type of case work oriented social work in Europe and other parts of the world including Africa. Most African countries emerged from colonial domination and it somehow impacted on growth and development of infrastructure. The little infrastructure that was created by the colonialists, such as transport and communication, water and drainage systems and power supplies, was for their own benefit, as large rural areas remain undeveloped (Noyoo, 2000:455). The industrialisation process resulted movement from rural to urban areas in most African countries and it adds to the increasing challenges of overcrowded housing conditions, unemployment, crime, dropping out of schools, domestic violence, alcohol abuse and poverty.

The majority of countries in Africa obtained independence from colonial powers in the 1960s and this was followed by a period of nation building and, in many instances, some degree of political volatility. For instance, by the late 1970s national debts for many African countries skyrocketed, and in the early 1980s structural adjustment programmes, as a way of curbing debt, were introduced worldwide by the international monetary fund and the World Bank, with support from various bilateral donors, such as Canada's CIDA (Canadian International Development Agency). Under structural adjustment, most countries in the continent had to cut back on social spending, lessen financial regulation and adopt exchange rates that are favourable to the North. In 2000 just nine countries had an income per head of more than R10 000 a year, which is less than R30 per head each day, and a mere five (Gabon, Seychelles, Botswana, Mauritius and South Africa) had an annual income per head of more than R25 000, or less than R70 per head daily (Heron, 2005:783).

The structural problems that African social workers regularly face are typically a result of political decisions and require political solutions. This means that different role players, which include government and politicians, determine the scope of social work practice in most African countries. The same sentiment is echoed by Mmatli (2008:299) who believes that in all African countries, other professional groups, politicians, economists and bureaucrats predominately define the social work agenda.

Fewer than half of African countries are elected democracies. Although Zambia, South Africa, Tanzania, Mozambique, Malawi, Kenya, Nigeria, and Sierra Leone became multi-party democracies in the 1990s. During this time, escalating wars and internal conflicts spread to one-third of the countries in the region.

In February 2005 the food and Agriculture Organisation listed 23 African countries among those requiring food assistance for climatic reasons (Heron, 2005:785).

The African continent is still faced with a lot of challenges regarding human development, such as hunger, disease, corruption, civil violence, illiteracy, squalor, and lack of meaningful opportunity (Mwansa, 2010:130). Most of the continent is confronted with extreme poverty, unemployment and starvation, and these compel the majority of people to move away from the rural areas to the cities seeking employment. There are also challenges of illiteracy, home-lessness, child streetism, ill-health, HIV and AIDS, abuse of human rights and civil liberties, civil conflicts and official corruption in most parts of the continent (Mmatli, 2008:297). All these challenges have an impact on the policy development and the psychosocial functioning of people on the continent which require social work intervention. Social workers now more than ever need to be actively involved in seeing to it that social development is realised because the value base of the profession obliges social workers to lift up the living conditions of marginal-ised population groups (Noyoo, 2000:453).

3.7 Social work education in Africa

The development of social work education was an important part of social work's profession-alisation. Social work education in Africa has been in existence for so many years, but its ideology was much more Eurocentric. For instance, the first school of social work in South Africa was in 1924 at the University of Cape Town and the University of Witwatersrand in 1931. (Mazibuko & Gray, 2004:129).

The initiative to form an organisation for social work education started in 1965, and culminated in the establishment of the Association of Social Work Education in Africa in 1971 (Mwansa, 2010:131).

The need for and problems of social work education in Africa have been of concern to eco-nomic commission for Africa and other UN (United Nations) agencies for some years (Neely, 1965:25). A seminar for social work educators, jointly sponsored by the UN bureau of social affairs and UNICEF (United Nations Children's Emergency Fund) with the assistance of the IASSW (International Associations of Schools of Social Work) was held in Alexandria UAR at the higher institute of social work from 14 August to 3 September 1965. It was directed by the social affairs officer of the UN Economic Commission for Africa, Dr Peter Omari (Neely, 1965:25).

The following were identified as common problems after each country presented its statement:

- Recruitment of candidates
- Shortage of qualified teaching faculty and field instruction supervisors
- Physical and technical deficiencies in buildings for schools of social work and training institutions, inadequate transport, and lack of text books, indigenous teaching materials and other equipment.

In order to address the above-mentioned challenges, the seminar recommended that:

- all schools of social work in Africa should be at the level of university or institute of higher learning
- the minimum educational requirements for admission to professional training should be from ten to 12 years
- practical work should occupy no less than one-third of the duration of training courses in schools of social work and in-service training
- national governments and national universities should concentrate upon providing the resources to make possible the provision of professional training of social workers at national institutions

- selection criteria and procedures for admission to schools of social work and to in-service training institutions should be examined and that a national committee in each country composed of representatives of universities, schools of social work, employing departments and in-service training institutions be appointed by the government department in charge of social affairs to study the problems of selection in the country with a view to standardising methods of selection
- one institution in Africa should be established by the economic commission for Africa to provide advanced level social work education to train the educators, social administrators and planners needed in the region
- one or two schools of social work in a sub-region, together with the Economic Commission for Africa should arrange some training seminars on field work counselling for selected staff in that sub-region.

A group of experts on social work training in Europe and their African colleagues were convened by the office of social affairs of the European office of the United Nations in Assistenziali Italiane e Internazionalle shortly after the seminar. The purpose of convening this expert group was to discuss European cooperation in training for social welfare work in Africa and to suggest ways in which European countries might strengthen the resources for training of African social welfare personnel. The expert group drew up some of the following conclusions.

- The need to transform the types of social work training which exist in Africa.
- The need for government to be involved in the expansion of social work training and programmes.
- The need to develop a social work training programme and structure relevant in preparing social workers in both Europe and Africa to perform different functions in Africa.
- The need to change the current training programmes in both European and African institutions to meet African needs.

The 1965 seminar for social work educators was a milestone for the state of the social work profession on the continent. There are different universities on the continent today that train social workers and their training is based on the mission encompassed in the profession which is to enable all people to develop their full potential, enrich their lives and prevent dysfunction

Social work education and training in Africa have to be transformed from models relying upon Western frameworks, philosophies, values and knowledge bases to Afro-centric models based on more indigenous knowledge systems, community-based interventions, and local values and practices (Mwansa, 2010:135).

3.8 The history of social welfare in South Africa

Social welfare in South Africa has been in existence prior the arrival of the Dutch in 1657. It was then based on the spirit of humanity (also known as *ubuntu*) when the responsibility of taking care of family members was taken on by the family and the community.

The Dutch settlers provided the first relief to poor white farmers in the mid-16th Century. This later developed into an institutional welfare resource, under the authority of the Dutch Reformed Church, which provided children and people with disabilities with social and economic assistance.

The history of the development of social welfare in South African history can be looked at in terms of three different phases, namely social welfare prior to the apartheid era, social welfare during the apartheid years, and social welfare in the post-apartheid years (after 1994).

3.8.1   Social welfare prior to the apartheid era

During the pre-colonial and pre-apartheid era, the responsibility of meeting the social needs in South Africa was largely taken on by families and society. This was mostly done in the spirit of humanity, also known as *ubuntu*. People's survival and social needs were taken care of by families and family members who did not expect anything in return.

The bio-medical model was applied during this era. It aimed at saving the lives of clients by protecting and relieving them from diseases and pain that impacted negatively on the normal human condition. The bio-medical model focuses on biological factors and excludes psychological and social influences.

Both colonialism and apartheid shaped the evolution of the nature, form and content of social welfare policy in South Africa (Patel, 2010:66). Colonial powers from European countries invaded the world from the Middle Ages until the nineteenth Century. They imposed a sense of superiority; those who come from other continents, other than Europe, were regarded as primitive and uncivilised.

South Africa developed quickly in the late nineteenth and early twentieth Centuries due to the discovery of diamonds and gold. This resulted in a need for a large labour force in the mining industries and many people (especially black males) were forced to relocate from rural to urban areas. Most families were separated due to the influx of family members to the cities.

The country saw an increase in social problems (such as child neglect, starvation, and poverty) due to this demographic transformation. Family responsibilities were left mainly with women. Women had to take care of the children, as men would be in the cities. In most African communities, families (especially extended families) and local communities also used to serve a very important role in seeing to it that people's basic needs were met.

Social welfare in South Africa was at a critical stage as a result of poverty and unemployment due to urbanisation and industrialism. The Commission of Inquiry was set up to investigate challenges and problems amongst whites, also known as the "poor white problem". The Dutch Reformed Church of South Africa organised a conference in Kimberley in 1937 to discuss a five-volume report from the commission. Two of the major recommendations from the Carnegie Report and the conference were the establishment of a social welfare department to overcome the piecemeal approach of the various departments which dealt with welfare matters and the training of social workers (Potgieter, 1998:21).

The first government office known as the Department of Social Welfare and Pensions was established in 1937. The first association for social workers was also established in 1937 after the first National Conference on Social Work that was held in Johannesburg. South Africa saw the formation of various welfare associations for various target population groups (such as the blind, deaf, and mentally ill) in the late 1920s and 1930s,

There was an influx of people to the cities during World War II (which lasted from 1939 to 1945). These people were even more vulnerable to poverty in the cities due to the fact that they were ill-equipped for life in a modern society.

3.8.2   Social welfare during the apartheid years (1948–1994)

The apartheid system came into effect in 1948, shortly after the National Party came into power. The white-only government introduced the apartheid policy, which was aimed at racial discrimination. Their main argument was that the integration of various races in the country would impose a threat to peace and freedom, and that development could only be attained through separateness.

It is for this reason that we are able to indicate that social welfare during the apartheid years in South Africa was characterised by inequality and unfairness.

The government introduced the Population Registration Act of 1950 which classified the population into four categories, namely black, white, coloured and Indian. The Act clearly stipulated different access and benefits to social welfare resources by different races. The white community enjoyed more decent access to social welfare, as compared to other races that were given limited social welfare access and benefits. The welfare needs of white people were prioritised and white people had more access to social welfare during the apartheid era. The black community welfare needs were mostly neglected.

The government later established separate welfare departments with the aim of addressing the social welfare issues of each racial group separately. The social welfare approach during this period was that of the **residual model** as it was characterised by minimal state intervention in providing and financing social welfare services and social securities. The residual approach requires the state or government to assist only when the family and the community fail to provide necessary support or assistance to its own members.

The rapid increase of migrant labour to the cities in the 1950s, due to the decline in subsistence, resulted in temporary migrants faced with high subsistence costs, as they had to support themselves and the families left behind in rural areas. Migrant labour, which was generally cheap labour, resulted in the emergence of the Independent African Trade Union movement in the 1970s and 1980s, which pressed for better wages.

The Group Areas Act (36 of 1966), promulgated by the government, led to severe family breakdown and impoverishment of African people in rural areas. This Act classified people according to racial groups. It included forcefully removing people from the specific areas they had occupied for many years. The non-white majority were given much smaller areas to live in than the white minority who owned most of the country.

The majority of people did not only lose their land, but also their houses, animals and so many other possessions.

The Group Areas Act also aimed to exclude non-whites from living in well-developed areas that were strictly for white people. As a result, non-whites were compelled to travel long distances to the cities for work.

With the banning of political parties, such as the African National Congress (ANC), people at grassroots level devised a variety of plans to ensure a form of indigenous self-help for black people, such as women's associations, youth groups, stokvels and burial societies, with the aim of mutual financial assistance.

The following are three Acts important to social welfare that were introduced in this era.

- The **National Welfare Act (100 of 1978)** made provision for the registration of welfare organisations, a South African Welfare Council and four specialist commissions.
- The **Fund-Raising Act (107 of 1978)** aimed to control fundraising from the public and at the same time provide for the establishment of a Disaster Relief Fund.
- The **Social and Associated Workers Act (110 of 1978)** made provision for a statutory council to regulate the conduct, training and registration of social and associated workers (Van Dyk, 2000:40).

South Africa introduced a new Constitution in 1983, making provision for the tricameral parliament with separate chambers for whites, coloureds and Asians, with the exclusion of blacks. This was followed by the national Population Development Programme (PDP), which aimed to stimulate development of communities at a local level and ensure a balance between population growth and available resources.

"The second Carnegie Inquiry into poverty and development, focusing on the country as a whole, was launched followed by a conference at the University of Cape Town in April 1984. There were lots of post-conference publications focused on needs and gaps identified at the conference." (Potgieter, 1998:23)

The South African social welfare context took a turn in 1990, shortly after the unbanning of the political organisations and the release of the late former president Nelson Mandela after 27 years in prison. This enabled the parties to come together in one accord for negotiations discussing the future of the country that was under apartheid for so many years. The negotiations' process itself was not an easy one as political violence spread from one part of the country to the other.

There was a feeling of uncertainty and fear amongst some citizens as they were wondering about the future of the country. There was an instant need to debate the welfare state of the country that was filled with injustice and unequal distribution of wealth prior to 1990. The debate yielded positive results, as it provided opportunities for different welfare organisations to shape the future of the country.

The first conference to engage in dialogue between the ANC and health and welfare role players took place in Maputo in 1990 and a Declaration of Health and Welfare in Southern Africa was adopted. The following conclusions were made by the conference:

• Transforming health and social services
• Promoting a new vision, and devising an appropriate welfare policy
• Prioritising primary health care, for the provision of health and welfare services. (Patel, 2010:87)

This was followed by the signing of the National Peace Accord in 1991, which brought an end to all the discriminatory laws in South Africa, such as the Group Areas Act, the Separate Amenities Act and the Population Registration Act.

A national welfare conference was held during November 1993 to debate plans for a new welfare system for the country, and a National Welfare Forum was established in 1994 (Van Dyk, 2000:42).

3.8.3   Social welfare in the post-apartheid years

The first democratic general election was held on the 27 April 1994. It saw the African National Congress winning the polls. As a result, the first black president, the late Mr Nelson Mandela, was inaugurated on 10 May 1994.

Various government departments, which included a single department of Welfare and Population Development (currently known as the Department of Social Development), were established in 1994. The Minister of Welfare and Population Development released a discussion document entitled: "*Towards a New Social Welfare Policy and Strategy for South Africa*" in 1995, providing an opportunity for South Africans to participate in the welfare debate.

One of the most important tasks the government was faced with was to transform the social welfare system in the country in the spirit of the Reconstruction and Development Programme (RDP). This resulted in the suggestion of drafting a white paper on social welfare. A white paper is a policy document which provides a broad framework, setting out the vision, mission, principles, approach and strategy of a policy. In other words, it guides the social welfare system in the country.

The white paper was drafted in consultation with the national department of welfare, provincial welfare departments and various welfare organisations. After many discussions with the stakeholders, the draft white paper for social welfare was accepted later in 1995 and published in the government gazette in early 1996.

The social developmental approach to social welfare policy was adopted. This approach evolved from the country's unique history of inequality and the violation of human rights due to colonialism and apartheid (Nicholas *et al.*, 2010:52).

There are five main features central to the idea of the social development approach:
1. It is rooted in a rights based approach to development, which includes the guaranteeing of a minimum standard of living, equitable access and equal opportunity for every citizen to receive services and benefits. The focus is on the disadvantaged.
2. It is concerned with harmonising economic and social policies. This means that it is based on the idea that economic growth alone cannot bring improvement without social investments in human capabilities, such as education, skills development and health care.
3. It emphasises the idea of promoting participation in development, which includes creating opportunities for citizens to be actively involved in promoting their own development and that of their own communities.
4. It is based on the partnership model, which encourages a partnership between individuals, groups, communities, civil society, donors, development agencies, and the private and public sectors to promote development.
5. It attempts to overcome the divisions that have existed historically between micro- and macro-intervention strategies.

The following are four main features distinguishing the developmental welfare service delivery model.
1. It is a **rights based approach to service delivery**, which seeks to promote, protect and defend the rights of those at risk and vulnerable. The focus is on needs and rights, and the developmental welfare service agencies would seek to:
   • protect the rights of the people
   • promote the rights by educating the people
   • facilitate access to rights
   • challenge policies that do not uphold rights.
2. It involves **integrated family-centred and community-based services**, whereby family and community based services, directed at people who are needy and at risk, are advocated.
3. It includes a **generalist approach to service delivery**, which seeks to embrace the generalist approach to social service delivery and social work practice. The generalist approach focuses on using a range of prevention and intervention methods in dealing with individuals, families, groups, organisations, and communities.
4. It involves **community developmental welfare services**, which is the intervention strategy aimed at addressing poverty and underdevelopment through community participation and empowerment, as well as social and economic development.

The social development approach is still considered today after more than 20 years of democracy in South Africa. It is important to indicate that despite numerous developments and transformation in the country, it is still facing its own challenges emanating from the past experiences. There are many South Africans who still believe that it should be the responsibility of government to provide basic needs to the people.

When the African National Congress came into power in 1994, it launched the Black Economic Empowerment programme (also known as BEE) with the aim of redressing the inequalities established by apartheid. It aimed at giving economic privileges to certain previously disadvantaged groups, namely blacks, coloureds, Indians and Chinese (who arrived before 1994). The introduction of the Black Economic Empowerment programme saw the black middle class benefiting more, and it is believed to have come with its own challenges as a result of fraud, corruption and the mismanagement of funds.

In the early 2000s, the economic situation of the country improved significantly and the social spending levels increased commensurately as compared to the slightly slow economic growth and poverty level in the mid to late 1990s.

Social spending on security, health and education increased significantly over the first decade of the twenty first Century. In 2008, the spending on social security and social welfare services was the second largest part of the budget, amounting to R70.7 billion. However, it was still not sufficient to address past backlogs in services, mass poverty, and the related effects of the HIV and AIDS epidemic (Nicholas *et al.*, 2010:57).

Democratic South Africa introduced a progressive Constitution, institution and legislative framework through which it would implement the transformation project from a pariah state of apartheid to a democratic prosperous, non-sexist, non-racial society. The South African agenda and the objectives set out in its development path embed the objectives of the Millennium Development Goals (MDGs) (Millennium Development Goals, 2013:13). South Africa developed the MDG reports in 2005, 2010, and 2013, which seek to provide an account of progress or regress on targets set out in the goals. The eight Millennium Development Goals are to:

1. eradicate extreme poverty and hunger
2. achieve universal primary education
3. promote gender equality and empower women
4. reduce child mortality
5. improve maternal health
6. combat HIV and AIDS, malaria, and other diseases
7. ensure environmental sustainability
8. develop a global partnership for development.

In the past, the National Coordinating Committee (NCC), the Technical Working Group (TWG) and the Sectoral Working Groups (SWGs), were responsible for drafting the MDGs reports, but the civil society feedback resulted in the expansion of responsibility for progressive improvement with the inclusion of the Report Drafting Team (RDT) and the Expanded Report Drafting Team (ERDT), which mainly comprised of civil society representatives.

Due to the past inequalities, emanating from race-based policies, the Constitution of South Africa, in its preamble, commits its leadership, citizenry and the state to undertake actions in reaching the fundamental outcomes, of which there shall be a normalised South African society that is prosperous, non-sexist and non-racial. To achieve this outcome the Constitution commits to:

- heal the divisions of the past and establish a society based on democratic values, social justice and fundamental human rights
- lay the foundations for a democratic and open society in which government is based on the will of the people and every citizen is equally protected by law
- improve the quality of life of all citizens and free the potential of each person
- build a united and democratic South Africa able to take its rightful place as a sovereign state in the family of nations.

To combat the challenges of poverty, hunger and unemployment, the South African govern-ment introduced the social wage policy aimed at reducing the cost of living for the poor. These social wages are packaged in different targeted forms, namely:

- free primary health care
- no-fee paying schools
- social grants
- RDP housing
- provision of basic and free basic services in the form of reticulated water
- sanitation and sewerage as well as solid waste management to households, particularly to those classified as indigent.

For instance, since 2001 the indigent household has been entitled monthly to a free six kiloli-tres of water, 50 kwh of electricity, R50 worth of sanitation, sewerage and refuse removal (Millennium Development Goals, 2013:22). About 3.5 million households were identified as indigent across the country and the local governments, through the integrated development programmes, took a leading role in the delivery of the social wage packages.

At the time of writing in 2014, the South African economic situation has changed since the inception of democracy in 1994, however, much remains to be done, since the country is still faced with lots of social challenges, such as unemployment, crime and poverty, which are neg-atively affecting the wellbeing of the people.

Protests by citizens are evidence that there is still a gap between the policy intentions and the actual delivery of government programmes.

 SELF-ASSESSMENT

1   List and discuss some of the important international legislations aimed at addressing the needs of the poor.
2   Briefly illustrate the most important development that occurred in South Africa, considering the:
    a   pre-apartheid era
    b   apartheid era
    c   post-apartheid era.

3.9 The global development of the social work profession

Social work has its origins in the centuries-old idea of charity, but in its organised forms it is a product of the political, social and public health effects of the Industrial Revolution (Sheldon & MacDonald, 2009:33).

It is believed that the first training in social work began at the University of Birmingham in 1895 and later at the London School of Economics. However, the number of graduates produced by these universities was very small.

"The professionalisation of social work over the 20th Century involved a number of different aspects and one was to define a body of theory to serve as the foundation for autonomy and respect of social work practice and its education. This theory has to a large extent been borrowed from the field of psychology, and, while initially highly influenced by the psychodynamic theory, now includes sociological theories, social learning theory, systems theory, social movement theory, structural theories, deviance theory, family theory, and feminism." (Earle, 2008:15)

There are many theories in social work training and the those mentioned above are only some of them.

The National Association of Social Workers (NASW) has conceptualised social work practice as having four major goals, namely:

1. to enhance the problem-solving, coping, and developmental capacities of people
2. to link people with systems that provide them with resources, services, and opportunities
3. to promote the effectiveness and humane operation of systems that provide people with resources and services
4. to develop and improve social policy.

3.10 The development of the social work profession in South Africa

"Social work in South Africa has allied itself with groups experiencing discrimination and social disadvantage, including people living in poverty and groups that have been alienated or mistreated because they were different in terms of race, ethnicity, gender, sexuality, religion, political viewpoint, or disability." (Barsky, 2006:7) In many areas, the profession of social work grew out of charitable work, such as volunteers who worked with abused, neglected or abandoned children (Mbedzi, 2011:17).

The social work profession is therefore aimed at addressing the social problems in the society/ community by means of capacitating and empowering people to deal with these social challenges more efficiently by themselves. It facilitates a move from dependency brought about by poverty to self-reliance and sustenance, while at the same time promoting and protecting the rights of the people within the society.

Social work has attempted to respond to diverse needs and social challenges in the process of developing a generalist approach, while at the same time promoting increased specialisation within specific fields of practice, such as child welfare, aging, disability, mental health and corrections.

Seven training institutions were established in the 1930s and they introduced degree and diploma courses in social work and in both practice and education. There was almost total adherence to models developed in Europe and North America (Potgieter, 1998:21).

In 1967, schools for social work organised the first Teachers Conference in Kimberley, combined with the meeting of the Joint Universities Committee for Social Work. The social work academics were provided with opportunities for face-to-face contact and to exchange ideas on curriculum issues and teaching methods and models (Potgieter, 1998:22).

The Social Work Act, first promulgated in 1978 when the council for social work was established, regulated the social work profession in South Africa and from this time on, social workers were required by law to register for practice. This resulted in the professional associations of social workers in South Africa to be developed as initiatives through which social workers could protect and give voice to their interests within social welfare.

The development of professional social work associations in South Africa was hampered and confounded by the establishment of the council of social work which is currently known as the South African Council for Social Service Professions (SACSSP). The major functions of the SACSSP are to:

• advance and protect the interests of the social work profession and its clients
• advise the Minister of Welfare on matters relating to the profession and on national and provisional policies relating to social work

- administer the registration of social workers, social auxiliary workers and student social workers
- determine and maintain standards of professional conduct
- determine and monitor minimum standards for education and training of social workers.

The development of social work education was an important part of social work professionalisation and the first school of social work in South Africa was at the University of Cape Town in 1924, followed by the University of Witwatersrand in 1931, and it was strictly open to white students. The social work training for other racial groups which includes, backs, coloureds and Indians, was introduced in the early 1940s and late 1950s in South Africa (Mazibuko & Gray, 2004:130).

The most dramatic event for social work education, and tertiary education as a whole, was when the Extension of University Education Act, 45 of 1959, was promulgated. This Act provided for separate university education for African, coloured and Indian people, and restrictions were placed on the admission of students other than white to the previously non-racial universities in Cape Town, Natal (now Kwa-Zulu Natal) and the Witwaterand (Van Dyk, 2000:38). The decision to separate the universities was justified on the basis that they would be separate but provide the same standard of education that would take into account the customs, norms, and traditions of various groups.

The former Minister of Social Development, Mr Zola Skweyiya, alluded to shortages of social workers in South Africa for the first time in 2003. The South African government shortly embarked on the process of recruiting prospective students to register with institutions of higher education to train as social workers. Until today, social work students are being offered bursaries through the national and provincial departments of social development.

The scarcity of professional social work skills in the country might pose threats to and difficulties for the government's ability to deal with the increasing number of social challenges, such as poverty, orphans and vulnerable children, HIV and AIDS, unemployment, family conflicts and marital disputes, teenage pregnancy, juvenile offenders, mistreatment of the disabled and elderly, as well as domestic violence. For these challenges to be addressed, professional social work skills are required and many professional social workers with competence and a strong theoretical background need to be produced by the training institutions.

It is estimated that there are 20 institutions of higher learning in South Africa that train social workers, and the admission requirements differ from one institution to another. The minimum duration of social work training in South African institutions today is four years.

A bachelor's degree in social work (BSW) is the most common minimum requirement to qualify for a job as a social worker in South Africa, however, some jobs, such as supervisory, administration/management, research, and staff training positions require an advanced degree such as a master's degree or a doctorate in social work.

This training should equip social workers with the necessary knowledge and skills to intervene at all levels in any setting and be able to deal with any challenge presented to them by the clients with the aim of capacitating clients to deal with their own problems.

 STOP AND REFLECT

1 Briefly discuss the main factors that led to the development of the social work profession.
2 Distinguish between social work and social welfare.
3 What is the background of social welfare and social work in Africa?
4 Briefly discuss the development of social work education in Africa.
5 Identify the most significant stages in the development of social work in South Africa.

3.11 **Conclusion**

Social welfare and social work originated so many centuries back, but still face adverse conditions that require transformation even in present times. There have been many circumstances that led to the development of these two important concepts (social welfare and social work), and the development processes differ from one country to the another, but they are mainly influenced by social, economic and political factors.

The Industrial Revolution played an important role in the transformation and development of a social welfare system, both internationally and in South Africa. As a result, there was an influx of people to the cities searching for employment in the manufacturing sectors. Families were left despondent and isolated, while having to deal with the after effects of the Industrial Revolution, such as poverty.

Families, volunteers and charity organisations, such as churches, played the most crucial role in meeting the social needs of family members before the development of social work as a profession.

The formalisation of social work as a profession enhanced social services in the sense that services were rendered by the most qualified professionals.

There were different dynamics that led to the development of social welfare and social work on the African continent. The development of social work education in Africa was mostly influenced by the European methods of practice and later a need to focus on the African methods was identified.

South African history has its own background that was filled with inequality and the distribution of unequal services to people of different races during the apartheid years. The welfare system in South Africa can be understood by referring to the historical factors that affected the social welfare of the country in the pre-apartheid, apartheid and post-apartheid eras.

The South African welfare system still faces some challenges of addressing the past imbalances, which are somehow caused by unstable economic factors, corruption, fraud and mismanagement of funds.

The above mentioned challenges need to be addressed, otherwise the development and growth in social welfare will be compromised.

End of the chapter questions

1. Briefly discuss the connection between social welfare and social work and how they apply on African context.
2. Describe the three approaches to social welfare policy and provide an example of each.
3. Discuss the development of social welfare and social work internationally.
4. What are the common factors that led to the development of social work and social welfare internationally and on the African continent?
5. What influenced the development of social work education on the African continent? Provide examples.
6. What was the nature of social welfare in South Africa during the pre-apartheid and the apartheid era?

Key concepts

- The **apartheid system** was a system (implemented in South Africa by the National Party government from 1948 until 1994) that promoted racial discrimination and segregation.
- **Social problems** are the challenges in a society that directly or indirectly affect the people. They can also be regarded as social conditions that are viewed by the community as undesirable. Social problems, for example, may include crime, teenage pregnancy, drug abuse and environmental problems.
- **Social welfare** refers to structured public or private services aimed at assisting the poor and disadvantaged groups. Social welfare focuses on the wellbeing of individuals, families, groups and the entire society, for example, the quality of the environment (air, soil, and water), the level of crime, the extent of drug abuse and teenage pregnancy, and the availability of essential social services.
- **Social welfare policy** is a set of principles, procedures and regulations that affect the social wellbeing of the people. It can also be regarded as the social services provided by government to its citizens in accordance with specific regulations and procedures, for example, assisting the needy with food benefits, housing assistance, unemployment insurance, and social security benefits.
- The **social welfare system** is a programme intended to provide assistance to poor and needy individuals, families, groups and communities. The type of welfare provided to individuals, families, groups and communities differs from one circumstance to another, for example: programmes such as poor relief, housing assistance, child care assistance, food stamps, unemployment compensation, and social grants.
- **Social work** is a helping profession that seeks to promote social change and problem solving in human relationships and the liberation of people to enhance wellbeing. Social work practice is aimed at assisting people (individuals, families, groups and communities), in enhancing and restoring their capacity for social functioning and creating favourable societal conditions to attain their goals. Social workers are employed in different settings, for example: private practice, government departments, non-governmental organisations, colleges and universities.
- *Ubuntu* is a Nguni word (which comprises of Zulu, Xhosa, Swati and Ndebele) and refers to the spirit of humanity. It affirms humanity in acknowledgement of others. It encompasses a general belief in a universal bond of sharing that connects all humanity, for example: members of a community may jointly take on the responsibility of taking a young boy, from the same community, to school without expecting anything in return.
- **Welfare organisations** are organisations (governmental or non-governmental) that provide welfare services to improve the conditions of the needy and disadvantaged people in society. They include social services provided by various government departments, such as the Department of Social Development and Correctional Services; and non-governmental organisations, such as child welfare organisations, care centres for the disabled, and care centres for the aged.

References

1. AMBROSINO, R., AMBROSINO, R., HEFFERNAN, J. & SHUTTLESWORTH, G. 2012. *Social work and social welfare: an introduction.* 7th ed. Canada: Thomson Brooks.
2. BARSKY, A.E. 2006. *Successful social work education: a student's guide.* Belmont: Thomson Wadsworth.
3. EARLE, N. 2008. *Social work in social change: the profession and education of social workers in South Africa.* Cape Town: HSRC Press.
4. HERON, B. 2005. *Changes and challenges: preparing social work students for practicums in today's sub-Saharan African context.* [Online]. Available: http:www.sagepublication.com [19 February 2015]
5. MACAROV, D. 1995. *Social welfare: structure and practice.* London: Sage Publications.
6. MAZIBUKO, F. & GRAY, M. 2004. Social work profession associations in South Africa. *International social work,* 47(1):129–142.
7. MBEDZI, R.P. 2011. *Exploring Social workers' Integration of the Person-Centred Approach into practice within different working contexts.* Pretoria, South Africa: Unisa. (Unpublished dissertation.)
8. MILLENIUM DEVELOPMENT GOALS. 2013. *The millennium development goals report: we can end poverty 2015.* New York: United Nations.
9. MMATLI, T. 2008. *Political activism as a social work strategy in Africa.* [Online]. Available: http://www.sagepublications.com [19 February 2015]
10. MWANSA, L.J. 2010. *Challenges facing social work education in Africa.* [Online]. Available: http://www.sagepublications.com [23 July 2014]
11. NEELY, A.E. 1965. *Social work education in a changing Africa: seminar for social work educators.* [Online]. Available: http//wwwsagepublications.com [21 February 2015]
12. NICHOLAS, L., RAUTENBACH, J. & MAISTRY, M. 2010. *Introduction to social work.* Cape Town: Juta and Co.
13. NOYOO, N. 2000. *Social development in sub-Saharan Africa: lessons for social work practice in South Africa.* [Online]. Available: http://www.sagepublications.com [19 February 2015]
14. PATEL, L. 2005. *Social welfare and social development in South Africa.* New York: Oxford University Press.
15. PATEL, L. 2010. *Social welfare and social development in South Africa.* New York: Oxford University Press.
16. POTGIETER, M.C. 1998. *The social work process: development to empower people.* South Africa: Prentice Hall.
17. SHAWSKY, A. 1972. *Social work education in Africa.* [Online]. Available: http://www.sage-publications.com [6 July 2014]
18. SHELDON, B. & MACDONALD, G. 2009. *A textbook of social work.* New York: Routledge.
19. VAN DYK, A.C. 2000. *Introduction to social work and the helping process: only study guide for SCK102-X.* Pretoria: Unisa.
20. ZASTROW, C. 2014. *Introduction to social work and social welfare: empowering people.* 11th ed. Canada: Brooks/Cole Cengage Learning.

Social work: Values, principles and ethics

Mimie Sesoko

CHAPTER OUTCOMES

By the end of this chapter, you should be able to:

✓ define social work values, ethics and principles

✓ define and outline the role of the South African Council for Social Service Professions

✓ describe the role of organisations in guiding and protecting social workers in practice

✓ describe and demonstrate an understanding of the Code of Ethics that governs social workers in their practice

✓ describe the practical professional ways in which social workers should and should not behave.

 Case Study 4.1

Molebogeng's friendship story

Molebogeng had two friends, Tshidi and Tsotlhe, who she trusted a lot and shared deep secrets with. Tsotlhe and Tshidi knew Molebogeng as a woman who loved them very much. One day she told them about her relationship with her new boyfriend and that she suspected that he, Kgotso, was HIV positive. She also indicated that he may have infected her as she was feeling very sick and had been vomiting blood since she started dating him. She was also losing weight and was afraid to go to the clinic, as she did not want to be told that she was HIV positive. Tsotlhe and Tshidi started spreading the rumour that Molebogeng was HIV positive.

The two friends saw Molebogeng as a danger to their lives. They decided to stay away from her, and so avoided her. They felt she might infect them. Molebogeng noticed some changes in her two friends' attitude towards her and wanted to know why they were avoiding her. Tsotlhe indicated that she wanted to focus on her studies and did not want to hang out with her anymore. Tshidi told her that she was busy at church and could not visit her. This made Molebogeng very sad, as she could sense that they were rejecting her. Then one day Molebogeng's neighbour told her that she overhead Tsotlhe and Tshidi talking about her in the bus. They said that she was HIV positive. Molebogeng was disappointed that her close friends were talking behind her back. This destroyed their relationship.

 STOP AND REFLECT

1   What, in your view, changed the relationship between Tshidi, Tsotlhe and Molebogeng?

2   If you were in Molebogeng's position how would you have responded if your best friends behaved the way Tshidi and Tsotlhe did?

3   If you were in Tsotlhe and Tshidi's position, what would you have done to help Molebogeng?

4   How do you feel about people who gossip or talk behind someone's back?

5   Define the concepts of confidentiality and being non-judgmental in a relationship.

6   Define your own values and principles, which you have developed over the years, around being a trustworthy friend.

7   What do you value or feel strongly about?

8   Do you think a social worker can behave like Tshidi and Tsotlhe? If not, state why.

After studying this case study and reflecting on your personal values, you will realise the importance of values in life. We all know the golden rule of treating others as you would like them to treat you. This is also important in life and especially in relationships. Young people learn this from their families and communities.

For social workers, this is part of their training. They are expected to respect their clients as they deal with individuals', families', groups' and community members' deep personal secrets and challenges. Social workers are not allowed to share a client's personal life story and challenges without their consent. Chapters 5 and 6 outline the helping process and how social workers build a professional relationship with individuals. The way a social worker behaves and respects clients' information is referred to as a professional value.

In this chapter we will discuss social work values and how they shape the way social workers relate to their clients and the communities they work with. Dominelli (2009:17) states that social work intervention has to occur within legislative parameters, an ethical framework and a code of professional ethics to ensure that social workers do not take advantage of people in vulnerable positions. In this chapter, we will look at the social work values, principles and standards. These will help us understand how social workers are expected to behave, act and perform their duties as professionals. We will further explore the role of the professional body that regulates the behaviour of social workers in South Africa and refer to similar international organisations.

4.1 Introduction

Within each helping profession, there are a number of fundamental principles that guide the actions that professionals in different fields must follow and honour when working with clients or communities. The focus of this chapter is on the social work profession. We will look at social workers', student social workers' and social auxiliary workers' expected personal conduct and behaviour in practice. In each country, social work professional bodies govern the way social workers are to behave in practice. These bodies develop what we refer to as a Code of Ethics. Social workers are expected to understand, know, remember and apply the principles and standards as outlined in their social work council's or association's Code of Ethics. This is because their conduct and behaviour is critical when offering social services to individuals, groups and communities. It is also critical in their relationship with fellow colleagues and the society at large. The code of conduct also looks at social work within the profession itself.

The work that social workers perform must be highly professional in nature and be guided by the social work values, ethics and principles. In South Africa, social workers must adhere to the guiding ethical principles stipulated by the South African Council for Social Service Professions (SACSSP). In this chapter, we refer to these guidelines and also refer to other international bodies, such as the National Association of Social Workers (NASW) and the International Federation of Social Work (IFSW).

4.2 Definitions of social work values, ethics and principles

The concept social work is defined in Chapter 1 of this book. The global definition refers to the principle of social justice, human rights, collective responsibility and respect for diversity as central to social work. Social justice is one of the core broader values of social work. This means that when social workers provide services, they cannot discriminate against any individuals, groups or communities. They are obligated to deal with unjust situations such as poverty, unemployment, lack of infrastructure, underdevelopment and many other social problems affecting vulnerable individuals and communities. In dealing with social injustices, the focus must be mainly on social change that will lead to development and empowerment of individuals and communities. Therefore, social justice as a value and principle does apply in all situations where social workers operate. A social worker cannot look at clients' circumstances and decide to cut corners or provide incomplete services. Professional values and principles are part and parcel of any social work setting. The social work values to be defined below apply in rural, urban, informal settlements, and to rich and poor individuals, families, groups and communities.

4.2.1 Social work values

In this section, we look at the different definitions of the concept social work values and refer to some examples to help you understand them. You will learn about the different definitions, so you are able to apply them to real life situations. We will refer to Montla's case study so you can practically conceptualise, define and describe the social work values as defined by different authors.

Values, ethics and principles are the cornerstone of social work. For any social worker in practice, it is important to apply the social work values as part of their day-to-day practice. As stated by Kirst-Ashman (2013:22) social work is a value-based profession and everything that social workers do must abide by the professional values. Social work values inform social work practice. Social work values also determine whether one's behaviour is acceptable or not. Different authors define social work values as follows:

Barlett (as cited in Bisman, 1994:45) defines values as those that are regarded as good and desirable. Social work values provide the basis for distinctions between good and bad. Bistek (as cited in Dominelli, 2009:18) initially voiced the traditional values that underpin social work's Code of Ethics as follows:

- Individualisation: A focus on the uniqueness of each individual's situation
- Purposeful expression of feelings: Using emotions to initiate behavioural changes
- Controlled emotional involvement: Maintaining a professional distance in relationships with service users
- Acceptance: Valuing a person in his or her own right
- Self-determination: Promoting service user independence and the ability to make decisions about their lives
- Confidentiality: Not disclosing information obtained in a professional relationship
- Non-judgmental attitude: Refraining from passing judgment on people

---

According to the National Association of Social Work (as cited in Corcoran, 2012:184), the basic values, ethical principles and ethical standards of social work can be defined as follows:
- A value is a simple statement about what is important to social workers.
- A principle is a general directive that describes how social workers act in accordance with social work values.
- A standard is a longer statement of a social worker's ethical responsibilities to clients, colleagues, practical settings, professionals, the profession and the society as a whole.

Therefore all social workers are expected to know their professional values as they provide guidance on how to respond to clients and communities during counselling and facilitation sessions. On the other hand, the principles guide how social workers behave as professionals. Both the values and principles are stipulated as part of the standards and norms of the social work profession. These are all clearly outlined in the social work Code of Ethics in different countries where social work as a profession has established professional bodies. In South Africa, the professional body that registers and regulates how social workers operate is known as the South African Council for Social Service Professions (SACSSP). All social workers in practice are required to register with their professional bodies, as this is a legal requirement by the professional body and the government. This means a social worker cannot practice without being registered. He or she cannot just do things without using his or her professional values and checking that he or she is doing them according to what is expected by his or her profession and the professional body. To do this, he or she has to know the values, standards and principles as stipulated in the Code of Ethics of the professional body he or she belongs too.

Grobler and Schenck (2010:38) refer to social work values as attitudes that the social worker, as the facilitator of change, can adopt to help him or her to treat clients with respect. They see values as an integral and continual part of the process of facilitation. They also emphasise that without the professional values, it would be impossible to create the safe environment necessary for a client's self-exploration. This therefore means that in their interaction with clients, groups and communities, social workers should be aware of the importance of the values that they reflect during the facilitation process.

Rogers (1987:21–31), and Grobler and Schenck (2010:38–44) describe the four basic professional values as: respect, individualisation, self-determination and confidentiality.

1. **Respect** is when the facilitator (social worker) shows respect and believes that the individual has sufficient capacity to deal constructively with all those aspects of his life that can come into conscious awareness. (For example: the family can solve their own problems if the facilitator believes and respects their opinions. The role of facilitators is to create a space conducive to family interaction. He or she therefore needs to use her or his communication skills to help the family members to talk to one another, and listen to their contributions. He or she needs to apply her communication skills to help them. (Refer to Chapter 1 on social work skills, knowledge and techniques.)

2. **Individualisation** is when the facilitator (social worker) perceives the client as the client sees him- or herself, sees each client as unique, and does not generalise and treat people with similar problems in the same way. (For example: the facilitator must see alcoholics not as one group, but treat each person with this problem as an individual who is different to others.)

3. **Self-determination** means the facilitator (social worker) must believe that he or she has the capability to determine what he or she wants for him- or herself. This is similar to respect, but in this case the social worker will encourage the client to believe in him- or herself and the social worker needs to draw on the strength and the self-determination of the client through his or her communication skills. (For example: the social worker must accept the principle that each person knows him- or herself better than anyone else does. The role, therefore, of the social worker is to apply the right skills, knowledge, techniques and theories to help the client rediscover who he or she is and what he or she wants.)

4. **Confidentiality** means that what has been said will remain private and will not be repeated to anyone else. This is sometimes difficult for a social worker who has to report his or her cases to a senior to get assistance. (For example: if you are going to talk to someone, be it your seniors at work, the client's doctor, parents or husband, you need to seek permission from the client first and explain why you need to talk to these people if they are part of the solution to a problem. When the social worker talks with no permission from the client it means he or she is breaking the client's trust.)

Rogers (1987:20) states that the facilitator's entire attitude and actions need to encourage the growth of the client as a person. Therefore this means that these four values are critical in the helping process as they determine how the client will be able to share his or her experiences and get to the bottom of his or her problems in order to change and drive his or her own development.

Corcoran (2012:183–184) and Kirst-Ashman (2013:35–36) describe six core values of social work as outlined by NASW along with supporting principles as shown in Table 4.1:

Table 4.1: NASW core values

Social work values	Supporting principles	Values emphasis
Service	Providing help, resources and benefits to people to help them achieve their maximum potential.	Social workers are to provide service to all people in need of help and not discriminate against anyone.
Social justice	Upholding the condition that in a perfect world all citizens would have identical rights, protection, opportunities, obligation and social benefits regardless of their background and membership groups (Barker, 2003:404–405).	Social workers are to promote social justice directly or indirectly through their services and as they connect clients to other services.
Dignity and worth of a person	Social workers respect the inherent dignity and worth of a person.	The dignity of clients and communities is to be respected at all times by social workers.
Importance of human relationship	Social workers recognise the central importance of human relationships.	Social workers are required to build professional relationships with clients and communities.
Integrity	Social workers behave in a trustworthy manner.	Social workers are required to have integrity in order to service clients and communities honestly and professionally.
Competence	Social workers practise within their areas of competence and development.	Social workers must be able to apply skills, knowledge, theories, tools and techniques to facilitate change. They should take responsibility to see to it that they have the required skills and knowledge.

 Case Study 4.2 **Montla**

Montla, a social worker who has just graduated from university, is employed at Bophelong Family Centre, which specialises in family therapy. A couple consulted with her, as they were experiencing conflict in their marriage. The husband, Jerry, reported that his wife, Suzan, was being reckless with the family finances. He talked about how his wife spent money on "luxury stuff" and did not buy the basic necessities. He complained about her overspending and laziness. Jerry felt Suzan came from a rich family and was very spoiled. He felt she did not take care of the household chores and the children. Jerry saw his three boys as spoiled kids who were just like their mother. He blamed all these problems on his wife. Suzan, on the other hand, complained about her husband cheating on her. She said she did not trust her husband's relationship with his secretary. She also felt overwhelmed by the household chores as she took care of everything, while her husband did nothing.

continued

Montla continued

Suzan felt that their three children needed Jerry's love, as they wanted him to be at their soccer matches and help them with their homework. She felt that she was doing her best to keep the family together.

Montla, the social worker, was very angry about Jerry's alleged behaviour and started adding her own words to Suzan's story. This couple's situation reminded her of her aunt's life. She saw Jerry as representing her uncle's behavior. She supported Suzan's story and expressed her anger towards Jerry as she felt irritated by cheating and felt that it was uncalled for. She called Suzan "poor Suzan", because she felt Suzan was over burdened with the household chores and the children. Montla expressed her feelings during an interview about men who cheat on innocent women. She got advice from her priest to tell Jerry to stop cheating on his wife and to take his marriage seriously. Montla reminded Jerry that he was a father and must support his children. She explained how he would be ultimately charged with maintenance if he did not care for his children. Montla took the priest's advice and ended the counselling by telling Suzan that she must prepare for divorce, as men who cheat don't change their behaviour easily.

 STOP AND REFLECT

1   After going through Montla's case study, create a table (as the example table 4.2 below) and describe which values system the social worker failed to respect or honour. Please substantiate your answer. Refer to the following authors' definitions of social work values.
    a   Bistek's five traditional social work values
    b   Corcoran and Kirst-Ashman's NASW five social work values
    c   Rogers', and Grobler and Schenck's four professional values

Table 4.2: Example table on values and social work behaviour

Social work values	Author	The social worker's behaviour (In this section, summarise what the social worker did or said and which value(s) she failed to respect or honour.)
1 Individualism	Bistek, Rogers, Grobler and Schenck	The social worker did not involve every member of the family in her counselling sessions. Her main interest in this family was Suzan. She focused on Suzan, as she felt sorry for her. She did not look at the other family members' issues and concerns. She did not explore how each one of them perceived their family problems. She never interviewed the children and did not know how they related to one another. She failed to treat each member as an individual within the family setting. She generalised the family problems as she had her own issues and failed to apply her value of individualism.

2   Describe why it is important for social workers to understand, know and apply their professional values.
3   What should individuals and communities do to protect themselves from the unethical behaviour of social workers?
4   What should social workers do to protect themselves from acting unethically?

4.3 The Code of Ethics and the social work profession

4.3.1 The Code of Ethics

There are many reasons why professions are guided by a Code of Ethics in their practice. For the social work profession in South Africa, as stated by the South African Council for Social Service Professions (2006:1), the code of conduct describes the standards of professional conduct required from social services practitioners in their daily professional activities. The Code of Ethics can therefore be referred to as the manual or the booklet for social work practice. It contains the standards, rules and regulations for practice. It therefore has a legislative and a moral function. The code also educates individuals and community members about what to expect from social workers, especially in their conduct and behaviour. Social workers are required to know the code by heart while the communities can refer to it to challenge a social worker's behaviour. Social workers are therefore expected to abide by the Code of Ethics and know it. They need to refer to it on daily basis as they apply their different skills and principles in their work environment. The council, as the professional body for the social services practitioners, is the custodian of the Code of Ethics.

As stated above, many countries like South Africa have developed codes of ethics for social workers. Dolgoff, Loewenberg and Harrington (2005:14), state that the social work profession has developed different codes of ethics to address specific fields of practice and country-specific social work issues.

These are a few social work organisations with their website links to their codes of ethics:
- The National Association of Social Workers (https://www.socialworkers.org/pubs/code/code.asp)
- The Clinical Social Work Association (http://associationsites.com/CSWA/collection/Ethcs%20Code%20Locked%2006.pdf)
- Canadian Association of Social Workers (http://casw-acts.ca/sites/default/files/attachements/CASW_Code%20of%20Ethics.pdf)
- American Association of Marriage and Family Therapy (http://www.aamft.org/resources/LRMPlan/Ethics/ethicscode2001.htm)
- South African Council for Social Service Professions (http://www.sacssp.co.za/Content/documents/EthicsCode.pdf)

Note: Do check the links and learn more about the above organisations' codes of ethics, as we will ask you to compare them with those of the South African Council for Social Service Professions.

4.3.2 The role of the South African Council for Social Service Professions (SACSSP)

As stated above, the social work profession in South Africa, like in many other countries, is regulated. This means social workers operate within a specific regulated setting that stipulates how they are expected to behave and conduct themselves while dealing with clients, other professionals, colleagues and the general community. The South African Social Services Profession (Act 110 of 1978) provides for the establishment of the South African Council for Social Service Professions and defines its powers and functions. This statutory council regulates the conduct, training and registration of social and associated workers.

The main objectives of the SACSSP as stated in the Policy Guidelines (2006:5) are to:
- protect and promote the interest of the professions
- maintain and enhance the prestige, status, integrity and dignity of the professions
- determine on the recommendation of the professional boards the qualification for the registration of social workers, social auxiliary workers and persons practising other professions
- regulate the practising of professions
- determine the standard of professional conduct
- exercise effective control over professional conduct
- encourage and promote efficiency in the responsibility with regard to the practice of the professions.

 STOP AND REFLECT

1 Select one of the above councils or associations through the links and compare the objectives or aims of that professional body with those of the SACSSP.
2 Describe the differences and state your opinion on the way the objectives are set out.
3 Do you think the social worker in that specific country and the social worker in South Africa are exposed to the same professional goals and objectives?
4 If so, describe in detail what you learned about the two professional bodies?

4.3.3   The social work profession and the registration process

According to the Social Service Profession Act (Act 110 of 1978) all practising social workers, social work students and social auxiliary workers are to register with the SACSSP.

The following is a summary of the requirements for the registration of each group as stipulated in the SACSSP guidelines:
- Student social workers are to register once, only at the beginning of the second year of their studies, and this is done via their training institutions. Their applications must reach the Council before 31 March of the relevant year. Because the student social workers get involved with field work practice at second year level, it is compulsory for them to register with SACSSP in their the second year. The registration continues to their third and fourth year of their studies. Then finally when they have successfully completed their degree, they can register as social workers with the same number allocated to them.
- Social auxiliary workers register prior to starting their studies, so by their first year as learners they are members of the council, and finally after completing their education and training. It is compulsory for social auxiliary workers to register when they are in practice and to use the designation, social auxiliary worker.
- All practising social workers (including social workers in private practice) must register with the council after graduating and display their SACSSP registration certificates in their work place. They are required to continue to be members of the SACSSP and pay their annual membership fees as council members for them to continue practising as social workers. Social workers who fail to register are not allowed to practise as social workers. For them to be allowed to practise again, they need to be restored. To be restored they are required to pay their outstanding annual membership fees. The council does not encourage late registration therefore members pay extra fees for failing to pay on time. It is therefore illegal for social workers in practice to provide services to clients and communities while they owe fees to the council. This is regarded as misconduct as they are not recognised as a social worker when they are not listed as members of the council. Should they be found with this kind of misconduct, they will be punished and reprimanded.

> **❓ STOP AND REFLECT**
>
> 1 Why do you think it is important for social workers to pay their annual SACSSP membership fees?
> 2 Do you think it is necessary for student social workers, who are in college or at a university, to register with the council while still studying and to pay SACSSP membership fees? If so, state your reasons.
> 3 We know that social auxiliary workers are supervised by social workers and do not handle cases. Why do you think it is necessary for them to register with SACSSP?
> 4 The university has a role to play in preparing student social workers to be professionals. Why should they get involved in ensuring that the student social workers in their second year register with the council? Is this their responsibility? What is your view on this?
> 5 Employers are to verify and ensure that social workers are registered with the council before they employ them. Why is this important?

4.3.4 SACSSP Policy Guidelines for Course of Conduct, Code of Ethics and Rules

The SACSSP Policy Guidelines for Course of Conduct, Code of Ethics and Rules for social workers was published and issued in April 2006.

> The two main purposes of the guidelines are:
> • to ensure that client systems receive an ethical and professional service
> • that the profession has an obligation to articulate its values and ethical principles.
> The ethical standards in the Policy Guidelines are divided into five sections, namely:
> • the profession
> • the client system
> • colleagues and other social workers
> • the practice setting
> • the broader society.
>
> Below is a summary of the ethical standards for social workers as outlined in the South African Council for Social Service Professions Policy.
> **Summary of SACSSP ethical standards**
> 1 Social workers' ethical responsibilities towards the profession
>   1.1 Integrity of the profession
>   1.2 Negligence
>   1.3 Dishonesty
>   1.4 Evaluation and research
>   1.5 Education, training and development
>   1.6 Competency
>   1.7 Incompetence of colleagues
>   1.8 Compliance with legislation, policies and procedure
>   1.9 Display of registration certificate
> 2 Social workers' ethical responsibilities towards client systems
>   2.1 Confidentiality
>   2.2 Professional relationship
>   2.3 Third party request for services
>   2.4 Gifts and incentives
>   2.5 Dealing with clients' money
>   2.6 Termination of the social worker–client relationship
>   2.7 Advertising and public statement

4.3.4.1   Ethical standards towards the profession

Social workers in practice are required to have knowledge and skills and apply social work theory and techniques as part of their intervention with individuals and communities. These skills are acquired through many years of training, both in class and through practice. Their behaviour and conduct is expected to be highly professional and to comply with the standards of their profession. In between practice and handling cases, group sessions and community work, some social work do behave in a manner that violates the ethical standards of the profession. This is referred to as misconduct.

The case in Example 4.1 below is an example of how a social worker's behaviour can be detrimental to his or her profession. He or she may be found guilty of being dishonest and having executed his or her professional duties in a manner that does not comply with the general accepted standards of practice in his or her profession.

EXAMPLE 4.1 EXAMPLE OF A CASE OF MISCONDUCT

My colleague! Wow I just read about a corruption case in social work. A social worker in practice is said to be making money from the foster care grant and child support grant. She cheats the system by helping some of her family members apply for the foster care grant.

Can social workers do that? I am surprised as I thought these are the people who should be protecting the children as they know the Children's Act and have been trained to serve the society in a just way. They also have corruption in their business of serving communities? Jo! Jo! We cannot trust them anymore.

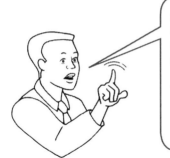

No! No! There are good social workers in our communities. I know Mrs Mmutle and Mr Mooi. They provide excellent service to our community. This particular social worker ... I cannot understand why she thought she could get away with this. She was trying to make money out of the foster care and child support grants, as she had financial problems and was desperate. But, guess what? She was reported to the SACSSP and she was charged. This did send a clear message to all social workers and social auxiliary workers about adhering to their Code of Ethics.

Yes, this is exactly what happened. She pleaded guilty and her case was further presented to the Office of the Minister of Social Development. The SACSSP cancelled her registration as social worker.

4.3.4.2   Ethical standards towards the client system

According to the SACSSP Policy Guidelines (2006:14), a social worker is required to respect the client's right to privacy and keep his or her information as confidential as possible. The client's information should not be divulged unless the social worker has acquired permission from the client. As part of this ethical standard, a client's information must be protected. The client may be a deceased person whose information the social worker has in his or her file. The social worker is required to explain what confidentiality or the right to privacy is for clients to exercise their right. Social workers need to empower clients by making sure that they know when they may be required to divulge information, and how the social worker will require the client's permission to do so. Clients must know when they should and should not give their consent to share their information.

The ethical standard clearly indicates that a social worker can be allowed to divulge a client's information when ordered to do so by a court of law. However, the social worker still needs the client's consent. If the client is a minor, his or her parent or guardian should give permission for information to be divulged. This also applies to the administration of a client's money. It should be done in an efficient and responsible way. No negligent manner is encouraged.

Furthermore, according to the SACSSP Policy Guidelines (2006), social workers are not allowed to:
- receive any bribe from a client in connection with any matter which is directly or indirectly related to his or her professional duties or practice
- discriminate against a client on account of social or economic status, sex, race, religion, language or nationality
- perform an act belonging to a professional field other than social work, including conducting psychometric tests, and diagnosing or providing therapy, unless he or she is properly qualified or legally authorised to do so
- prevent clients from procuring advice or assistance from other persons who are authorised by law to advise or treat persons concerning their social welfare.

EXAMPLE 4.2 AN EXAMPLE OF A VIOLATION

In the rural village of Eersteveld, Sophie, a social worker was well respected by community members and the traditional leadership. She was running farmers' groups and also supporting the community with their poultry projects. She managed over the years to get funding from different departments for the village projects. The community praised her for her good service. Her facilitation role was well accepted by members of the different groups. Instead of allowing the agricultural committee to drive the economic development projects on their own (as they were now well established), she decided to stay with the projects as they were making more money than she had expected. She did not allow the community to drive their own projects (value of self-determination) and to be independent from her. Sophie had facilitated change in the Eersteveld farmers' projects and they were empowered. She felt she was entitled to rewards from the projects. The committee ended up giving her ten percent of their profit as a gift. She received a lump sum of money and praised herself for being the best social worker in the region. This matter was reported to the organisation and to the council by one of her colleagues and she was called to the disciplinary committee for forcing communities to pay her for her service. This was misconduct, as she forced the community to give her a gift for a job that she was already paid for.

4.3.4.3   Ethical standards for social workers towards colleagues and other professional persons

The social work profession encourages colleagues to work in peace with one another and to support each another. This is not easy to achieve, especially when colleagues come from different racial, ethnic and cultural backgrounds, and also hold different positions. In a multi-disciplinary setting, where different professionals are required to work as a team and complement each other's skills, one may find issues relating to class, status and position as very challenging.

In an organisation, directors are senior to managers and coordinators. Social workers should respect and work well with other colleagues, and should avoid criticism and negative judgments.

According to the Policy Guidelines (2006) the following acts or omissions of a social worker regarding behaviour towards colleagues and other professional persons are classified as unprofessional or improper conduct. If a social worker:

- directly or indirectly criticises the work of a colleague, or another professional person, in a manner that does not build that person, especially if the criticism is done during her or his duty-bound hours in the presence of clients or other people
- directly and indirectly openly reflects on the professional reputation, skills, competence, knowledge or qualifications of a colleague or of such other professional person in a negative way.

EXAMPLE 4.3 AN EXAMPLE OF COMPLIANCE

Bontle, a social worker at Koopies Welfare Centre, has 20 years of experience and has acquired a wealth of experience in working with councillors, social auxiliary workers and community development workers. She has learned over the years to always look at the bright side of the programmes and appreciate each member's skills and knowledge. She is a positive team leader. Xoliswa, who has just graduated with her doctoral degree in community development, felt that she wanted to fast track all development in Koopies, as everyone was so slow. Bontle talked to her during supervision sessions to develop the team and learn from other members even though they were young and were her subordinates. Bontle advised Xoliswa to spend more time with each team member in order to get to know their strengths. Xoliswa was fascinated by the wealth of experience in the team and was able to learn from everyone. Within a period of six months, Koopies Welfare Centre was able to set new goals and achieve them, because Xoliswa took Bontle's advice very well. Yes, instead of criticising the team she worked with them and from their frame of reference. Xoliswa used the strength based approach where she looked at the assets of the organisation and applied them to the organisation's advantage. The wealth of experience that existed over the years in the welfare organisation helped Xoliswa to facilitate change.

4.3.4.4   Ethical standard of social worker towards employers and partners

The social work profession requires that the environment in which social workers operate facilitates growth for both the client and the social workers. If there is unethical behaviour within the environment, it will discredit both the profession and the social workers as professionals. Therefore, the activities that take place in the counselling setting, and where the social worker performs other activities, such as group work, community work, teaching and research, should reflect what the profession stands for.

The SACSSP Policy Guidelines (2006) stipulate the following acts or omissions of a social worker regarding behaviour towards employers and partners as constituting unprofessional or improper conduct.
- Social workers practising and carrying other businesses, trade or work apart from social work during office hours without prior consent or arrangement with the organisation and the council.
- Social workers partnering and practising with a person who is not registered in terms of the Act, or sharing their office with such a person, except with the prior written consent of the council and subject to such conditions as the council may determine.

EXAMPLE 4.4 AN EXAMPLE OF COMPLIANCE

Kgomotso was recruited by a mining company to provide social work services to the Marikane mine workers in the platinum belt. The area is new to her and she has not worked in the business sector before. She was not sure what her job would entail and so consulted the Human Resource Manager in the company to outline her job description, especially with regard to the mineworkers who are continuously on strike. She then approached the SACSSP to get guidance on her new role in the business sector. She was guided on how to work in a multidisciplinary setting. She also looked for a mentor in the same field. Rosina, a social worker with vast experience and expertise in the business environment, agreed to mentor her. Kgomotso has started settling in and is sure that she will have support from the council, her mentor and other colleagues in business.

CHECK YOUR PROGRESS

1 Relook at the different definitions from the following authors in Section 2.1. Then describe and explain how the ethical standards in the example above fit with the values.
  a Bistek's five traditional social work values
  b Corcoran and Kirst-Ashman's NASW five social work values
  c Rogers', and Grobler and Schenck's four professional values
2 Choose a case where a social worker complied, and one in which she or he did not comply, with the ethical standards. Explain the values that the social worker had applied, or failed to apply, in dealing with the client systems, colleagues and the profession.

4.3.4.5   Ethical standards of social workers relating to the broader society

The work of a social worker is not only with individuals, groups and the community as this can compartmentalise the social work services in a society with broad needs. The broader socio-economic and political challenges of the society are part of the responsibilities of the social work profession. Social issues are huge in South Africa, hence it is important for social workers to understand social policies and programmes implemented by the government.

Social development, as the new paradigm shift for South Africa, is very challenging and social workers are required to contribute towards defining this paradigm. Patel (2005) outlines how the social development paradigm will slowly shift from a welfare approach to an integrated developmental approach. Social work professionals operate in environments where they deal with vulnerable communities. They are required to facilitate change and empower communities to drive their own development process. Communities have vast needs and challenges, but they also have strengths and a wealth of indigenous knowledge. Therefore they are to make a contribution to the social welfare and social policy framework in South Africa.

The ethical responsibilities of social workers towards the broader society of South Africa, as outlined in the SACSSP Policy Guidelines (2006:42), are as follows.
- Social workers are required to engage in social and political actions that facilitate change for the large part of the society.
- They have to ensure that vulnerable members of the society have access to resources, opportunities and information for them to make the right choices.
- They must provide support and guidance in public emergency situations and be aware of resources to support such situations.
- They must promote development for all.

EXAMPLE 4.5 AN EXAMPLE OF COMPLIANCE

The aim of the South African National Development Plan (NDP) is to address the standard of living of all South Africans through the elimination of poverty and inequality. When the NDP was developed, a number of experts who represent different disciplines and professions were appointed as commissioners to work on the plan. These were experts with knowledge on development and who understood the South African development arena. One of these experts was a social worker. For her to make a meaningful contribution to the team, she consulted other social workers to get their input so that she could represent the views of social workers in South Africa. The social workers have, therefore, through one of their colleagues made a vast contribution in shaping the policy framework of the NDP. This is what is expected in their profession. They are also expected to participate in the implementation process of this plan and monitor whether the goals of the NDP are achieved. What is more critical in their involvement is to ensure that the policy framework of the NDP addresses the needs of the vulnerable community. If not, they are challenged as a profession to make more of a contribution towards policy changes. Social workers, therefore, are to participate in policy development processes of the country in order to address the broader needs of the society.

4.4   Conclusion

In this chapter we looked at the importance of social work values, principles and standards and how they guide social workers, students and social auxiliary workers in the intervention process. The role of the SACSSP was defined and the manner in which the statutory body protects the profession and social workers, students and social auxiliary workers servicing vulnerable communities was explored. Case studies were used to illustrate the importance of the social work profession and the ethical behavior expected from the professionals in the helping profession. The Code of Ethics and the guiding principles are guided by the Social Service Profession Act 110 of 1978. This provides an understanding of the legal mandate of the SACSSP and the behaviour expected in providing services.

End of chapter questions

Study the Code of Ethics of the SACSSP and NASW to answer the following questions.

1. As a group, choose three sections from the five ethical standards and responsibilities of social work (as outlined in the box with the heading "Summary of SACSSP ethical standards" on page 80). Discuss each point as a group, and give practical case examples (that you know of, have read about or can imagine) of a violation of the standard.
2. Then role-play the procedure the SACSSP will follow to charge each case. (Refer to the Policy Guidelines and Act.)
3. As a group, choose three sections from the five standards of the ethical responsibilities of social work (as outlined in the box with the heading "Summary of SACSSP ethical standards" on page 80). Discuss each point as a group, and give practical case examples of compliance to the standard.
4. In a group, discuss the role and function of the South African Council for Social Service Professions and state why it is important to have a regulatory body for social service practitioners.
5. In an essay, write why it is important for you to be a member of the SACSSP. Explain how you will you benefit from it.
6. Compare and contrast the SACSSP and NASW Codes of Ethics. Use the website link provided on page 79 to download the NASW Code of Ethics.
7. After comparing the two professional bodies in Question 6, do you think social workers in South Africa and internationally are treated in the same way when it comes to the implementation of the Codes of Ethics of social work as outlined in NASW and SACSSP. Provide a full explanation with reasons for your argument.

Key concepts

- **Social work values** refer to a set of moral or ethical principles, such as respecting a client's right to privacy.
- **Social work principles** refer to the way social workers act in accordance with social work values, for example, for the value of social justice, the supporting principle would be that social workers are to challenge social injustice.
- A **Code of Ethics** is a set of moral principles that guides the professional conduct and professional practice of social workers and other professions, for example, the SACSSP Code of Ethics and the NASW Code of Ethics.
- **Ethical standards** refer to the ethical responsibilities that the social work professional has to clients, colleagues, society, the profession and practice setting.
- Integrity of the profession is an example of an ethical standard for the social work profession. It implies that social work professionals must work towards maintaining and promoting a high standard of practice.
- A **legal statutory body** is a body that is established through an Act of Law, for example, the SACSSP is an association that was established through the Social Service Profession Act (Act 110 of 1978).

References

1. BISMAN, C. 1994. *Social work practice.* Belmont, California: Brooks/Cole Wadsworth Inc.
2. BISTEK, E.P. 1961. *The case work relationship.* London: Allen and Unwin.
3. CORCORON, J. 2012. *Helping skills for social work direct practice.* New York: Oxford University Press.
4. DOLGOFF, R., LOEWENBERG, F.M. & HARRINGTON, D. 2005. *Ethical decisions for social work practice.* 7th ed. Belmont CA: Brooks/Cole Thomson Learning.
5. DOMINELLI, L. 2009. *Introducing social work.* Cambridge: Polity Press.
6. GROBLER, H. & SCHENCK, C.J. 2010. *Person centred facilitation process, theory and practice.* 3rd ed. Cape Town: Oxford University Press.
7. KIRST-ASHMAN, K. 2013. *Introduction to social work and social welfare critical thinking perspectives.* 4th ed. University of Wisconsin, Whitewater: Brooks/Cole.
8. PATEL, L. 2005. *Social welfare and social development in South Africa.* Cape Town: Oxford University Press.
9. ROGERS, C.R. 1987. *Client centred therapy, its current practice, implication and theory.* London: Constable.
   Services Profession Act 1978 (110 as amended). South Africa.
10. SOUTH AFRICAN COUNCIL FOR SOCIAL SERVICE PROFESSIONS. 2006. *Policy Guidelines for Course of Conduct, Code of Ethics and the Rules for Social Workers.* [Online]. Available: http://www.sacssp.co.za/Content/documents/EthicsCode.pdf [6 September 2013]
11. SOUTH AFRICAN COUNCIL FOR SOCIAL SERVICE PROFESSIONS. 2009. *Social Auxiliary Workers Registration.* (Newsletter.) Vol. 2. May–June 2009. Pretoria.
12. SOUTH AFRICAN COUNCIL FOR SOCIAL SERVICE PROFESSIONS. 2009. Student Registration. (Flyer). *South African Council for Social Service Professions.* Pretoria.

PART
2

Chapter 5
The helping process in social work

Chapter 6
Case work: Social work with individuals

Chapter 7
Group work

Chapter 8
Community work: A social work method

The helping process in social work

5

Johannah Sekudu

CHAPTER OUTCOMES

By the end of this chapter, you should be able to:

✓ define the important concepts in the social work helping process

✓ describe the social work helping process from the generalist perspective

✓ describe the different steps involved in the helping process

✓ explain the importance of assessment in the helping process

✓ discuss the importance of cultural sensitive social work in the helping process

✓ describe the common theories, models, approaches and perspectives in social work practice.

 Case Study 5.1 **Lesego**

Lesego is a 54-year-old woman, living in a rural village in the North West Province of South Africa, Segwaelane near Brits. She is a single mother of three children, aged six, eight and 19, and employed at a vegetable farm not far from her home. The older child is a male, who is not attending school and is involved in abusing *nyaope*. (*Nyaope* is a combination of cocaine and marijuana commonly abused by teenagers in townships. It affects their functioning in all spheres of their lives and could lead to death if used over a long period of time.) He is also receiving hostile treatment from the community members due to his criminal behaviour. He stole a lot of his mother's belongings that he sold to get his daily fix of *nyaope* as he is not employed and depends on his mother for survival. The younger two sisters are still at school, but do not perform well as they always feel their security is threatened, due to their brother's behaviour. Lesego and her family depend on a child care grant that she receives for her two younger children and her meagre salary from her employer, as her children's father does not contribute towards their upbringing. This makes it difficult for her to meet their needs. The family is staying in a one-roomed shack without any amenities, such as running water, electricity and sanitation facilities. Lesego has been admitted at a nearby hospital and diagnosed with depression. She has also been referred to a social worker for assistance.

5.1 Introduction

Social work training in South Africa is based on enabling social workers to intervene in people's troubled situations as generalist practitioners. Generalist practitioners are expected to be equipped with a variety of skills and techniques to meet the needs of their clients at a basic level. Furthermore, generalist practice is the application of an eclectic knowledge base, professional values and a wide range of skills to target systems for change within their contexts. An eclectic knowledge base refers to a social worker possessing the basic social work knowledge, which includes the professional values, principles and goals of social work, basic social work skills as well as the different theoretical frameworks. These enable him or her to intervene in problems that a client presents to him or her. With this knowledge base, the social worker is able to select the appropriate techniques to facilitate the process of change in the client system's problematic situation. It is important to always take the client system's environment into consideration so as to understand the interaction that exists between the two that might have contributed to the problematic situation.

Understanding the interaction between the client system and the environment assists the social worker to identify the problematic areas and together with the client come up with appropriate intervention strategies to address them. The process of establishing the appropriate intervention strategies requires the full involvement of the client system, as indicated by the developmental approach, which will be discussed in detail later in this chapter. The involvement of the client system encourages the client to own his or her problem and be committed to finding a workable solution. It is important to always remember that the client system is the expert on his or her situation and in the process of change, he or she will bring in these expertise to enable the process to unfold with ease.

As a generalist practitioner, as explained above, the social worker is equipped to address the needs of his or her clients at all the levels of intervention, namely, at individual, group and community levels. This requires the social worker to be able to use the professional values and basic skills to select relevant aspects of the theoretical frameworks to facilitate the process of change in the client systems' problematic situation. As this intervention process unfolds, the social worker assumes a number of roles, depending on the client system's needs and capabilities to engage in the helping process. It is from this background that the helping process in this chapter is discussed, because it is always important to realise that a person who is experiencing difficulties in his or her life cannot be helped without considering the environment that he or she is part of, as there is continuous interaction between the person and his or her environment. At the entry level in social work practice, the social worker must be able to intervene as a generalist and be able to recognise the situation that needs specialised intervention to connect the client to such services.

As this is an introductory text for social work students, it is important to study this chapter with an understanding that it prepares you for basic social work intervention at an entry level of practice. The case study provided above shows the complexity of problems that clients can bring to the social worker for assistance, and calls for the well-equipped social worker to address the situation adequately, based on the client's strengths and willingness to participate in the helping process. This will ultimately lead to the empowerment of the client. The social work intervention process must have a beginning and an end, meaning that the goal must always be to ultimately have an empowered client, who can be self-reliant in future, and not depend on the social worker's assistance for the rest of his or her life. This is confirmed by the definition of social work as given by NASW (The National Association of Social Workers) in Kirst-Ashman (2013:6): "Social work is the professional activity of helping individuals, groups or communities enhance or restore their capacity for social functioning and creating societal conditions favourable to this goal." This definition has further been refined and the new one was adopted in 2014 at the IFSW conference in Melbourne as: Social work is a practice-based profession and an academic discipline that promotes social change and development, social cohesion, and the empowerment and liberation of people. Principles of social justice, human rights, collective responsibility and respect for diversities are central to social work. Underpinned by theories of social work, social sciences, humanities and indigenous knowledge, social work engages people and structures to address life challenges and enhance wellbeing.

5.2   The helping process

It is important to note that different social work authors use different concepts to address the social work helping process. It is, at times, referred to as the change process or the problem-solving process. For the purpose of avoiding confusion in this chapter, it will be referred to as the helping process.

The helping process unfolds within the given theoretical framework adopted by the social worker at a given time. With this in mind, it becomes important to highlight the theoretical framework for this chapter, to assist students in understanding the process clearly.

5.2.1 Theoretical framework

Social work practice in South Africa has been for decades heavily influenced by theories from the United Kingdom and United States. The other influence on how social work services were rendered emanated from the government principles, characterised by segregation, that were adopted for a long time. The recent move is the call to use the developmental approach to social work practice, as outlined in the *White Paper for Social Welfare* (1997). This paradigm emphasises the importance of social and economic development of human beings, through empowerment as well as recognition of their strengths, to enhance the helping process. The developmental approach goes together with the strengths-based approach as well as empowerment. The strengths-based approach emphasises the fact that every person is born with strengths that they bring to the helping process. This requires the social worker to recognise these strengths when interacting with the client and ensure that they are enhanced. A focus on the strengths of the client system assists in minimising the weaknesses, and leads to the empowerment of the client. More details on the developmental approach, strengths perspective and empowerment are given later in this chapter when the theoretical frameworks are discussed. The paradigm also takes into consideration the environments that human beings exist in, which makes the person-in-environment theory relevant for social work practice. Cultural sensitive social work practice is also important when intervening in clients' problematic situations because culture influences how people behave as they interact with their environments. This makes it impossible for the social worker to facilitate change in the client's life without taking the cultural context into consideration.

(The different theories, models, approaches and perspectives are discussed in detail later in the chapter)

5.2.2 The steps in the helping process

The social work helping process is defined by Sheafor and Horesji (as cited in Kirst-Ashman, 2013:113) as "the process that involves the development and implementation of a strategy for improving or altering some specified condition, pattern of behaviour or set of circumstances in an effort to improve a client's social functioning or wellbeing." This is a social work effort to assist the client systems in identifying needed change in their lives, helping them to develop strategies to make the needed change through the empowerment and assistance of client systems to implement these strategies. It is also important for the social worker to monitor and evaluate progress throughout the helping process to ensure that the desired change is achieved. It is clear that the helping process is aimed at bringing improvement in the client system's life circumstances, and it unfolds through specific steps that have to be mastered with the full participation of the client.

The helping process that is adopted in this book is the one outlined by Kirst-Ashman (2013:117–124) and efforts to apply the steps to the case study provided at the beginning of this chapter will be made. This process unfolds in six primary steps.

Before the steps are discussed, it is important to include a brief discussion of the intake phase in the welfare organisation. Intake refers to the phase when the client system makes his or her first contact with the social work service. How this phase unfolds depends on the practical set up of the particular welfare organisation. In some organisations there are intake workers, who are social workers who screen the client systems' presenting problems and then refer them to the relevant social worker who will engage them in the process of change. This phase is very important to ensure that the client's confidence is won for him or her to believe that he or she will be assisted to deal with the problematic situation he or she is facing. The intake worker uses the social work values and principles and basic skills to engage the client. This enables him or her to identify the client's problematic situation so that he or she can be linked with the relevant social worker who will take the process further.

In other organisations there are no intake workers. The social worker does the intake and then proceeds to the intervention process. Let us now focus on the different steps of the intervention process.

5.2.2.1   Step 1: Engagement/Exploration

This is the initial step in the helping process when the social workers introduce themselves to the problem at hand. This step is referred to as "social study" by Ambrosino, Ambrosino, Heffernan and Shuttlesworth (2012:106), while Kirst-Ashman (2013:117) refers to it as "engagement". It is referred to, in other social work literature, as the "exploration phase". It is during this step that the social worker has to establish a helping relationship with the client, to assist the client to relax and share his or her problem. The establishment of the helping relationship depends on the appropriate use of social work skills and techniques (as discussed in Chapter 1 of this book), social work values (as outlined and discussed in Chapter 4), social work theories (discussed in this chapter), as well as cultural sensitive social work skills.

The helping relationship is seen as the door to the helping process and if it is not well established, it is unlikely to unfold satisfactorily to meet the needs of the clients. In establishing this relationship the social worker uses the verbal and non-verbal cues to communicate unconditional acceptance of the client as an important human being who needs to be helped. Warmth has to be communicated to the client so as to create an environment that says to the client "you are seen as important and you are not judged for your situation". The client must be made to feel safe, and free to share his or her situation without any fear of being judged. He or she must experience the social worker as someone who is willing to listen and assist. All the communication skills (discussed in Chapter 1) and techniques (discussed in Chapter 6) must be used to ensure that the helping process takes place.

It is always important for the social worker to realise that the client cannot simply open up and share his or her situation with a stranger without experiencing difficulties. It is also important to remember that the client is troubled by his or her situation, that he or she might have struggled with it for some time, and that he or she had to find the courage to approach the social worker's office. This situation in itself is anxiety provoking, and calls for the social worker to be respectful, tactful and sensitive. This will ensure that the client calms down and is able to talk about his or her troubled situation. Social workers must make an effort to facilitate the process of developing a helping relationship characterised by trust.

EXAMPLE 5.1

This client was hesitant to visit the social work office. She did not feel confident enough to sit down, let alone talk. She is also a shy person.

Client:	Good day, madam. *(in a low tone of voice)*
Social worker:	Good day, Ms X. *(leaning forward towards the client, with a smile)* How is the day treating you so far? You may need to sit down, so that we can talk about your visit today.
Client:	Ai, I really don't know where to start. Things are just a mess in my life. Are you well, social worker?
Social worker:	Oh, I see. I am well. I can see that it is very difficult for you to talk about your situation, which is understandable. You may start anywhere and just share with me what made you visit our office today.

The above responses can be used to show the client that his or her visit to the social worker's office is an important step towards resolving the problematic situation he or she is faced with. After the initial effort to establish the helping relationship, the social worker is able to engage the client in the process of talking about his or her situation. It is very important to mention here that the helping relationship is ongoing throughout the helping process. It only ends when the helping process has been concluded. This first step of talking about the situation is thera-peutic for the client, as the social worker has to use communication skills to address the client's feelings about his or her situation.

As indicated by Dubois and Miley (as cited in Ambrosino *et al.*, 2012:106), this step must assist the social worker in answering the following questions:

- Who is the client?
- What is the nature of the needs and problems as seen and experienced by the client?
- What has the client done to alleviate these needs and problems?
- How effective were the efforts?
- What other individuals or groups are affected by the needs and problems, and how is the client associated with them?
- What are the client's strengths and weaknesses?
- How motivated is the client to work towards solutions to address these needs and problems?

The answers to these questions will assist the social worker in gaining a better idea of what the client is dealing with, the context in which the problem is experienced, as well as the nature of the problem at hand. In the given case study, Lesego has been referred to the social worker, so the first task facing the social worker is to have the above questions answered. The social worker can either visit Lesego at the ward, depending on her physical wellness, or call her to an office, where privacy is guaranteed. Given Lesego's situation, it will not be easy to simply share her situation with the social worker, therefore the social worker needs to use basic communication skills, such as attentive listening, empathy, observation, and non-verbal cues, to have the above questions answered. Using cultural sensitive social work practice, the social worker has to com-municate respect to Lesego. This will deepen the helping relationship and set the tone for the successful problem-solving process. Empathy must also be used by the social worker to enable Lesego to talk about her problems. This will ensure a warm and accepting environment. By using empathy, the social worker can paraphrase what Lesego is telling her, without sounding like a parrot, through skilfully reflecting the content as well as the feelings about what Lesego is going through. This will also confirm whether what the client is saying is heard and under-stood correctly. (The concepts of cultural social work practice and empathy used in social work practice are discussed further in Chapter 6.)

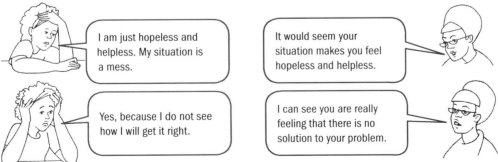

Figure 5.1: Social worker using empathy

The responses in figure 5.1 illustrate that the social worker is listening to Lesego and is trying to understand how she feels about her situation. When using empathy, the social worker reflects his or her understanding of the client's feelings and the content of what he or she has presented back to the client. This helps the social worker to make the client aware that he or she is listening and an effort is being made to understand what is being presented. In this manner, the client realises that the social worker is taking him or her seriously and is willing to help him or her address the problem at hand.

5.2.2.2   Step 2: Assessment

Successful execution of the first step ushers in the second step known as assessment. Ambrosino *et al.* (2012:106) see this step "as a process of making tentative judgements about how the information derived from the first step affects the client system's behaviour and the meaning into the particular behaviour." This is a process not an event, in which the information gathered during the exploration phase is analysed and synthesised to provide a concise picture of the client and his or her needs and strengths. Assessment requires thorough attention to ensure that the actual need or problem that motivated the client's visit to the social worker's office is identified. If this is not done thoroughly, the remaining steps in the process of intervention will be affected, specifically the planning phase that entails setting goals. If the actual problem or need is not known, inappropriate goals – that will not assist in addressing the client's needs – will be set.

In assessing the client's situation, the social worker has to take aspects of diversity into consideration, as they have a serious impact on how the client will interact with the social worker. Ignoring these aspects could lead to a failure in establishing the helping relationship. Aspects of human diversity such as age, class, colour, culture, disability, ethnicity, gender, gender identity and expression, immigration status, political ideology, race, religion and sexual orientation, are very important in social work practice and they demand that the social worker be sensitive to them. According to Sheafor and Horesji (2012:125) "'it is critical for the social worker to first develop self-awareness and strive to understand how these aspects have shaped his or her own views". This will assist the social worker in not making judgements based on bias but on the actual situation of the client. This will also assist the social worker in not generalising towards the client, but dealing with him or her as unique as he or she is. It also becomes important for the social worker to learn about the cultural context of the client that he or she serves and never assume that the client's situation is determined by their cultural background, as this might hinder the objective assessment of the client. If the social worker does not communicate understanding and respect towards the client's diverse aspects, the client could see him or her as someone who is disrespectful and insensitive, and this could affect the helping process negatively. For example, in some black cultures, a young person must never look an older person directly in the eyes when talking, as this is viewed as disrespectful. This is contrary to the social work way of doing things, where maintaining eye contact is seen as a technique used to communicate attentive listening to the client. In this situation the social worker has to be well aware of this difference for him or her to respond appropriately towards the client within the cultural context of the client. It is very important for the social worker to realise that he or she can learn about the culture of the community he or she is serving through interacting with them and asking them to share more about it. Aspects of a culture in a particular community must be learned from the community, so the social worker is able to demonstrate respect to the community members he or she is serving. This will facilitate common understanding and effective intervention.

Assessment is a dynamic process that is modified and updated as the social worker gains more insight, information and experience in working with the client system. This continuous modification becomes very important because it is not always possible to get all the information from the client during the first step of the intervention process. Ambrosino *et al.* (2012:106) suggest that assessment should answer the following basic questions:

- What factors are contributing to the client's unmet needs?
- What systems are involved?
- What is the effect of the client's behaviour on interacting systems and vice versa?
- What is the possibility for initiating a successful process of change?

These questions illustrate the important role played by the person-in-environment perspective in social work practice. This is the case because the interactions that the client is having continuously with his or her environment have a bearing on how he or she sees the problem and how he or she will be motivated to address the problematic situation.

It could be concluded that assessment is the process within the helping process that enables the social worker to identify the variables that are involved in the client's situation. This identification facilitates the process of clarifying the actual problem (the real problem) from the presenting problem (the problem that the client will share whilst checking if he or she could trust the social worker with his or her real problem). Because it is not easy for clients to state their problems, many feel more comfortable talking about something that is not always the actual problem that pushed them to seek help. This is what makes the assessment phase an important one in the helping process, because with accurate assessment, the client and the social worker are able to develop appropriate strategies to address the situation effectively. You will learn more about how assessment is done as you progress with your social work studies.

In Lesego's case, the social worker has to establish what had contributed to Lesego's current situation, in other words, how did Lesego find herself in her current situation (being admitted into hospital for the treatment of depression, having left her young children alone with no one to care for them). All the other systems that are involved in the problem have to be established. Lesego's strengths and weaknesses must be established as well, to ensure that she is engaged at her level and assisted in growth. The social worker focuses on the client's capabilities and does not assume that she or he knows everything and will do things for the client. This can lead to a situation where the client fails to search and recognise her strengths and then becomes dependent on the social worker for each and every problem she comes across. When adopting the developmental approach, the social worker is challenged to ensure that at the end of the helping process, the client has developed some skills and is able to face life without leaning on the social worker for direction.

It is very important to realise that assessment sets the stage for the intervention, by identifying the problems and strengths of the client. The following step, known as planning, is seen as a step that specifies what should be done to address the client's identified need. It is also important for the social worker to realise that assessment is continuous throughout the helping process, because as the process unfolds and the helping relationship becomes stronger, the client is able to give more information that could require the focus to be modified.

To ensure meaningful assessment is accomplished, the social worker uses the basic skills as indicated earlier. Empathy will be a skill that the social worker will have to use at all times to ensure that the client is aware that he or she is understood. A social worker cannot do thorough assessment without using listening skills and observing the client's non-verbal communication. There are times when what the client says verbally differs from what he or she is portraying non-verbally. This is the reason behind utilising all the communication skills to ensure that the crux of the problem is understood, and the appropriate intervention strategies are developed. As indicated earlier, these intervention strategies are developed in collaboration with the client as he or she understands his or her situation far better than the social worker. He or she will also know what can work and what cannot work in addressing the problem.

5.2.2.3   Step 3: Planning

After identifying the actual problem or need of the client together with the client in the assessment phase, the social worker is in a position to plan the actual intervention with the client. This step is made successful by the accurate assessment in the previous step. The following aspects have to be taken into consideration when planning for intervention:

- The social worker should work with the client and not dictate to the client.
- The social worker, together with the client, should prioritise the problems so that the most critical problem is addressed first.
- The social worker must identify the client's strengths, to provide appropriate guidance in the planned change process.
- All the systems that are in interaction with the client need to be identified and involved in the helping process.
- Any course of action to be taken must be evidence-based, to check the effectiveness thereof.
- The client must be assisted to evaluate the pros and cons of the planned course of action before its implementation.

The social worker must involve the client in ascertaining intervention options that have a potential to address identified needs. Involvement of the client facilitates the helping process because the client learns to own the process and not be a spectator. In this step, it becomes very important to review all the possible options so that the most appropriate ones for the client are determined and agreed upon. This is the reason behind the full involvement of the client. After determining the most appropriate options, the social worker now set goals together with the client. It is also important to set realistic and achievable goals. They must be in line with the client's strengths that have been identified during the assessment phase and the specific targets for change.

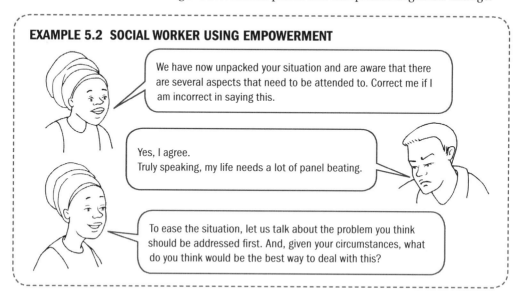

EXAMPLE 5.2 SOCIAL WORKER USING EMPOWERMENT

We have now unpacked your situation and are aware that there are several aspects that need to be attended to. Correct me if I am incorrect in saying this.

Yes, I agree.
Truly speaking, my life needs a lot of panel beating.

To ease the situation, let us talk about the problem you think should be addressed first. And, given your circumstances, what do you think would be the best way to deal with this?

The responses in example 5.2 from the social worker are aimed at making the client see him- or herself as the leader in having his or her problematic situation resolved. This goes together with empowerment, which is defined by Zastrow and Kirst-Ashman (2013:12) as the "the process of increasing personal, interpersonal or political power, so that individuals can take action to improve their life situations." In this way the client systems do not depend on the social worker for direction but take the lead in the unfolding of the helping process, according to their capabilities that were identified during the assessment phase of the helping process.

After this has been established, the social worker and the client systems have to agree on a contract that will outline how the actual intervention is going to be implemented. This must clearly state the set goals, and the timeframe and responsibilities of all people involved in the intervention process. These clarifications assist in facilitating the intervention process without any person having to assume what has to happen. When the contract is made based on the client's strengths, the implementation process tends to unfold smoothly, because all the persons involved know what has to be done, by whom and how. According to Ambrosino *et al.* (2012:107) "the contract entails the agreement between the social worker and the client systems to work towards the identified intervention goals." The contract further serves as a framework to assess the intervention progress periodically. The contracts agreed upon by social workers and their client systems are not cast in stone. They are constantly renegotiated, depending on any new information that may arise as the process unfolds.

If applying this step to Lesego's situation, the following should be done. After establishing what the problem is, the social worker should engage Lesego in prioritising the aspects of her situation. Due to the fact that she is in hospital, the social worker should attend to her immediate emotions by assisting her in identifying the stressors in her life and then prioritising the one that needs to be attended to first. No matter how helpless the client might seem, the social worker should enable him or her to realise his or her worth and capabilities in order to address the problematic situation, while the social worker plays the role of facilitator.

 STOP AND REFLECT

Use Lesego's situation to formulate the exact aspects that need to be agreed upon, according to their priority, in order to alleviate the stressful situation. Focus on the responsibilities to be addressed by Lesego as well as those needing to be addressed by the social worker.

5.2.2.4   Step 4: Implementation/Intervention

Based on the clearly stated tasks and responsibilities in the contract, the implementation process has to unfold. Implementation is seen by Kirst-Ashman (2013:124) as "the process whereby the client systems and the worker follow their plan to achieve their goals that have been identified and agreed upon in their contract." This is the step during which the actual intervention is done based on the contract between the worker and the client system. This step is further directed to meet the established goals and calls for the social worker to perform different roles that have been discussed in Chapter 1 of this book. The social worker might be a negotiator, where he or she assists the client system in accessing some services outside the agency. He or she could also be an advocate, where he or she speaks on behalf of the client system to access the needed services, both within and outside the agency.

The activities during this step, depending on the client's need, may include:

- counselling to improve the client's self-concept
- engaging other community resources
- establishing support groups to enhance the client's personal growth
- developing resources, such as the establishment of income generating projects
- finding alternative-care resources
- encouraging family involvement
- offering play therapy.

The implementation phase has to be used to assist the client system to reach an acceptable resolution of the problematic situation. This step calls for the social worker's skills in ensuring that the client systems are involved in the whole process, as this fosters empowerment and development of the client systems.

In Lesego's case, her son can be involved in a long-term process of counselling to assist him in dealing with his addiction. To address the issue of the family's inadequate accommodation, the social worker could approaching the local government structures to advocate for the family to be considered for a RDP house. The client's younger children could be involved in play therapy, to assist them in dealing with the circumstances at home by empowering them to develop coping skills. Lesego can also be empowered by linking her to support groups in the area where she will be able to share her situation with members who are in similar situations. This will lead to the development of coping skills. Developmental projects could be established, after consultation with the relevant stakeholders, to involve community members in the process of their own development and empowerment by generating some income for their families. In all these activities, full involvement of the client systems will lead to a successful intervention process.

As the intervention process unfolds, it becomes important for the social worker and the client system to check if any progress has been made towards achieving the set goals. This is informed by the agreed upon goals and it has to be an ongoing process

5.2.2.5   Step 5: Evaluation

Evaluation is an ongoing process in which the social worker and the client system review intervention activities and assess their impact on the client system's problem situation after the intervention phase has been introduced. According to Kirst-Ashman (2013:124) "evaluation is a process of analysing, monitoring and determining the effectiveness of the intervention in relation to the goal." This step becomes very important to ensure that the efforts made since the engagement step are benefitting the client system. It is important to note that the client system becomes involved in the whole process from the beginning. This makes it crucial to also get involved in this step, as it is the client system that will tell if the efforts are yielding some positive results. The social worker must ask him- or herself the following questions:

- Do the agreed upon intervention strategies work?
- Which one is not working?
- Are the client system's circumstances changing for the better or not?
- If there is no change at all, what went wrong?
- How does the client see his or her situation now, after the process has been initiated?
- Which intervention strategies need to be changed?
- Is there a need to get other resources to address the client system's problematic situation?

To answer these questions, the social worker needs to involve the client system. If he or she does not, the social worker may proceed under the false impression that there has been positive progress, according to the client systems' perspective. If the client system is left behind, the agreed upon contract may be abandoned by the client system.

Through evaluating the progress made, the social worker is also proving his or her accountability to the agency that employed him or her. The agency needs to be convinced that he or she is assisting the client systems to change their circumstances, through empowerment and development. It has to be born in mind that the social worker's actions within an agency reflect on how the agency is performing, in as far as affecting change in the lives of people is concerned. As indicated in Chapter 4, ethics play an important role in providing the ethical framework that guides social workers in their efforts to affect change in the lives of their client systems. Without evaluation, it will be impossible to establish if the ethical obligations of the social service agency are met or not.

5.2.2.6   Step 6: Disengagement

The social work intervention process must come to an end. This is the phase where the worker and the client system agree to end the helping relationship that was established at the beginning of the helping process. This disengagement follows the evaluation stage, where the progress was measured.

It is important for the social worker to ensure that termination is discussed at the beginning of the process, i.e. during the contract stage, to ensure that the client system is aware that this relationship is temporary. This will facilitate the process in that all efforts will be geared towards achieving the goal within the agreed upon timeframe. This does not mean that the client should be pushed to reach the goal, but the process must be allowed to unfold step by step for the benefit of the client system.

Disengagement might come abruptly, in cases where the client system is not satisfied with the progress made in the intervention process, and decides not to continue with the helping relationship. This situation might arise because the social worker did not involve the client in the planning of the intervention process, failing to engage the client system in setting the goals by ensuring that the contract is mutually agreed upon. If the social worker is not yet experienced, there is always a need to work under supervision to prevent the development of such situations. The supervisor must always be an experienced professional, who will be able to provide guidance on how the social worker has to operate to ensure that the problematic situations of the client systems are addressed satisfactorily.

The other situation that could lead to unplanned termination is a social worker's irresponsible behaviour or lack of commitment and accountability. This might arise if a social worker does not honour appointments or also does not adhere to professional values and principles (as discussed in Chapter 4). It can also arise if a social worker does not allow the client system to own the intervention process through active involvement from the beginning. This might lead to the social worker determining what the client system's needs are and also establishing how they have to be met. This could lead to the client system losing interest and going to another agency, or giving up on the social work intervention.

It can also happen that the client system's needs are not wholly met at the end of the agreed upon activities, because the agency does not have the resources to meet the needs. This calls for the social worker to be knowledgeable about the resources in the community that he or she serves, to ensure that he or she links the client systems with the necessary resources at the appropriate times. This is confirmed by Zastrow (2014:50) who states that "one of the goals of social work is to link people with systems that provide them with resources, services and opportunities." Referral must be done appropriately and the referring social worker must ensure that the client system is referred to the appropriate resource. (Referral is discussed in Chapter 6.)

In Lesego's case, the social worker has to make appropriate referrals to the relevant resources in the client's environment to ensure that the remaining aspects of the situation, that were not met within the hospital setting, are attended to. The issue of counselling with the aim of rehabilitating Lesego's son can be referred to SANCA (South African National Council on Alcohol and Drug Dependency) offices in her community. The social worker in the area where Lesego stays can be requested to attend to the younger children's problems regarding their academic work as well as their psychosocial wellbeing. As indicated earlier on, the local government authorities can be the other resource where Lesego can be referred to have her accommodation problem attended to. The whereabouts of the children's father is known to Lesego, so she could be linked with the nearest magistrate's offics to claim maintenance, with the aim of alleviating her financial strain. Since Lesego is already receiving child grant support, it may be an indication that this aspect has already been attended to. This should be verified with her.

Termination of the helping relationship must be informed by the outcomes of the evaluation stage. It can happen that the evaluation reveals that the client system has not yet developed the necessary coping skills to go on without the social worker's assistance. In this instance the contract has to be renegotiated to include the unmet needs of the client system, the timeframe in which to accomplish them, as well as the strategies to be used to address them. This must be approached with care to avoid a situation where the client system is unable to end the helping relationship because of a dependency that might develop. Empowerment and development of the client system must always be the aim of the social worker from the beginning of the helping process. In an effort to achieve this, social work skills and professional values and principles must be used effectively.

 STOP AND REFLECT

1 Why is the understanding of the person-in-environment so crucial in the social work helping process
2 To establish the helping relationship with the client, which skills do social workers need?
3 Why is it so important for the social worker to establish the helping relationship with the client at the beginning of the helping process?
4 What is the role of the engagement/exploration step in the helping process?
5 Assessment is found to be fundamental in the helping process. Explain why.
6 What makes it so crucial for the social worker to engage the client throughout the helping process?
7 In setting goals with the client, which aspects have to be taken into consideration?
8 Which specific circumstances could lead to termination of the helping process (planned and unplanned)?

5.3   Models, theories, approaches and perspectives

Models, theories, approaches and perspectives are used in social work practice to assist the social worker in understanding the client systems better, so as to pave the way for appropriate intervention. Different authors use these concepts interchangeably, although they might have different meanings. It is important to remember that with all the approaches, theories, models and perspectives used in the social work helping process, the helping relationship plays an important role. The social worker must always begin with establishing this professional relationship using the professional values and principles, skills and techniques, in order to ensure that trust in the client system is developed. This relationship facilitates the helping process, for the benefit of the client systems at all levels of intervention, namely at individual, group and community levels.

Due to the limited scope of this text, not all the social work theories can be discussed.

5.3.1   Developmental approach

The discussion of the theoretical framework in social work practice in South Africa is based on the developmental approach. You have already learned about the developmental approach in Chapters 1 and 3, and earlier in this chapter. This is the approach that was adopted by the government of South Africa after the dawn of the democratic elections in 1994. This approach was adopted to ensure a shift from the residual and institutional paradigms (fully discussed in Chapter 3). The developmental approach takes the social and economic development of clients into consideration, with the aim of empowering them. This approach is defined by Midgley (as cited in Zastrow, 2014:9) as a "process of planned social change designed to promote the well-being of the population as a whole in conjunction with a dynamic process of economic development." This definition presents the developmental approach as beneficial to clients because it encompasses empowerment. This means that the client has to develop some skills that will assist him or her to face future problematic situations without seeking the assistance of a social worker. This approach can be used at all the levels of social work intervention, namely at individual, family, group and community levels. When using this approach, the practitioner engages the client system in a process of development towards an improved quality of life, emanating from improved social functioning.

5.3.2   The strengths perspective

Social work has been, for many years, practised from the medical model, which denied the client systems the opportunity to be empowered. In the medical model the client systems became the recipients of the services and were not involved in the process of exploring and planning the change process. This led to dependency that made the client systems rely on the social worker and unable to develop any skills to equip themselves to address their own problematic situations in future. This could have been the case because of the individualistic approach that was used to address the client systems' problems. This entailed a focus on the client alone without considering the social context. Social work has now shifted from this individualistic approach to address the client systems' problems within their social contexts and consider the inherent strengths that every person possesses.

The strengths perspective challenges social workers to see every person as having some inherent strengths, regardless of the nature of the problem he or she might be experiencing at the time when contact is made with the social worker. In considering these strengths, the client system is regarded as the expert who will assist the social worker in understanding his or her situation better, by sharing personal experiences with the social worker. The medical model sees the client system as having an "illness" or "weakness" that needs to be diagnosed and fixed, while the strengths perspective sees the client as having strengths that need to be uncovered and then used to change the problematic situation they are experiencing. The social worker uses his or her professional skills and knowledge to assist the client system to explore these strengths, as well as those in the social environment, and then use them to address the problematic situation. In the process of identifying the strengths of the client system, the weaknesses are also identified. The social worker has to assist the client to maximise the strengths and minimise the weaknesses. A focus on the weaknesses is found to impair the worker's capacity to identify the client systems' potential to grow (Zastrow, 2014:52). In this process clients are helped to enhance their self-esteem, which is so important for them to go on in life, and not see themselves as failures.

According to Saleeby (as cited in Zastrow, 2014:53; Kirst-Ashman, 2013:63) there are five principles that guide the strengths perspective. They are as follows:

1. **Every individual, group, family and community has strengths**.

    Every person is born with strengths, which may be suppressed by the unfavourable circumstances that they are exposed to in life. It then becomes important for the social worker to bear this in mind when working with clients, irrespective of where they come from or what they are experiencing. By seeking social work intervention, the client needs to be assisted in discovering these strengths so that there can be an improvement in their life situation.

2. **Trauma and abuse, illness and struggle may cause pain and suffering but they may also be sources of challenge and opportunity.**

   Traumatic situations push people to grow because during the process of dealing with them, new coping skills are developed. Therefore, it becomes important to note that people tend to develop after experiencing trauma. It is rare that a person will emerge out of a traumatic situation still the same. Trauma is painful and not wished for, but it challenges the person to grow. It is after the crisis that a person is able to do things differently, because the experience forces him or her to develop some new ways of dealing with things that are unpleasant. With this in mind, the social worker is able to enable the client to use the traumatic situation to develop new skills, instead of giving up on life.

3. **Social workers should assume that they do not know the upper limits of the capacity to grow and change, and take individual's, group's, family's and community's hopes and dreams seriously.**

   With this principle it becomes clear that as much as the social worker has knowledge and skills, he or she is not equipped to measure the desire and the capacity of the client systems to change. The social worker must ensure that the vision and hopes of the client are explored and that every effort is made towards achieving them is taken with the involvement of the client. This will encourage the client to develop hope in the change process and in a way become motivated to work towards that desired change.

4. **Social workers best serve clients by collaborating with them.**

   In the helping process, the social worker needs to see him- or herself as a partner with the client, to avoid the relationship being characterised by superiority-inferiority. This type of relationship makes the client see him- or herself as a victim and the social worker as the rescuer, which does not allow the helping relationship to foster growth. In a collaborative relationship, the client owns the process and sees the social worker as a facilitator of the desired change. This can motivate the client system to develop ownership of the problematic situation and the process of having it resolved, with the help of the social worker.

5. **Every environment is full of resources.**

   No matter how intense or serious the problematic situation, there will always be resources in the environment that can be utlised to assist the helping process. This calls for the social worker to explore and identify these resources and ultimately link the client systems with them. At times these resources are within the client him- or herself but obscured by the problematic situation. This is the reason why the client's strengths need to be explored and then maximised.

These five principles highlight the importance of recognising clients as partners who need to be assisted to improve their life situations, and considering clients' social contexts as they have an impact on their lives. The shift from pathology to strengths assists the social worker in recognising the inborn strengths of the client and maximising them for the benefit of the client. The strengths perspective is closely linked to the idea of empowerment.

5.3.3 Empowerment approach

Empowerment is a process of helping individuals, families, groups or communities to increase their interpersonal, personal, political and socioeconomic power. Social workers can empower clients:

- personally, by helping them to take control of their lives through changing their personal thinking patterns, feelings and behaviour
- interpersonally, by assisting them to manage their relationships more effectively
- politically, by helping them to change their manner of interacting with larger systems.

According to Parsons (as cited in Walsh, 2010:24), empowerment has the following three aspects:
1. It is a developmental process ranging from individual growth to social change.
2. It is in part a psychological state characterised by feelings of self-esteem, self-value and control over one's life.
3. It may involve liberation from oppressive aspects in the client's life.

The social worker should help the client to become aware of internal (within him- or herself) and external (in his or her social environments) conflicts and tensions so as to enable the client to free him- or herself from those constraints.

Lee (1994:27–28) found the principles of the empowerment approach to be as follows:

- **All oppression is destructive of life and should be challenged by social workers and clients.**
  It is clear that oppression has been one of the characteristics of the South African nation, leading to division and disempowerment of the majority of the citizens of the country. With this in mind, the social worker must always aim to assist clients to regain their power through engaging them in a process of developing skills so that they can believe in themselves. It is important for every person to believe in his or her inner ability to do things for him- or herself, for him or her to ultimately stand up for his or her rights.

- **The social worker should maintain holistic vision in situations of oppression.**
  With the history of division in South Africa, the majority of citizens are still oppressed by poverty and economic inequality. Again, with the high level of poverty in the country, many people are still not in control of their lives. They depend on the government for survival through the social grants that they receive. These are the people who make up the bulk of social workers' case loads, therefore the social worker needs to ensure that he or she maintains a clear vision when interacting with these people. The vision should be to liberate them from their state of helplessness by empowering them. Empowerment of these people could be achieved by engaging them in social and economic development, which could assist them in believing in their innate ability to take charge of their lives and not depend on the government. In this case, the social worker could involve these people in income generating projects that could ultimately empower them economically. The social worker can also use growth groups to facilitate growth in these people.

- **People empower themselves; social workers should assist.**
  It is true that people have the ability to empower themselves, they only need the social worker to facilitate this process of change. This principle goes together with the self-determination principle as one of the social work principles. In this process of change, the social worker should allow the client to take control by assisting him or her in identifying his or her strengths and focusing on them. If these strengths are identified and maximised, the client will be able to take a lead in the process of change.

- **People who share common ground need each other to attain empowerment.**
  As it has been indicated above, the social worker can use group work and community work as the means to facilitate change leading to empowerment. (These methods are discussed in detail in Chapters 7 and 8.)

- **Social workers should establish an "I and I" relationship with their clients.**
  As it has already been emphasised in the helping process earlier, the relationship between the social worker and the client plays an important role in the process of change. This relationship must be one in which the client feels he or she is a unique and respected human being who has the right to share his or her views without any fear of being judged.

- **Social work should encourage the client to state his or her situation in his or her own words.** The social worker has an important role to play here in ensuring that the client is able to talk about his or her situation in his or her own words, according to how the problematic situation is experienced (and not to say what he or she believes the social worker has to hear). There has to be an environment that says to the client "you are free to express yourself for your problem to be clearly understood".
- **The social worker should maintain a focus on the person as victor and not a victim.** In the process of empowerment, the social worker should focus on encouraging the client to see him- or herself as someone who has the ability to overcome the undesirable situation he or she finds him- or herself in. The client must be able to believe in him- or herself as having the ability to change and not see him- or herself as a victim of circumstance, waiting to be rescued. In this principle the social worker has to effectively use the enabler role. (The enabler role is discussed in Chapter 1.)
- **The social worker should maintain a social change focus.** With this focus in mind, the social worker will be able to encourage the client to focus on the process of change through believing that he or she has the ability to change, as has been alluded to above.

These principles show how the empowerment process has to be allowed to enable the desired change to unfold in the client's life. In using them, the social worker will be able to guide the process of change for the benefit of the client and at the end of the process the client will be able to stand on his or her own and not depend on any person to deal with his or her challenging situation.

It is a fact that most of the client systems approaching social workers for assistance are from vulnerable groups, as identified in the White Paper for Social Welfare (1997). With poverty being a serious problem in South Africa and the current economic state of the country, social workers have to deal with people who have experienced a prolonged period of lack of resources leading to their impaired social functioning. They also lack the power to change their circumstances or their environments, sometimes having reached a point of apathy, where they feel helpless and hopeless. Focusing on the weaknesses of such people reinforces the feeling of helplessness, therefore, the social worker has to create an environment for the client systems to realise that they have the capacity to change their situation, with the help of a social worker. Empowerment gives clients hope and motivates them to focus on changing their life situations. At the time of termination of the helping process the client system must be able to stand and move forward with confidence that developed from the interaction with the social worker.

5.3.4   Ecological-systems perspective

The ecological-systems perspective is widely used in social work because it assists social workers in understanding their client systems in totality. It refers to a combination of the concepts of the systems theory with those of the ecological theory. In this perspective the client system is viewed as an entity that is in constant interaction with its environment being influenced and also influencing the environment. According to Segal, Gerdes and Steiner (2013:150) "the ecological-systems perspective requires the social workers to understand their client systems in the context of the social systems and people that they interact with." The social worker has to make all the efforts to understand every system that the client system interacts with and the impact of the interaction on the client system. The social context of the client system plays an important role in the helping process because there is no point in the client's life where the social context can be removed. It keeps on changing but is always part of the client's life. As a result, during the exploration step discussed earlier on, the social worker has to ensure that all the systems that the client interacts with, as well as the impact they have on each other (client and the social environment), are explored. This assists the social worker in making the correct assessment that will guide the helping process accordingly, and ultimately set goals that are appropriate to meeting the needs of the client system.

The ecological-systems perspective is used by generalist social work practitioners, where different roles are used to address the needs of the client systems. In the case study above, some of the roles and how they could be used have been indicated. The generalist practitioner using this perspective is able to make an indepth assessment of the client system's problematic situation, which is so crucial to ensuring intervention that is responsive to specific needs.

It is also important to see the individual client as a system, because a person has a number of dimensions that influence his or her behaviour. A person has a physical dimension, an emotional dimension, a psychological dimension, and a spiritual dimension. All these dimensions are in interaction with one another and further influence how the client will react to certain situations. It then becomes very important to attend to these dimensions during the exploration and assessment steps of the helping process.

5.3.5   Problem-solving approach

The problem-solving approach is a step-by-step thinking and acting process that involves moving from an undesired to a desired state. It is important to note that this theory was influenced by the cognitive theory as well as the psychoanalytic understanding of human behaviour. With this theory in mind the social worker recognises the clients' capacities to use their ability to think in order to attain the goals they desire and value. In this process the clients are able to use the information obtained from the environment to design ways of meeting their needs, with the help of the social worker. This theory focuses on the belief that every person has a desire to have his or her needs met, and this makes it a widely used approach in social work practice. It takes the client's input into consideration. This approach is relevant to the developmental approach, because it focuses on the social worker facilitating change in clients by first recognising their innate ability to address their own problems.

This approach is said to have originated and developed from the work of Helen Harris Perlman in the 1950s, who later published a book in 1957, titled *Social Casework*: *A Problem Solving Process*, which made a great contribution with regard to this as a recognised social work theory (Turner & Jaco,1996:503). This approach emphasises the process of helping the client to change his or her problematic situation and this process unfolds in steps. In the problem-solving approach the client is required to move from simply talking and identifying his or her problematic situation, towards taking action to resolve the situation. According to Ambrosino *et al.* (2012:110) "this approach holds that the success of this process depends on the motivation, capacity and opportunity of the client to change." Without motivation the client is unable to make progress towards change.

According to Shier (2011:366), the problem-solving model has been refined by Compton and Galaway in their work of 1994 and the model unfolds as follows:

5.3.5.1   Step 1: Contact phase

During this phase, problem identification occurs. The problem is firstly identified by the client, who then approaches the social worker. Together they agree on what the problem to be addressed is. After defining the problem the goal to be achieved is then set, having taken into consideration the resources available to be used in addressing the problem. The contract is then agreed upon, which clarifies the agency's resources and commitment to addressing the identified problem. Also during this phase the social worker has to explore the client's motivation, available opportunities as well as the capacity to address the problem. Without the client's motivation to affect change in the problematic situation, it will be next to impossible for the social worker to facilitate the change process.

5.3.5.2   Step 2: Contract phase
The assessment and evaluation are said to take place during this phase. Efforts are made by the social worker to understand the client system's problem clearly. This is followed by the formulation of the plan of action, where the social worker tries to set attainable goals, examine the alternatives and their likely outcomes and then clarify the roles to be played by the client and those to be played by the social worker. At this stage, it is also for the social worker to evaluate the hope of attaining the set goals based on the available resources and the client's motivation and capacity to change.

5.3.5.3   Step 3: Action phase
It is during this phase that the actual carrying out of the contract, which was agreed on in the previous step, takes place. Again, during this phase the social worker needs to explore the available resources as well as the different roles to be played and the relevant role-players to play them, in order for the problem to be resolved. After the plan has been carried out, the social worker and the client have to evaluate whether the problem has been resolved, what helped and what did not help in the process, as well as what needs to be done to maintain this positive change. The social worker together with the client has to explore the support systems that are available for the client to maintain the attained results. This is followed by the termination of the process.

The above process begins with a problem and ends with a solution, but it does not unfold in a linear fashion. This means that the social worker together with the client may go back and forth between the stipulated phases. For example, it might happen that at the action phase some information is lacking that was supposed to have been collected during the contact phase. Then the best way would be to explore that information, and to ensure that the process becomes responsive to the real problem of the client. This becomes possible because of the continuous evaluation that forms part and parcel of every intervention process. Evaluation assists in ensuring that appropriate actions are taken at the appropriate times.

The problem-solving process as presented here must not be confused with the helping process that has been presented earlier on in this chapter. This process is unique to the problem-solving approach and the process presented earlier is relevant for generalist intervention and does not focus on a particular theory.

5.3.6   Task-centred approach

"The task-centred approach is said to be born out of the work of William Reid and Laura Epstein in 1972" (Healy, 2005:108). It was intended for therapeutic intervention with individuals and families who voluntarily commit to the social work intervention process, but has later been extended to a broader range of settings, including statutory work. Task-centred social work can be seen as a short-term treatment approach that is aimed at achieving specific tasks within a stipulated timeframe. It demands that social workers and clients concentrate to a greater extent on having the problem resolved. This is accomplished by putting focus on specific tasks that are aimed at having the problematic situation resolved. Its emphasis is on the careful selection of specific tasks that have to be accomplished within a specific timeframe, to ensure problem solving. Teater (2010:178) sees the fundamental nature of task-centred social work intervention to be "a collaborative process between social workers and their clients to alleviate explicit problems that are acknowledged and understood by both parties." In this process, the parties establish goals that are personally meaningful to them and develop tasks to be completed in an effort to alleviate the problem. The task-centred theory helps clients to build confidence and self-esteem through experiencing small successes in completing tasks along the journey of alleviating their problems. Ambrosino *et al.* (2012:112) see the task-centred approach as "an action model designed to engage the client quickly and meaningfully in the identifying, confronting and acting on the problem."

There are specific key principles and characteristics that are put forth as unique to the task-centred approach (Healy, 2005:113–117). These basic principles and characteristics are discussed briefly as follows:

5.3.6.1   Seek mutual clarity with service users
It is always important to ensure that there is clarity regarding the purpose of the interaction between the client and the social worker. This fosters the development of a well-grounded, helping relationship that is based on trust and mutual understanding. The social worker has the responsibility to facilitate the process of clarifying the purpose of the interaction as this leads to appropriate intervention efforts. It is also important to ensure that there is an establishment of a contract between the social worker and the client to ensure that they know exactly why they are interacting and who is responsible for which tasks. This enhances the positive progress towards resolving the agreed-upon problem.

5.3.6.2   Aim for small achievements rather than large changes
With this principle, the focus is on breaking down the goal into smaller tasks for the client to address one at a time within a specific timeframe. As illustrated in the case study at the beginning of this chapter, the client system that approaches the social worker is sometimes experiencing complex problems that cannot be addressed entirely at one time. Due to the complexity of these problems, client systems become overwhelmed and sometimes reach the point of helplessness. It then becomes the social worker's responsibility to engage them in a process of helping them to regain their self-worth. Agreeing with the client on the small tasks assists the client to believe in him- or herself once these small tasks are successfully accomplished.

5.3.6.3   Focus on the 'here and now'
The social worker facilitates the process of change in the client's life by focusing on the 'here and now'. This shifts the focus from the past history of the client and focuses on the present to ensure that change takes place. The social worker focuses only on the aspects of history that have an influence on the current state of affairs to affect change.

5.3.6.4   Promote collaboration between worker and service users
This principle emphasises the importance of the participation of the client in the helping process. The social worker and the client have to form a partnership in the whole intervention process. Each has specific tasks that he or she has to accomplish in order for the problematic situation to be resolved. With this partnership the client is helped to develop and be actively involved in the change process. When the client sees him- or herself as a valued partner it becomes easy to own the process and ensure that it succeeds.

5.3.6.5   Build client capacities for action

The social worker uses this principle to assist the client in developing some new problem-solving skills. It has to be remembered that before the client decides to approach the social worker for professional help, he or she has tried several strategies to address the problem that might have not yielded the desired results. This can lead to the feeling of helplessness which has to be done away with through the helping process. This then calls for the social worker to facilitate the process of developing new skills in the client, for these skills to be used to address the problematic situation. This is beneficial for the client when considering the fact that some of the problems experienced by clients originate from their environment, for example unjust structural conditions created by the political sphere of the clients' environments.

5.3.6.6   Planned brevity

This principle refers to a well-planned programme aimed at addressing and changing the client's problematic situation. This planned programme stipulates specific goals and tasks to be attained, including the specific timeframe. The well-planned programme assists the involved parties to focus on what has to be done, within the stipulated timeframe. Both parties benefit from this well-planned programme because the service provider organisation will save costs and the client will have the problematic situation changed within a short space of time.

5.3.6.7   Promote systematic and structured approaches to intervention

The aim of this principle is to ensure that the intervention process is well-structured and time limited. The intervention process also proceeds systematically and sequentially because of the clarity between the social worker and the client that has been established at the beginning of the helping process. It is also important to realise that the utilisation of scientifically tested intervention strategies facilitates the change process within a short space of time.

5.3.6.8   Adopt a scientific approach to practise evaluation

Due to the responsibility that goes together with social work intervention, the practitioner has to ensure that accountability is upheld throughout the intervention process. This can be achieved by constantly reviewing and monitoring the helping process, using the scientifically tested methods. This calls for social workers to always be accountable to their clients as well as their employers by ensuring that the service they provide brings change in the client's life within a stipulated timeframe. It must not be assumed that the helping process has brought about change – this has to be scientifically ascertained.

It is clear from these basic principles of the task-centred approach that the social work intervention process within this theoretical framework has to be specific and time-limited, with the active involvement of the client.

5.3.7   Psychosocial theory

Psychosocial treatment in social work originated from the work of Mary Richmond and transformed through the integration of new and evolving knowledge in the human sciences. According to Robinson and Kaplan (2011:387) "the psychosocial treatment was also transformed by the integration of a set of empirically derived treatment procedures that have now become the standard techniques of both generalist and advanced social work practice." This notion refers to the utilisation of what is known as fundamental to the social work profession, namely:

- the technique of engagement
- the importance of empathy and the helping relationship
- factual exploration of the client's problem
- the importance of thorough assessment
- the importance of understanding human development and behaviour
- transference in the helping relationship
- the important role played by the social environment in the person's problematic situation.

The psychosocial theory is based on systematic thinking and affords the social worker the opportunity to adopt a comprehensive way of addressing the clients' problematic situations, utilising a variety of techniques. The intervention process is always based on the needs of a particular client at a particular time. The needs are explored and agreed upon between the social worker and the client, as well as the goals to be achieved. This is a collaborative process between the social worker and the client. Robinson and Kaplan (2011:389) are of the opinion that "the social worker has to motivate and facilitate clients to be self-directed and active participants in the process of change."

The psychosocial approach takes into consideration the relationship between the client and his or her environment. This emphasises the important role played by the interaction that the client is always engaged in with his or her environment, which has an impact on his or her behaviour at a given time. This approach is closely linked to the ecological-systems perspective discussed above, where the person-in-environment becomes the focus when dealing with the problematic situations of the client. The interaction between the system and its environment cannot be overemphasised because there is no point in a person's life when he or she can be divorced from his or her environment.

5.3.8 Person-centred approach

The person-centred approach was initially known as the client-centred approach and was conceptualised by Carl Rogers in the 1940s. These two concepts are sometimes used interchangeably. Person-centred approach deals with the self or identity of the individual, group or community. According to Sharf (as cited in Kirst-Ashman, 2013:419) "the person-centred approach takes a positive view of individuals, believing that they tend to move towards becoming fully functioning." The focus of this theory is not to change people but to create an environment in which people can feel safe to explore themselves and then decide if they want to change. The role of the social worker using this model is to facilitate the change process.

Grobler and Schenck (2009:4) indicate that "this theory looks at those experiences that the client cannot allow into his or her conscious mind, because they threaten the client's perception of who he or she is." In order for the client to ultimately deal with these experiences the social worker needs to create a safe environment and unconditionally accept the client. In this safe environment the client will be relaxed and then begin the journey of self-discovery, followed by the reconstruction of the self to a more acceptable perspective of the self. The worker is seen as the facilitator of change in the whole helping process and must assist the client in dealing with the experiences that threaten the self through the use of basic and advanced communication skills, propositions as well as the professional values.

According to Patterson (2012:225) "the person-centred model uses three basic theoretical principles" discussed below:

5.3.8.1   Human nature

This principle indicates that practitioners adopt a way of intervening influenced by his or her anthropological background. Rogers' theory is based on the intrinsic, inherent and fundamental organismic drive of the human being to live to his or her fullest potential. It is therefore important for the social worker using this model to take human nature into consideration when engaging in the helping process with clients. This inherent drive must be explored and used for the benefit of the client.

5.3.8.2   Core conditions sustaining person-centred theory and the role of the therapist

According to this principle, people are born with the ability to understand themselves and direct their lives positively, depending on the relationships they are engaged in. This notion then calls for the practitioner to ensure that he or she establishes a professional relationship with the client (discussed in Chapter 6). These conditions are said to allow the practitioner and the client to be engaged in a shared journey of self-discovery of their humaneness and participate in a journey of growth together. It is only in a safe environment that the client will be able to explore him- or herself and identify the needs to be changed, followed by efforts towards change.

5.3.8.3   Self-actualisation

Self-actualisation is a life-long process, inherent in every human being, of realising one's full potential. It is believed that every person is born with the resources for personal growth, so when the person is experiencing problematic situations in life, the social worker has to facilitate the process of uncovering these resources. This is achieved through establishing a conducive environment for the client to feel free to explore and then begin the journey of self-development.

The person-centred theory assists the social worker in realising the inherent desire and capacity of every person to grow. This enables the social worker not to see the client as a hopeless case and then assume all the responsibility towards change. The social worker's role is only to facilitate the process of self-discovery and the change process.

5.3.9   Crisis intervention

Crisis intervention is a process of intervention that is based on the crisis theory, which states that individuals have the capacity to cope with their stressful situations, but in some instances these stressful events could be so intense and beyond the coping capabilities of individuals, leading to a state of disequilibrium. When an individual is in this state, he or she needs external assistance to assist him or her in improving the coping capability. According to Teater (2010:196) the goal of crisis intervention is to address the crisis with coping strategies, and to help individuals to draw upon newly identified strengths, resources and coping mechanisms when faced with stressors in future. It is also important to mention that crisis intervention is a short-term intervention process that is aimed at addressing the crisis as perceived and experienced by the client system.

Crisis intervention as a theory and method was developed by American psychiatrists in the 1940s namely Erich Lindemann and Gerald Caplan (Teater, 2010:197; Walsh, 2010:302). This theory was developed based on the research that was conducted on the reactions and grieving processes of the survivors and families who lost their loved ones in the Coconut Grove night club fire in Boston. From this research it was concluded that the length and outcome of a grief reaction depend on the person's time to mourn, adjustment to the changed environment and eventually the development of new relationships. This confirms the notion that from a crisis situation a person develops new strengths and coping mechanisms. It could be argued that the crisis that is experienced by a human being creates an opportunity for growth. Even if it is not pleasant, it shakes a person to move from his or her comfort zone. This can be linked to the strengths perspective that states that crisis and pain challenge the individual to develop new coping skills, as the current ones are not always able to assist.

5.3.9.1   Basic assumptions of the crisis theory

According to the crisis theorists Golan; Parad and Parad; and Roberts (as cited in Teater, 2010:199–200) the following are the basic assumptions of the crisis theory:

- Systems encounter stressful events throughout their lifespans, challenging the systems to utilise existing strengths, resources and coping mechanisms to address events to decrease the negative impact thereof.
- Each system uses its strengths, resources and coping mechanisms, when faced with difficulties or stressful events, to maintain its balance.
- Systems can encounter a stressful event that is beyond their usual experience of stressful situations. Trying to reduce the negative impact of the event can lead to a disturbed balance, known as a crisis state.
- A crisis state is overcome by intervening in the acute state and building on the system's strength, resources and coping mechanisms, which can be used to lessen the negative impact of the event and also be used to deal with future stressful events.

These assumptions attest to the fact that each system makes an effort to maintain its equilibrium, in the event of stressful events that are so inevitable in the lifespan of each system. Each system has its inner strengths and coping mechanisms that are utilised when stressful events are encountered, and when they fail to alleviate the negative consequences of these events, there is a need for the system to be assisted to develop new coping skills and inner strengths. This can be achieved through the use of crisis intervention theory.

5.3.9.2   Major concepts in the crisis intervention theory

It is important to discuss the major concepts in this theory to facilitate the understanding and application thereof.

5.3.9.2.1   Stress

Stress is defined by Lazarus and Lazarus (as cited in Walsh, 2010:304) as "an event in which environmental or internal demands tax or exceed a person's coping resources." The event might be social (disruption in the social structure), biological (disruption caused by a sudden illness), or psychological (cognitive or emotional). All these disturbances interfere with the stability that the individual was enjoying, resulting in a crisis situation, where the coping patterns are shaken. How a person experiences stress depends on the biological makeup of the person as well as previous experiences in managing stressful situations. Vulnerability to stress is related to the social state of a person within the social structure, for example a person experiencing poverty is exposed to unbearable conditions that make him or her prone to stress.

5.3.9.2.2   Crisis

Crisis can be defined as an individual's perception or experience of an event as an intolerable difficulty. The intensity thereof depends on the perception of the individual experiencing the event, who finds him- or herself lacking in inner strength and coping capacity. It is important to note that in a crisis situation, each individual's response will always be unique, challenging the social worker intervening in the person's situation to observe the principle of individual-isation at all times. When the crisis is experienced, the individual tries to address it, but fails to overcome it. The increase in internal tension leads to an openness to external assistance.

5.3.9.3 Types of crises

It is also very important to refer to the different types of crises, namely, developmental, situational and existential crises (Walsh, 2010:305). These types are discussed briefly as follows:

- Developmental crisis emanates from the normal developmental stages of life, where the individual experiences internal stress due to the changes in his or her life. An example of the situation that might lead to a crisis is when a person leaves home for the first time to further his or her studies after passing matric. For a person who has been staying with his or her parents for the whole of his or her life, it may be traumatic to go and stay at a students' residence. The intensity of this crisis depends on the perception that the person has of his or her new situation. If it is perceived as scary, then the crisis will be intense, and the person will need to be assisted to develop new coping strategies to survive.
- Situational crisis emanates from an uncommon event that a person could not foresee. This situation happens abruptly and disturbs the person's equilibrium. For example, no person anticipates illness, sexual assault, loss of a loved one or loss of a job. These situations unsettle a person, and existing coping strategies are rendered inadequate. This calls for external intervention for the person to be assisted to develop new coping mechanisms.
- Existential crisis is experienced when a person faces an escalating inner tension related to issues of purpose in life, independence, freedom or commitment. Sometimes in life a person may have regrets regarding the choices that he or she has made. These choices may be seen as having influenced the individual's current life situation, and a sense of lack of purpose might be intense. For example, recently we have seen a number of reported cases of Satanist activities, where young people were engaged in activities that resulted in the death of one of them, and then some of them regretted their involvement. Some of them experienced intense conflict to the extent of contemplating suicide.

James and Gilliland state that individuals may respond in three patterns to a crisis situation (as cited in Walsh, 2010:305):

1. One individual may freeze, meaning that the person does not improve but makes adjust-ments that may be harmful to his or her life, for example abusing substances in order to escape the reality of his or her situation. This person will find it difficult to address his or her situation, leading to an escalated crisis situation.
2. Another individual may adopt the growth pattern, where new coping skills are developed with the help of a professional helper. This person will be able to cope with other stressful situations in future because of the new coping strategies and skills that were developed due to a crisis.
3. The last pattern of responding to a crisis is the equilibrium one, where the person returns to the pre-crisis state, without any improved functioning. There is no change in this indi-vidual except that he or she survived the crisis.

5.3.9.4 The stages in the crisis intervention model

The following is the seven-stage crisis intervention model as indicated by Teater (2010:200–203).

5.3.9.4.1 Stage 1: Plan and conduct crisis assessment

This stage involves a thorough biopsychosocial assessment of the client's state, including all the aspects that might be part of the client's state. The client must be assessed for the use of any substances as well as any self-inflicted harm or any intention of harm, including suicide. The social worker must be clear regarding any suicidal thoughts by attentively listening and analysing what the client is saying and exploring whether there is any plan in place to be implemented. The available resources and support in the client's environment must also be explored, so as to utilise them to assist the client in drawing some strength.

5.3.9.4.2 Stage 2: Establish the therapeutic relationship

This stage is very important to enable the social worker to collect information from the client. It therefore takes place in conjunction with the first stage. Of importance is to remember that there cannot be any assessment before information collection and information collection cannot happen before the establishment of the therapeutic relationship. The social work basic skills (in Chapter 6) and professional values (in Chapter 4) are used to establish this relationship.

5.3.9.4.3 Stage 3: Identify the dimensions of the presenting problem

It is important to collect information regarding the crisis situation as seen by the client and any precipitating events. The core of this stage is to get clarity regarding what the client is going through, whether the current situation has been experienced before, and if so, how it was handled, and what is different about the current situation that led to the state of the client.

5.3.9.4.4 Stage 4: Explore and address feelings and emotions

During this stage, the focus is on exploring the client's feelings and emotions, pertaining to the experienced situation, and addressing them. This happens in conjunction with the previous stage, where the focus is on gathering information because the information cannot be separated from the feelings and emotions. What the client is experiencing is accompanied by feelings and emotions, so it becomes very important to take cognisance thereof. In doing this, the social worker utilises active listening as well as all the other basic communication skills (discussed in Chapter 6).

5.3.9.4.5 Stage 5: Generate and explore alternatives

The social worker focuses on generating and exploring alternatives that could address the client's situation. This becomes possible if the strengths and previous coping skills have been established, because the focus is on enhancing the client's existing strengths and coping capacity. In going through this stage the social worker has to ensure that the client's feelings and emotions pertaining to each alternative are explored and attended to. Of importance is to note that this is a collaborative process that calls for the total involvement of the client.

5.3.9.4.6 Stage 6: Develop an action plan and its implementation

After the alternatives have been generated and explored, then the action plan is agreed upon and implemented. In some cases the social worker might have to take action, based on the inability of the client to make a decision. For example, when a client is mentally unfit to make decisions, the social worker has to implement the action of having the client hospitalised. In this stage, it can also be that an agency or person is identified, where the client will continue to receive assistance and support.

5.3.9.4.7   Stage 7: Establish a follow-up plan and agreement

After the action plan has been implemented it becomes necessary to follow up on the client's state after the intervention, so as to ensure that the crisis state is resolved. This can be done through telephonic or face-to-face contact. It is important for the social worker to establish whether his or her intervention efforts assisted the client in alleviating the negative impact of the crisis in the client's life.

Crisis intervention is a short-term process aimed at assisting the client in attaining a state of equilibrium (that was disturbed by a crisis situation or event). It taps into the client's existing strengths and coping mechanisms, with the aim of maximising them.

5.4   Conclusion

This chapter focused on the helping process in general, without focusing on any specific model, approach, perspective or theory. It addressed the important concepts in the social work helping process, the social work helping process from the generalist perspective, the different steps involved in the helping process, the important role of assessment in the helping process, the importance of cultural sensitive social work in the helping process, as well as the common theories, models, approaches and perspectives used in social work practice.

End of chapter questions

1. Select one theory, perspective or approach that you believe is most suitable to address Lesego's situation.
2. In your application of this theory, perspective or approach, identify the important aspects that are more applicable to this case.

Key concepts

*   **Social work intervention** refers to the efforts made by the social worker to assist the client in addressing his or her problematic situation, through employing the necessary social work knowledge, skills and professional values
*   **Assessment** refers to the process of scrutinising the information given by the client to ultimately identify the actual problem that the client has brought to the social worker's attention
*   The **helping process** refers to the process that unfolds as the social worker and the client attend to the problematic situation that the client has brought to the attention of the social worker. This process begins with the intake phase and ends with the disengagement phase, when the social worker and the client agree on terminating the process.
*   **Crisis intervention** refers to the helping process that the social worker and the client embark on in the case of the client experiencing a crisis that has disturbed his or her balance.
*   **Generalist social work practice** refers to social work practice in which the social worker is able to intervene in clients' problematic situations using a variety of skills from different social work theories. This intervention can take place in any field or setting of social work practice. It is different from specialist social work practice.
*   **Eclectic knowledge base**, in social work terms, refers to an integrated approach to social work practice, in which the social worker employs knowledge and skills from different social work theories in an effort to engage the client in the process of change.

- The **helping relationship** is the professional relationship that the social worker has to establish with the client to ensure that the helping process unfolds in an environment characterised by trust
- **Cultural sensitive social work practice** refers to a situation in which the social worker recognises the importance of respecting the client's culture in the process of intervention. This requires the social worker to have gone through a process of self-awareness in as far as different cultural practices are concerned, for him or her to recognise his or her own biases and prejudices.
- **Empathy** is a skill that a social worker has to always use in the intervention process in an effort to understand the client's feelings as well as the content of the problematic situation. When using this skill, the social worker communicates his or her understanding to the client to confirm whether what he or she heard and observed is correct according to the client's understanding.
- **Empowerment** is a concept often used within the developmental approach and it refers to an effort of ensuring that the client is assisted to develop new skills and knowledge to enable the client to address future problems without relying on the social worker's intervention.

References

1. AMBROSINO, R., AMBROSINO, R., HEFFERNAN, J. & SHUTTLESWORTH, G. 2012. *Social work and social welfare: an introduction.* 7th ed. Canada: Thomson Brooks.
2. GROBLER, H. & SCHENCK, R. 2009. *Person-centred facilitation*: process, theory and practice. Cape Town: Oxford University Press.
3. HEALY, K. 2005. *Social work theories in context: creating frameworks for practice.* New York: Palgrave MacMillan.
4. KIRST-ASHMAN, K.K. 2013. *Introduction to social work & social welfare: critical thinking perspectives.* 4th ed. Canada: Brooks/Cole Cengage Learning.
5. LEE, J.A.B. 1994. *The empowerment approach to social work practice.* New York: Columbia Press.
6. PATTERSON, C.A. 2012. Person-centred theory. (In Thyer, B.A., Dulmus, C.N. & Sowers, K.M. *Human behavior in the social environment: theories for social work practice.* Canada: John Wiley & Sons. p. 225–259.)
7. REID, W.J. 1996. Task-centred social work. (*In* Turner, F.J. *Social work treatment: interlocking theoretical approaches.* 4th ed. New York: The Free Press. p. 513–532.)
8. ROBINSON, H. & KAPLAN, C. 2011. Psychosocial theory and social work treatment. (*In* Turner, F.J. *Social work treatment: interlocking theoretical approaches.* 5th ed. New York: The Free Press. p. 387–400.)
9. SEGAL, E.A., GERDES, K.E. & STEINER, S. 2013. *An Introduction to the profession of social work: becoming a change agent.* 4th ed. USA: Brooks/Cole Cengage Learning.
10. SHEAFOR, B.W. & HORESJI, C.R. 2012. *Techniques and guidelines for social work practice.* 9th ed. New Jersey: Allyn & Bacon.
11. SHIER, M.L. 2011. Problem-solving and social work. (*In* Turner, F.J. *Social work treatment*: *interlocking theoretical approaches.* 5th ed. New York: The Free Press. p. 364–373.)
12. TEATER, B. 2010. *An introduction to applying social work theories and methods.* New York: Open University Press.

13. TURNER, J. & JACO, R.M. 1996. Problem-solving theory and social work treatment (*In* Turner, F.J. *Social work treatment: interlocking theoretical approaches.* 4th ed. New York: The Free Press. p. 503–522.)
14. WALSH, J. 2010. *Direct social work practice.* 2nd ed. Canada: Wadsworth Cengage Learning.
15. ZASTROW, C. 2014. *Introduction to social work and welfare: empowering people.* 11th ed. Canada: Brooks/Cole Cengage Learning.
16. ZASTROW, C.H. & KIRST-ASHMAN, K.K. 2013. *Understanding human behavior and the social environment.* 9th ed. China: Brooks/Cole Cengage Learning.

Case work: Social work with individuals

Johannah Sekudu

CHAPTER OUTCOMES

By the end of this chapter, you should be able to:

✓ describe case work as one of the primary methods of social work

✓ discuss the development of social work with individuals (case work)

✓ identify and apply the basic skills needed by social workers to intervene in clients' troubled lives on an individual level (micro-level)

✓ describe and apply the intervention strategies used in social work with individuals

✓ apply the different theories used in social work intervention with individuals.

 Case Study 6.1 **Tsakani**

Tsakani is a 55-year-old lady from a rural area in Limpopo. She recently had to relocate to Diepsloot, near Johannesburg, in search of better economic opportunities. She is a single mother caring for her four grand-children, whose mothers are unable to secure employment due to their lack of skills and the high unemployment rate in the country. The social worker is a young person who was born and raised in an urban area where no strict cultural practices are observed by community members. She completed her schooling and tertiary education in an area where distinct cultures are diluted due to the integration of people from many different cultures. A unique culture in this particular community emerged and was adopted by community members as acceptable. Tsakani arrived at the social worker's office in her traditional XiTsonga attire and when offered a chair she declined as she preferred to sit on the floor. When the social worker tried to persuade her to accept the chair, she felt offended and told the social worker that she is disrespectful. The social worker ignored the comment and tried to focus on why the client visited her office. In an effort to use the social work skills to build the helping relationship, the social worker maintained eye contact with the client, which also offended the client, as this was also seen as disrespectful. The social worker became irritated and her tone of voice changed from a soft and professional to loud and harsh.

6.1 Introduction

This chapter addresses one of the three primary methods of intervention in social work, namely intervention with individuals. The other two, group work and community work, are addressed in Chapters 7 and 8 respectively. In the past, intervention with individuals was commonly known as case work, but now it is referred to as social work intervention with individuals, families and couples. This is social work intervention at the micro-level, which means, intervention on a one-on-one basis with clients and their families. It is important to note that intervention in an individual's life must always include the family, as the person is always in interaction with his or her family members.

The discussion is based on the generalist practice, as a requirement for social work training in the global social work community. This requires training institutions to ensure that at completion of the social work qualification, students are able to practise as generalists, meaning that they must be equipped to address the social issues or problems that clients bring to their attention, using the relevant skills and techniques irrespective of the field they may be employed in.

As generalist practitioners, social workers do not practise as specialists but are equipped with a broad range of social work knowledge, skills and intervention strategies to address any case that is brought to their attention. In cases where the problem requires specialised intervention, the client is referred to a relevant agency. Details on generalist social work practice are given in Chapter 5.

6.2 Case work as a primary method in social work

Mary Richmond is regarded as the founder of case work as a method of intervention in social work. She also formulated the term social case work, which refers to an effort by the social worker to work directly with individuals, on a one-on-one basis, or families, to enhance their wellbeing and social functioning. It is important to realise that an individual cannot be helped without taking his or her family into consideration, because of the continuous interaction that exists between every individual and his or her family. This calls for an involvement of the individual's family throughout the whole helping process to ensure effective intervention. It can be that the individual is experiencing a problematic situation because of his or her interaction with family members, therefore intervention with the individual without the involvement of the family will not yield sustainable solutions. This makes the client's family a very important component in the helping process.

Case work refers to social work intervention at the micro-level, where the social worker intervenes on a one-on-one basis with a single client, including his or her family, who is experiencing some challenges in his or her social functioning. The aim is to help the individual resolve his or her personal and social problems, but sometimes it can be that the individual has to be assisted to adjust to the social environment or the environment has to change to be in harmony with the client's needs. There are times when the imbalance in the client's life emanates from the social environment, demanding intervention in that particular area of the client's life. The point in the life of a client that needs to be the focus of the intervention process is always determined through assessment (as discussed in Chapter 5), when the necessary information pertaining to the client's situation is collected. This emphasises the importance of including the client's social environment in the helping process, which is an approach in social work commonly known as person-in-environment. The client's social environment refers to the immediate people that a person interacts with on a regular basis, for example family members, play mates, school mates and teachers, and colleagues. When there is an imbalance between the individual and his or her social environment, the individual develops some discomfort, and requires professional assistance in dealing with and overcoming the situation. It might be that the individual needs to be assisted in developing some coping skills, or that the environment needs changing, to restore the balance.

Case work is geared towards helping individuals within their families to identify solutions to their problematic situations. It encompasses a variety of activities, depending on the problem that the client presents to the social worker, which is confirmed by a thorough assessment process. It becomes very important for the social worker not to stop at the presenting problem but to go further and explore the client's situation to ultimately reach the actual problem. The presenting problem is the problem that the client presents at the beginning of the helping relationship, before a relationship of trust has been developed. The client uses the presenting problem to test if he or she is accepted by the social worker before he or she moves on to share the actual pain he or she is experiencing. Remember that the social worker is a stranger to the client, so it will not be easy for a client to simply share before a trust relationship has been established. The actual problem is the real problem that brought the client to the social worker's office.

The social worker determines this through careful exploration and assessment of the client's situation. For example, a client could begin by telling the social worker that she is experiencing problems with her children who are troublesome. The social worker may only find out after thorough exploration that the actual problem is an unhealthy relationship between the mother and her children. For the intervention process to be successful, the social worker has to confirm the actual problem with the client.

The intervention process begins with the establishment of the professional relationship, sometimes referred to as the helping relationship, that is discussed in detail in Chapter 5 of this book. This relationship paves the way for the development of trust that enables the client to share his or her problematic situation with the social worker. The steps in the process depend on the theoretical framework adopted by the social worker in addressing the particular problem. (The different theories, perspectives, approaches and models are discussed in Chapter 5.) Of importance is the assessment that has to be done thoroughly to ensure that the actual problem is identified, as indicated above, for appropriate intervention to be effected.

As a primary method in social work, case work is practised in all fields of social work service delivery. (The different fields are discussed in Chapter 9.) It could be said that it forms the basis for social work intervention, but must not be seen in isolation from the other two primary methods, group work and community work.

6.2.1   The development of social work intervention with individuals (case work)

In order to understand case work as a method of intervention in social work practice, it becomes very important to know its beginnings. This will assist in understanding the specific aspects that led to the development of case work as a primary method of intervention in social work. It is also important to note that social case work shares the social work values and principles as well as the communication skills with the other two primary methods of intervention, namely group work and community work. Each method is characterised by specific and unique skills and techniques, which have to be mastered for a person to distinguish him- or herself as a specialist in either of the methods.

Figure 6.1: Social worker addressing a group

According to Daniş and Kirbaç (2013:703) "social work with individuals emerged before social work with groups and community work methods." These primary methods are said to have developed in England and USA before they were adopted in other countries. Mary Ellen Richmond is seen as the person who constructed the foundations for social case work, in her book titled *Social Diagnosis*. "This book marks the beginning of social work intervention with individuals, where the focus was on investigating the causes of poverty and social exclusion in individuals' lives" (Steyaert, 2013). *Social Diagnosis* is seen as the basis for the psychosocial approach in social work intervention with individuals. (The psychosocial approach is discussed in Chapter 5.) In her book, Richmond demonstrates the fact that an individual's problematic situation cannot be understood without taking his or her environment into consideration, which is emphasised by the systems-ecological model as discussed in Chapter 5.

6.2.2   Basic skills and techniques in case work

Basic interpersonal skills form the basis for social work intervention at all levels, including at the micro-level (case work). These skills include culturally competent communication, verbal and non-verbal communication, listening and active listening, warmth, empathy and genuineness. It is important for the social worker to master these skills for him or her to be able to engage with clients in a productive manner and assist them to deal with their problematic situations. The social worker uses these skills to establish the helping relationship that is so crucial in the helping process. In the initial stage of the helping process, clients expose themselves to a stranger (the social worker), so it is not easy for them to open up and share their problems. The social worker must communicate in a way that will develop the client's trust, so that he or she can share his or her story without any feelings of intimidation. Professional values and principles are also important in building this relationship, because clients do not want to be judged, but need to be accepted as they are and be reassured that their stories are not going to be shared with anyone outside the helping relationship. (The professional values and principles are discussed in Chapter 4.) The basic skills and techniques will be discussed one by one to facilitate clear understanding.

6.2.2.1   Culturally competent communication

South Africa is a country characterised by a variety of cultural groups and this is the environment that the social worker has to practise in. This challenge is for the social worker to be well informed of the cultural practices within the community that he or she practices. The social worker has to be culturally respectful and competent to ensure that he or she is able to understand the meanings attached to the cultural practices, as this will enable him or her to establish the helping relationship that is so crucial for effective intervention. After the successful establishment of the helping relationship, cultural competent communication is still essential for the intervention process to unfold positively and benefit the client.

Culturally competent communication refers to a situation in which the social worker is aware of the cultural context within which he or she is practising social work. This requires self-awareness with regard to the social worker's own culture and the culture of the community that is being served. It becomes important for the social worker to be aware of his or her biases and prejudices regarding the cultural group he or she serves, so that he or she is able to deal with them before interacting with clients. With this self-awareness the social worker is able to know what to avoid when interacting with clients from a particular cultural group. It is human not to like some cultural practices from other people's cultures, and sometimes your own culture, but if you are not aware of what you do not like you may find yourself unable to interact appropriately with clients who observe their cultural practices. According to Kirst-Ashman and Hull (2012:26–27) "cultural competency for social work practitioners is based on the professional Code of Ethics, and involves the following six dimensions:

1. Development of an awareness of personal values, assumptions and biases
2. Recognition that cultural values and differences directly shape life experiences
3. Understanding that stereotypes, discrimination and oppression may have direct negative effects on various diverse groups
4. Commitment to ongoing learning about clients' cultures
5. Establishment of an appreciation of other cultures, recognition of their strengths and nurturance of attitudes that respect differences
6. Acquisition of effective skills for working with people from other cultures."

The social worker must always be aware of his or her own culture and the specific aspects he or she cannot accept, so as to be aware of the fact that in all the cultures there are some aspects that are difficult to accept and internalise. With this awareness the social worker is able to guard against prejudices when the clients refer to their cultural practices (value differences) that might be different to those of the social worker. This awareness develops as the social worker interacts with the community in a process of learning to know the community, leading to ultimately developing the necessary knowledge regarding the cultural practices as well as the cultural differences that are observed within that particular community. Knowing the community that you serve is the first step towards understanding how things are done so that you do not bring your own prejudices and biases that could interfere with the intervention process.

South Africa is a country characterised by many different cultures that guide the behaviour of people. With this in mind, studying and practising social work in South Africa challenges everybody to be culturally competent, to ensure appropriate and acceptable service to the client systems. LaFromboise, Coleman and Gerton state that a culturally competent social worker "possesses a strong personal identity, has knowledge of the beliefs and culture, displays sensitivity to the affective processes of culture, communicates clearly in the language of the cultural group, performs socially sanctioned behaviour, maintains active social relations within the cultural group and negotiates the institutional structures of that culture" (as cited in Lum, 2003:6). This notion means that the social worker must make efforts to learn the language of the community he or she is serving, behave appropriately according to the cultural expectations of the community and display sensitivity and respect when interacting with community members. For example, if a female social worker renders services to a traditional community that does not approve of women wearing trousers when in the company of males, she will have to make an effort not to offend the community as she will never be accepted without observing the cultural practices. In this type of community, once entry is negotiated with the traditional leaders, the social worker must ensure that she dresses in an acceptable manner, by not wearing trousers or mini-skirts or showing her hair and complicated hair styles.

Efforts have to be made to attain cultural competency because it is not inherent. The social worker must always remember that by staying in his or her office and waiting for the client to come in, he or she will not learn how the community does things. This is the reason behind adopting an integrated approach towards rendering social work services in a given community. Through community work, engaging with communities or networking, the social worker needs to get involved in the community and interact actively with members. This is the only manner that the culture of a community can be learned. This challenges social workers not to see themselves as case workers only, but also as all-rounded practitioners who are able to use all the social work methods to render services to the communities. It is also important for the social worker to ask community members about their cultural practices so that he or she is able to be sensitive in his or her interaction with them. This will also demonstrate respect to clients, which will strengthen the helping relationship.

6.2.2.2 Verbal and non-verbal behaviour

Human interaction is always characterised by both verbal and non-verbal behaviour that carry a particular message at a given time. Verbal communication refers to what is being said in words to another person and then understood, while non-verbal communication refers to what is being said in actions, such as facial expressions, hand movement, eye contact, the way the person sits and the distance maintained during the communication process. Verbal and non-verbal communication can take place at the same place, and non-verbal communication can be used to confirm words that are spoken at the same time.

According to Cournoyer (2008:137), "a great deal of human communication is non-verbal", challenging the social worker to be on the look out for this type of communication as he or she interacts with clients. In professional encounters with others, the social worker's body language must always be congruent to the verbal language used at the same time. For example, if the social worker tells the client that she understands what he or she is saying, it must be clearly communicated by a relaxed, straight face. If the client can observe that the social worker seems confused about what is being said while claiming to understand, the client will not trust the social worker, and the helping relationship will be disturbed. This calls for the social worker to demonstrate genuineness, when interacting with the clients, to ensure that the helping relationship is strengthened. The conscious use of non-verbal cues by the social worker will encourage the client to trust the social worker and lead to a better understanding of the problem without any obstacles. The social worker has to make the client aware if he or she does not understand what the client is saying in order to communicate genuineness that is so necessary to develop a healthy helping relationship. In many instances, clients will be able to detect a discrepancy between verbal and non-verbal messages from the social worker. This congruency is also important on the part of the client to ensure that the correct message is received by the social worker in the interaction process. If the social worker and the client lose one another, the helping process cannot unfold successfully for the benefit of the client. Our non-verbal behaviour should be respectful towards the client. It is important for the social worker to also observe the non-verbal cues of the client as they assist in understanding what the client is communicating at a given time. For example, a client may share that something happened which made him or her happy while his or her tone of voice is low and he or she is frowning. The social worker should address this immediately in order to assist the client in keeping in touch with his or her real feelings.

Eye contact is very important when establishing the helping relationship. How eye contact is maintained differs from culture to culture, which calls for the social worker to be aware of the cultural context of the client systems he or she is serving. For example, in South Africa there are cultures that perceive eye contact between a younger person and an older person as disrespectful. It is very important for social workers to be aware of this, especially since most social workers begin practising at a young age. If a social worker is not sensitive to this and maintains eye contact, the client might lose interest, because people are offended by disrespect. The appropriate use of eye contact facilitates the process of establishing the helping relationship. Eye contact in professional interaction assists the social worker to communicate interest in the client but this has to be done with sensitivity. Eye contact is different form staring, which is when a social worker looks at the client without any meaning. Staring can be intimidating for the client or scare the client, resulting in a disturbed helping relationship. The client can also interpret staring as lack of understanding or interest in what is being shared. This challenges the social worker to be aware of his or her non-verbal cues and use them to confirm the verbal language and strengthen the helping relationship. The social worker must always aim to communicate respect for clients as this will strengthen the helping relationship and enable a process of positive change.

 STOP AND REFLECT

1 Use the case study at the beginning of this chapter to:
  a give your own opinion on the client's behaviour and the social worker's response in relation to culturally competent social work practice.
  b list all the elements that can be associated with culturally sensitive social work practice in the case study and give your opinion on how the social worker should have related to the client. Take into consideration the age of the client as well as that of the social worker.
2 Respect is one of the important concepts in building the helping relationship. In your own opinion, how can the social worker demonstrate this respect for the client? Elaborate.

6.2.2.3   Listening and respectful attentive listening

Attentive listening is another aspect of non-verbal communication. It is the ability to hear and comprehend what is being said. The social worker must be aware of the barriers that could disturb the reception of the correct message. In most cases, this happens when the social worker's attention is divided. The client will be able to detect this, as it is often demonstrated by inappropriate responses, and might lose interest in the whole helping process, because he or she might come to the conclusion that he or she is not taken seriously. No person will feel accepted and respected if they are attended to with divided attention. Divided attention will also lead to the social worker missing important information given by the client. Another barrier to attentive listening is the external environment, where there could be a lot of noise and other distractions. It is because of this that the social worker must ensure that the interview occurs in an environment that is free from any distraction, so that the interaction will flow freely and the client to be able to express him- or herself. For example, the social worker could put a note on the outside of the door requesting not to be disturbed. Imagine sharing your deepest secrets while people come and go as they please in the room. It is easy for a client to believe that he or she is not respected, which is the most important value in social work. Kirst-Ashman and Hull (2012:54) agree that "listening is not a simple thing as it demands concentration, perceptiveness and the use of a range of interviewing skills." (These interviewing skills will be discussed later in this chapter.)

Listening and understanding what a client is sharing facilitates active involvement in the whole helping process, because the client will feel motivated to share further information. With this kind of sharing, the social worker will be able to determine the actual problem easily and quickly, leading to a facilitated helping process. By listening attentively, the social worker will be able to retrieve what has been shared and use it to benefit the client. It is very important for the social worker to keep on checking whether he or she has understood the client correctly. The social worker should not just depend on on his or her own understanding. This is referred to as empathic understanding. Empathic understanding is useful in assuring the client that the social worker is making an effort to understand him or her. This will encourage him or her to share more about the problematic situation.

6.2.2.4 Facial expressions

Facial expressions are used to send a message and sometimes used to confirm what is being communicated verbally. It is important for the social worker to be aware of the facial expressions he or she is using at all times, specifically when interacting with clients. It is also important to ensure that facial expressions are consciously used to confirm the verbal message given at a particular time to avoid confusing the client. For example, when a client is met with a smile and warmth as they enter an office, they will feel free to relax and share their stories. This has to be done in a professional manner that communicates respect for the client. It is important for social workers to acknowledge that they are also human beings, so as not to jeopardise their interaction with clients. Pretending to be someone or something else can lead the client to believing that the social worker is artificial, which could bring an end to the helping relationship without the client benefitting at all. No person would like to be assisted by someone who is not in touch with him- or herself, because this person will not be able to meet the client at his or her level. Social workers must not behave in a mechanical manner, but rather always acknowledge their own emotions. By doing this, they will be able to use their facial expressions appropriately to strengthen the helping relationship.

6.2.2.5 Body posture

Body posture can also be used to give a message, so it has to be used consciously. The social worker must sit in a way that communicates acceptance of the client and also a way that says to the client "I am here to listen to you. This time is yours." (See Figure 6.2). The client will feel respected, leading him or her to relax and be able to communicate clearly about what is bothering him or her. Sheafor and Horesji (2012:101) are of the opinion that "leaning slightly forward towards the client communicates attention and interest," and this could be done to facilitate smooth communication during the interview process. Folding your arms may communicate a lack of interest in the client, so it could hamper the helping relationship. On the other hand, the social worker must not be too relaxed, as this might communicate to the client that it does not matter what happens in the session. For example, if the client, after being offered a chair, moves his or her chair closer to the social worker, the client may assume that they have a friendly relationship and not focus on the professional relationship. This could lead to a situation in which the client may forget that he or she approached the social worker to request assistance regarding his or her disturbed social functioning. Young social workers can also be attracted to their clients, if they are not always consciously aware of the reasons why they are interacting with them.

Figure 6.2: An example of appropriate body posture

6.2.2.6   Tone of voice

The tone of voice used during an interaction always reveals the emotions felt at that particular time. A loud tone may be used to communicate anger, aggression and a sense of control, while a meek and scarcely audible tone may communicate fear and submission. The social worker must always be aware of his or her tone of voice so as to ensure that the communication with the client is not misinterpreted. It is also important for the social worker to observe the tone of voice used by the client so as to detect his or her emotional state, as this will help in responding appropriately after acknowledging the real state of the client's emotions. For example in the case study at the beginning of this chapter, the social worker could not control her emotions when the client accused her of disrespect. This would not only disturb the establishment of a helping relationship, but could also stop its development before the process begins.

6.2.2.7   Warmth

Warmth can be communicated to the client both verbally and non-verbally. It is a way of communicating interest, concern and affection to another individual. In social work, it is used to show the client that he or she is welcomed and accepted by the social worker. Ushering the client into an office with a smile and enthusiasm communicates warmth and will assist the client in relaxing and being able to open up. Warmth promotes a sense of comfort and wellbeing, and it goes a long way in strengthening the helping relationship. For example, it is common knowledge that people living in the streets struggle to get themselves clean leading to an unpleasant odour. Based on the principle of acceptance, the social worker would have to communicate warmth to a client such as this, regardless of his or her personal hygiene. The social worker should have a welcoming expression on his or her face. The client's hygiene can be addressed once unconditional acceptance and warmth have been communicated, so that the client feels accepted as a human being.

To communicate warmth verbally the following statements can be used:

- "Good morning, I am pleased to meet you this morning."
- "Please come in and have a seat."
- "Good morning mam, the weather is so pleasant today."

STOP AND REFLECT

1 Use the case study provided at the beginning of the chapter to think about how you would practically address this situation without sounding disrespectful and judgemental towards the client.
2 Give your opinion regarding initiating a helping relationship with the client in the case study, using the basic skills and techniques you have learned up to this point.

6.2.2.8   Empathy

Empathy is the ability of the social worker to attempt to understand the client's world the way it is seen by the client and then communicate that understanding to the client. Kirst-Ashman and Hull (2012:56) indicate that "empathy involves not only being in tune with how the client feels but also conveying that to the client." Letting the client know that you understand how he or she feels and sees his or her world is very important in strengthening the helping relationship. Empathy allows the social worker to acknowledge the real feelings of the client and lets the client know that his or her real feelings are observed and understood. It does not matter whether the feelings are positive or negative, but they have to be acknowledged and communicated to the client. For example, if a frustrated mother relates how she sometimes feel hatred towards her teenage daughter whose behaviour is unacceptable, it is important to acknowledge that and respond empathetically, to show the client that her feelings are not judged, but understood in the context they are experienced. The social worker can respond by saying: "It can be difficult to stay with a child who does not cooperate with you." This statement is non-judgemental and shows the client that she is understood. Communicating understanding of the feelings and content of what the client is sharing allows the client to feel accepted and supported in his or her problematic situation. The client will feel as if he or she has someone who is willing to travel the journey with him or her towards changing the situation.

When using empathy, the social worker has to also reflect on the content of the information shared by the client to ensure that it is understood correctly according to the client's perception. This is used to avoid a situation in which the social worker attaches his or her own interpretation to what the client is sharing. This could lead the client to believing that the social worker is not interested in his or her story nor interested in helping him or her. If content is reflected, the client will be in a position to confirm or correct the social worker and this will foster mutual understanding and facilitate the intervention process. Clients would like to be seen as important in the helping process, so it is essential that they see the social worker making an effort to communicate empathy, and not sympathy, to them. To be empathetic, the social worker must make an effort to fully understand what the client is going through. Being sympathetic, on the other hand, means to feel pity. Demonstrating empathy will tell the client that the social worker is feeling *with* him or her; displaying sympathy will convey that the social worker is feeling *for* the client. This can be patronising. The client needs to be shown that he or she has the right to feel the way he or she is feeling, and can be helped to overcome what he or she is facing. Feeling pity for the client does not take the helping process further and could lead to the client disengaging from the process.

It is important to note that continuous use of empathy throughout the helping process becomes an important tool in the whole intervention process, as the client needs to be reassured that the feelings and information he or she is sharing are fully understood. The social worker must guard against falsely communicating understanding to the client because this can destroy the helping relationship, as the client will doubt the genuineness of the worker. It is also very important for the social worker to let the client express his or her feelings and perceptions of his or her situation clearly so that they can be correctly understood. Once the client knows that he or she is understood, he or she will feel relieved and motivated to be genuinely involved in the process of achieving the aspired change.

The examples in Figure 6.3 of responding empathetically to a client show the client that he or she is not judged, and that the social worker understands what he or she is going through at that particular time. The social worker must always be careful to choose the right words as they may harm the process instead of facilitating it. Non-verbal cues can also be used to communicate empathy, such as leaning forward towards the client, maintaining eye contact, and nodding the head with a genuine facial expression. There are times when a client is unable to proceed in sharing his or her story and this calls for the social worker to be observant and use minimal encouragers to encourage the client to share more. A relationship characterised by empathy requires minimal encouragers to motivate the client to proceed. Minimal encouragers are non-verbal cues used to encourage the client to continue sharing his or her story. The social worker can nod his or her head with a straight and genuine facial expression, responding with, for example "mmm" or "ok", to show the client that he or she is still listening and understanding, and would like the client to continue.

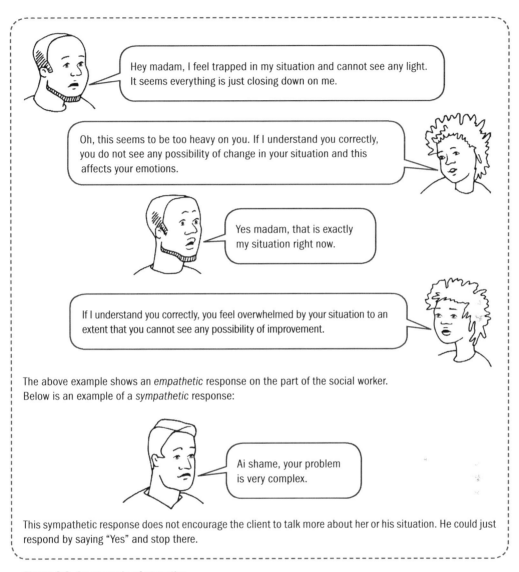

The above example shows an *empathetic* response on the part of the social worker. Below is an example of a *sympathetic* response:

This sympathetic response does not encourage the client to talk more about her or his situation. He could just respond by saying "Yes" and stop there.

Figure 6.3: An example of empathy

6.2.2.9 Genuineness and congruence

Genuineness in the helping relationship requires the social worker to maintain an honest, open and natural expression of self at all times. Genuineness means that the social worker is always him- or herself despite the fact that the interaction is geared towards achieving a goal for the benefit of the client. Being genuine challenges the client to be wholly involved in the helping process knowing that he or she is in interaction with a real person, who is also honest. The social worker must never pretend to be someone that he or she is not, because this can betray the trust of the client and result in a short-lived relationship. If the client detects that the social worker is not genuine, the helping relationship can be destroyed and the intervention process derailed.

For example: A client visits a social worker and expresses her problem of dealing with her husband's addiction to gambling and the social worker brushes it aside as trivial. This may be because the social worker is experiencing the same problem.

There are times in a helping relationship that require a social worker to self-disclose, but this has to be done with extra care. The social worker must have dealt with his or her situation and no longer have negative feelings attached to it. This self-disclosure must be done only when the social worker is convinced that it will facilitate the helping process. It must also be done when the helping relationship is strong enough to avoid feelings of vulnerability. In self-disclosure the social worker uses his or her own experience to help the client see that he or she is a real human being who also experiences difficulties. Furthermore, self-disclosure is used to encourage the client to see that problematic situations can be overcome, just like the social worker managed to overcome his or her own problem.

Genuineness can also be communicated non-verbally by confirming verbal communication with corresponding facial expressions, body posture and eye contact.

6.2.2.10 Concern for others (*ubuntu*)

It is common to hear students, in their first year of social work training, stating concern for others as their sole motivation for choosing social work as a career. Some even go a step further to share how they are involved as volunteers in their communities. Concern for others is necessary for a social worker to serve beyond the call of duty, and it has to come from within and not be a mechanical exercise stipulated by the profession. The concept of *ubuntu* is unique to South Africa and referred to in the *White Paper for Social Welfare (1997)* as "the principle of caring for each other's wellbeing and a spirit of mutual support." It is further stated in the *White Paper for Social Welfare (1997)* that "people are people through others", meaning that it is through the recognition of others as human beings and interacting with them as such, that a person can be seen as a human being. This notion challenges social workers to realise that their interaction with clients must be characterised by concern for others for them to also be recognised as human beings. Caring for others is learned through socialisation and enhanced by the training that social workers receive before qualifying. The social worker needs to be passionate about helping others beyond the call of duty to facilitate the helping process.

The above skills and techniques are not inherent, as a result the social worker must make an effort to master them. This journey begins when social work is selected as a career of choice, enhanced through training and further nurtured after qualifying, when the newly qualified social worker's skills are guided and refined through supervision. It is also important to realise that these skills and techniques are not used exclusively in social case work, but also at the other levels of social work intervention. The above skills are used with the framework of social work ethics to ensure that clients feel respected throughout the helping process. As alluded to earlier on, respect is the foundation of the whole helping process because if the client is deprived of it the helping relationship will not be established. Without the helping relationship, the helping process cannot unfold as the client will not feel free to express him- or herself in an environment where he or she is not respected.

6.3 Strategies to facilitate change

In facilitating change within the client system's problematic situation, the social worker can use a variety of strategies and techniques to gather relevant information, assess it, plan the intervention process, implement it, evaluate it and then terminate it. These strategies are discussed hereunder within the framework of generalist social work practice.

6.3.1 Interviewing

"An interview is a person-to-person interaction that has a definite and deliberate purpose that is recognised and accepted by both participants." (Kadushin & Kadushin, 2013:6) It constitutes a conversation that is designed to meet a specific purpose. Due to the fact that it is designed to meet a specific purpose, it has to be well planned. It is different from an ordinary conversation in the sense that it has a specific purpose. In an interview, the social worker facilitates the direction of the process to ensure that the purpose is achieved, This means that there will always be an interviewer (social worker) and an interviewee (the client). Even if the social worker guides the direction of the interview, the client's full participation allows the process to unfold towards reaching a goal. It is important to remember that the client is the expert of his or her problematic situation, but needs to be assisted to share information so that a solution can be determined. This is achieved by creating an environment in which the client feels free to share his or her experiences. The social worker is the professional expert that has to work hand in hand with the client (who is the expert on his or her context) to unpack the challenging/problematic situation, so that the client's wellbeing can be enhanced.

Planning for the interview plays an important role in ensuring that the purpose of the interview is achieved. The interview can take place in a variety of settings, depending on the organisation in which the social worker works. (The variety of fields in which social work is practised are explored in Chapter 9.) In some instances, the social worker does not have control over the setting at all, for example in a hospital, where the client can be interviewed while on his or her bed. In an office the social worker needs to be very sensitive to the setting to ensure that the client feels safe to talk. The dress code of the social worker must also be appropriate, so as not to intimidate the client. In a situation where the interview is a follow up, it is important to prepare psychologically and physically, so that confidence and competence are portrayed to the client. In a situation where the interview takes place in a client's home, the social worker will not have control on the setting, but should try by all means to uphold the professional values, so that the client is able to share the necessary information to facilitate change.

The client will always be anxious when coming to the social worker's office, especially if it is the first time he or she has approached a social worker. The social worker must, therefore, make an effort to alleviate his or her anxiety by effectively using the necessary skills and techniques. Cultural competence must never be forgotten, and the communication skills discussed above have to be mastered for the interview to be successful. Due to budgetary constraints in many welfare organisations in South Africa, specifically in NGOs, we find that creating a conducive environment for these meetings can sometimes be impossible. Because of the problem of overcrowding in social work offices, social workers often have to share offices, sometimes with social auxiliary workers, and this could be intimidating for the client. To minimise the negative impact, the social worker should make an effort to look for a space conducive to privacy and confidentiality.

The social worker must ensure that the environment in which the interview takes place is free from any form of disruptions. For example, a sign on the door indicating that no one should disturb the interview will go a long way in minimising disturbance. The social worker must also ensure that the phone is off the hook, unless he or she is expecting an emergency call. if it happens that during the interview the office phone rings, the social worker has the obligation to minimise the negative impact of this disturbance by explaining to the client why he or she has to take the emergency call during the interview. The social worker must make a point of communicating that the call is of importance and work related. All personal calls must be avoided during an interview, so cell phones should be switched off or on silent mode to avoid any disturbance, as the client might feel disrespected,. Imagine if you were sharing your personal problems to a social worker and the social worker receives a personal call from a friend and continues to chat to him or her. The client will feel unaccepted, disrespected and taken for granted, leading to a disengagement from the whole process, maybe even before it begins.

Remember, the client needs to feel safe, respected and accepted during the interview, for him or her to feel free to share the actual reason that initiated his or her contact with the social worker. Demonstrating respect to the client facilitates the helping process, because the more relaxed and safe the client feels, the more he or she will be able to share vital information required for a thorough assessment of the problematic situation to take place.

Social work interviews are mostly used by the social worker to assist the client in sharing the story that led him or her to contact the social worker. The process of gathering information facilitates the social worker's and the client's understanding of the problematic situation. The developmental approach requires the social worker to ensure that the principle of client participation is upheld throughout. The interview marks the beginning of the intervention process, that is, during the initial contact that the client makes with the social worker, after the helping relationship has been established. It is also important to note that information gathering does not stop after the first interview, as it often happens that more information is shared after the helping relationship has been established through the careful application of skills, professional values and principles (as discussed in Chapter 4).

6.3.2 Counselling

After the client's difficult situation has been unpacked during the interview, it is then important to agree with the client on specific aspects that need to be attended to. These aspects are negotiated and recorded in a contract, as discussed in Chapter 5 (the whole helping process is discussed in Chapter 5). There are times when the client's problematic situation does not require any tangible intervention like the removal of a child from an unsafe home, or the provision of food parcels to a hungry family. This is established in the assessment process that follows the gathering of information on the client's situation. The assessment of the client's problematic situation could determine that the intervention needed is counselling. Counselling is explored in the following discussion.

Counselling entails a process that is facilitated by the social worker to empower the client to develop skills and knowledge that will enhance his or her wellbeing. According to Egan (2014:12), "counselling helps the client to diffuse and manage their acute problem situation and also helps them to develop basic problem-solving skills, through engaging them in the helping process as partners." Through counselling, the client is assisted in seeing him- or herself from the correct perspective in relation to the situation he or she is experiencing in order to faciliate the process of change. Understanding the client's perceptions of his or her situation is very important for the social worker, as it enables him or her to facilitate the process of change appropiately, for the benefit of the client. In most cases, a client's perception of him- or herself within the problematic sutuation is distorted. This distortion is addressed through counselling. Changing the way the client perceives him- or herself empowers him or her. Empowerment also requires the client to develop coping skills that will equip him or her to face future problematic situations with confidence, and not return to the social worker for assistance. Through empowerment the client's capabilities are enhanced. Counselling assists the client in becoming independent and in using his or her strengths to face life's challenges. (Empowerment and the strengths perspective are discussed in Chapter 5.)

Counselling is beneficial to clients in that it helps them to develop new skills that will assist them in understanding themselves better, and in interacting more effectively with their environments. It is through counselling that the client comes to realise some of the aspects of his or her life that might have led to the problem situation he or she is facing. This realisation equips the client to be mindful of these factors in future, to avoid a repetition of a similar problematic situation. In other words, it could be said that through counselling, clients are empowered and helped to experience personal growth. Counselling creates an awareness in the client's mind of his or her situation and future situations, as people's experiences are never static, but continuously changing. Counselling helps the client to develop a new perspective that enables him or her to use his or her newly developed knowledge and skills to deal effectively with his or her current and future challenges.

All social work skills, professional values and social work techniques are needed for a successful counselling process to facilitate the change process. Counselling cannot take place without the creation of a safe environment for the client and a helping relationship that is characterised by trust and respect, including all the characteristics discussed above. In this process the social worker becomes the facilitator of change and the client becomes the owner of the process. It is very important for the social worker to ensure that all barriers to successful interviewing are addressed, as indicated above. It is crucial to be totally committed to the client's needs at the time of the interaction to entice him or her to also be committed. This can only be achieved through the use of all the appropriate social work skills.

The counselling process must always be guided by a contract that should be respected by both the social worker and the client. The contract must clearly stipulate the following aspects clearly:

- The specific issues to be addressed through the process
- The timeframe needed to complete the process
- The parties to be involved in the process
- The evaluation tools to be used to assess progress
- The terms agreed upon regarding lack of progress should it occur
- The follow up framework needed after the termination of the process
- Final termination of the whole process.

The contract becomes necessary to ensure that all the involved parties bring their part to the process for it to be successful.

6.3.3   Recording

Recording is a process of writing down every activity that takes place between the social worker and the client. During the interview, the social worker has to inform the client that he or she needs to take notes (or record information) in order for him or her to write a comprehensive report (process notes) on what took place, as required by the profession. There are different reports used in social work practice, namely, intake report, process report, progress report, evaluation report, court report and placement report, just to mention few. Since this book is at an introductory level, these different reports are not discussed.

Record keeping in social work is one of the essential techniques that has to be mastered by every practising social worker. It is demanding and time consuming, but social work practice cannot do without it. O'Bourke (2010:1) states that "attitudes towards case recording are generally negative, which might be because of the demanding nature of this task, leading to no one being enthusiastic to do it." Social workers do not have a choice but to learn to master record keeping because of the professional ethics that govern their work. It is through accurate and detailed records that social work service delivery can be continuous, regardless of ever changing personnel. It is therefore crucial for social work students to be introduced to this important technique, which has been a vital part of social work practice since its origin (when it was still a charitable activity). According to O'Bourke (2010:2), "recording in social work started during the time of Octavia Hill, and it was no more just an administrative process, but an integral part of social work intervention."

Recording in social work ensures accountability of the agency's service delivery to its clients. For the social worker who is employed by an agency, he or she needs to account for what he or she is doing to deserve a salary at the end of the month, and it is through record keeping that evidence of the social worker's work can be seen. If an agency has to convince government to fund it, the agency will need to account for every cent that it has received to ensure further funding. If the agency is unable to keep appropriate, accurate and detailed accounting records and records showing how it benefits the community, the government will not be keen to continue to fund it.

It is also important to keep records to ensure continuity in the process of bringing about change to a client's matter, should it happen that the social worker who started with the helping process had to leave the agency. Through the correct and detailed records the new social worker will be able to take the process further. Staff turnover is an unavoidable factor in every work environment, including the social work field of practice. Imagine a situation in which a client goes to a follow-up session at a particular agency, only to find a new social worker who does not know anything about his or her problematic situation dealing with his or her case. The relationship of trust that was already developed will be broken, especially when the client has to start telling his or her sory all over again. This might lead to the client disengaging from the process or giving up on ever getting professional assistance from the social work profession. When a new social worker takes on an established cased, it cannot be easy for the client to have confidence in the agency or in the social work profession, but with accurate and detailed record keeping the new social worker will be able to know where to start, what has already been accomplished and what still needs to be addressed.

Recording also assists the social worker in remembering what has been accomplished with the client and what has to be done in the future, hence facilitating appropriate planning. It is important to note that the social worker in a particular agency deals with a variety of clients with a variety of problematic situations, which makes it difficult for the social worker to remember every detail of each client's situation. Proper record keeping will keep the social worker up to date and well informed of each unique case. It is essential for the social worker to record the information after each interaction with the client, while it is still fresh in his or her mind, so that records are as accurate as possible.

Record keeping is also used to gather information that will assist in compiling reports for outside organisations, such as courts or institutions of care, specifically because it is not always possible to collect all the required information in one contact with a client. Social work practice utilises reports to communicate with the outside world regarding clients' problematic situations that have to be addressed. Due to the fact that some issues that clients bring to the attention of a social worker cannot be addressed by the social worker in isolation, accurate and detailed records need to be kept to inform other stakeholders who have the expertise to proceed with the intervention. It is important to note that social workers operate within multi-disciplinary, multi-sectorial and multi-professional settings, where a number of members bring their expertise to provide the appropriate intervention to the client. The tool that is used to communicate to other team members is the report. It has to provide all the necessary information on the client's problematic situation for appropriate intervention to take place. The aspect of the need for involvement of other stakeholders in the process of rendering a comprehensive service to the client is also discussed in other chapters of this book, for example in Chapters 3, 7 and 8, where it is made clear that social work cannot be practiced in isolation. In some instances, an agency cannot assist a client further and a referral is required. If the social worker at the next agency is not given enough detailed information, the client would be subjected to another exploration of his or her problem situation by a social worker. This could be traumatic to the client and also detrimental to the helping relationship, resulting in the client losing confidence in the social work profession.

The purposes of recording can be said to practise continuity, administration, training and research. The purposes of practice and administration have been discussed in detail above. With regard to training, student social workers are exposed to learning how to keep records, through their engagement in the practical work that they have to do in the different years of study. Students' progress in learning how to use the social work skills is assessed through the reports that they write. There are different types of reports that the students have to learn to write during the training process, as mentioned above.

In research, it is impossible for the researcher to complete a research project without keeping records of the whole process. In this instance, records are kept from the writing of the proposal and data collection (especially when the qualitative research approach is used, because interviews are conducted and observations made to collect as much information as possible in order to ultimately answer the research question) to the last step of the research process. The details of this process are also beyond the scope of this text, but it is important to always remember that for social workers to provide appropriate services to their clients, they have to continually engage in research.

6.3.4   Referral

Referral is the process of connecting clients with the appropriate resources that will assist them in resolving their problematic situations, as not all problems can be addressed successfully by only one welfare agency. Before a referral can be made, it is important for the social worker to assess the client's motivation and ability to utilise the resource referred to. This becomes crucial, as some clients might be unable to follow through on the referral due of various factors. For example, it might be that a client has to travel a long distance and spend a lot of money to reach the new resource. If it happens that the amount of money needed for travelling is unavailable, the client will not follow up on the referral. This will impact negatively on the client's life. It can also be that the client is not motivated to begin a new helping relationship with another professional after struggling to engage with his or her current professional. If the social worker is sensitive to these aspects and addresses them, the referral process could benefit the client, because the client will receive the service he or she is in need of at that particular time. Together with ascertaining the client's motivation and ability to follow through on a particular referral, the social worker must also assess the ability of the resource to provide the required service to the client. This calls for the social worker to be knowledgeable of the resources in the area he or she serves and also be aware of the actual services they offer. This will ensure that clients are referred to resources that will address their needs appropriately, and not be subjected to additional stress or trauma.

It is common knowledge that many social welfare agencies are unable to provide the services that they set out to render, due to financial constraints aggravated by the current economic situation in the whole world, South Africa included. Many non-governmental organisations are struggling to retain social workers due to this economic situation, leading to their inability to maintain quality services, at the expense of clients. If an agency that a social worker is working for does not provide the service that his or her client is in need of at that particular time, the social worker should refer the client to another agency.

Sometimes social workers are not comfortable working in certain areas. As professionals, social workers need to subject themselves to a process of self-discovery during their training period to establish the areas that they are not comfortable working in. This will avoid 'pass the buck' practice. For example, a social worker who hates interacting with people who abuse substances will find it very difficult to assist a client presenting with such a problem, unless he or she identified this during training and made an effort to deal with it. It has to be clear that referral is never a way for a social worker to shift his or her responsibility onto someone else, because he or she is not keen to deal with the type of problematic situation the client is presenting to him or her. Referral is not a simple activity and it needs to be done with extra care to ensure its success in benefitting client systems.

Since referral is not a way to pass the buck to another professional, Sheafor and Horesji (2012:40) are of the opinion that "the social worker must also make a follow up after referring the client, to establish if the client is receiving the services that he or she was referred for." In cases where the client's needs are not met, the social worker has to establish what the problem is and make an effort to assist the client further. This will ensure that the client maintains confidence in the social work professional as a change agent, working from the framework of professional values and principles.

6.4   Conclusion

This chapter addressed case work as one of the primary methods in social work, the development of social work with individuals (case work), the basic skills and techniques needed by social workers to intervene in clients' troubled lives at the individual level (micro-level) as well as the intervention strategies used with individuals in social work.

End of chapter questions

1. How would you describe case work as a primary method in social work practice?
2. List and describe the skills and techniques needed in social work intervention with individuals.
3. Cultural-sensitive social work practice is an important aspect in social work practice. Discuss the rationale behind this statement.
4. Discuss interviewing, recording, counselling and referral as important techniques in social work practice.

Key concepts

- **Case work** is one of the primary methods in social work and it is implemented on a one-on-one basis with individuals and their families as well as couples.
- **Social work skills** are the skills used by social workers to intervene in the problematic situations of their clients.
- **Cultural sensitive social work practice** refers to a situation where a social worker recognises the importance of respecting the client's culture in the process of intervention. This requires the social worker to have gone through a process of self-awareness in as far as different cultural practices are concerned, for him or her to recognise his or her own biases and prejudices.
- **Empathy** is a skill that the social worker has to always use in the intervention process in an effort to understand the client's feelings as well as the content of the problematic situation. When using this skill, the social worker communicates his or her understanding to the client to confirm whether what he or she has heard and observed is correct according to the client's understanding.
- **Empowerment** is a concept strongly used within the developmental approach and it refers to an effort of ensuring that the client is assisted to develop new skills and knowledge to enable the client to address future problems without relying on the social worker's intervention.
- **Interviewing** is a process of interacting with the client with a purpose of collecting information regarding the client's problematic situation to enable the social worker to facilitate change towards the improved wellbeing of the client.
- **Counselling** is a process of assisting the client to see his or her situation from the right perspective and proceed to develop coping skills for future use as well.
- **Recording** is a process of writing the details of every encounter a social worker has with a client, for several reasons that are aimed at enhancing the wellbeing of the client as well as for the benefit of the agency.
- **Referral** is the process of linking the client with the appropriate service that will assist him or her in finding a solution to the problematic situation experienced at the particular time.

References

1. AMBROSINO, R., AMBROSINO, R., HEFFERNAN, J. & SHUTTLESWORTH, G. 2012. *Social work and social welfare: an introduction.* 7th ed. Canada: Thomson Brooks.
2. COURNOYER, B.R. 2008. *The social work skills workbook.* 5th ed. USA: Brooks/Cole. DANIŞ, M.Z. & KIRBAÇ, A. 2013. *The historical development of social work practice with individuals. Middle-East Journal of Scientific Research,* 14(5):703–711.
3. DEPARTMENT OF SOCIAL DEVELOPMENT. 1997. *White paper for social welfare.* Pretoria: Government Printers.
4. EGAN, G. 2014. *The skilled helper: a problem-management approach to helping.* 10th ed. USA: Brooks/Cole.
5. KADUSHIN, A. & KADUSHIN, G. 2013. *The social work interview.* 5th ed. New York: Columbia University Press.
6. KIRST-ASHMAN, K.K. & HULL, G.H. Jr. 2012. *Understanding generalist practice.* 6th ed. USA: Brooks/Cole.

7. LUM, D. 2003. *Cultural competent practice: a framework for understanding diverse groups and justice issues.* 2nd ed. USA: Brooks/Cole.

8. O'BOURKE, L. 2010. *Recording in social work: not just an administrative task.* Great Britain: The Policy Press.

9. SHEAFOR, B.W. & HORESJI, C.R. 2012. *Techniques and guidelines for social work practice.* 9th ed. New York: Allyn & Bacon.

10. STEYAERT, J. 2013. *History of social work.* [Online]. Available: http://historyofsocialwork. org/eng/details.php?cps=6 [28 January 2014]

Group work

Lulu Qalinge

 Case Study 7.1 Mothers' group

A social worker working for Bantubonke Non-Governmental Organisation (NGO) decides to run a group of mothers of young children abusing drugs and alcohol. Her rationale for running the group was prompted by the number of mothers coming to the office concerned about their children who abuse substances. According to the mothers, the children steal from the family, have abandoned school, stay out for most of the day, do not at sleep home and are most of the time under the influence of either alcohol or drugs. They are worried about their children's safety out on the streets and are also concerned about their hygiene and eating habits. The parents feel depressed, frustrated, overwhelmed, and desperate to help their children. They simply cannot cope with their situations.

As one of her intervention strategies, the social worker negotiates with the mothers to form a group. The reason for forming the group is to afford mothers an opportunity to share views and experiences with one another about their children and to find ways of coping with the situation they find themselves in. The mothers had the option of participating or refusing to participate because the social worker, though knowing the value of group work, did not force or impose the group on the mothers. However, all 12 mothers agreed to be part of the group.

The social worker, together with the group members, decided on the group's goals, norms and standards to control and direct members' behaviour. They also decided together on the activities that will help them achieve the goals.

7.1 Introduction

At different intervals within this chapter you will be asked to reflect on the above case study, and to analyse it based on what you have learned. Your analysis and your reflection will depend on your understanding of the group work method. You are therefore encouraged to read and engage with the chapter with understanding and not to simply regurgitate information that is in the book. You should use some of your own personal experiences for better understanding. Remember that we all belong to different groups throughout the different stages of our development. As a young person you belong to a certain group of peers. You may belong to a church group, a group of sports lovers, and of course to a family group. However, at times we find some of these groups not responding to our needs and aspirations, thus creating discomfort, psychological pressure and challenges that may affect our normal social functioning and wellbeing.

These are some of the conditions that may call for professional intervention, which may occur within a therapeutic group setting.

A social work group, as you can imagine, is different from the above-mentioned groups. The difference is social work groups are formed to help group members deal with the socio-emotional challenges they experience whereas the other groups are naturally occurring. A detailed explanation of these groups will be given later on in the chapter.

You may ask, why the use of groups in social work? The answer to this question is that social work uses three basic methods of intervention (refer to Chapter 1 of this book), which are: case work, **group work** and community work. Each of these methods is discussed in different chapters.

Looking at the above case study, the questions that probably come to mind as a first year social work student are: What is group work? What is a group in the context of social work practice? Why a group? What will participants gain from this group? What is the role of a social worker in the group? How do social work groups work?

The following sections will assist you in answering the above questions.

7.2   Groups and social work groups

All human beings are born within a group, which determines their socialisation and shapes their perceptions of life. Drower (as cited in McKendrick, 1987:85) emphasises that survival is linked to the interrelationships formed among human beings, starting with the family we are born in. It is through the initial socialisation into the family group followed by other group experiences, such as a peer group, a classroom group, a church group, and a work group, that psychosocial competency is achieved and maintained throughout the life cycle. These are what we call natural groups, because they occur naturally and give people a sense of belonging. In some instances, we do not choose to belong to a group, but become part of it by virtue of being born and socialised into it. Examples of these types of groups are family groups, clan groups, traditional groups and religious groups. The list is endless. Consequently, since individuals spend most of their time interacting in groups, many of their problems and misconceptions are likely to emanate from these very interactions. Vinter (as cited in Garvin, 1981:35) refers to this as interactional view of deviance. Due to this fact, coupled with the healthy group experiences, it can be acknowledged that many concerns and difficulties we face in life can easily be resolved within a controlled structured group system. This is the basic rationale for using groups as a method of intervention in social work practice, hence the use of social group work. The difference between what we call natural groups and social work groups is that social work groups are not naturally occurring groups, because they are normally formed by a professional social worker for the purpose of assisting group members to meet their needs. Social work groups exist under the auspices of an organisation or institution, which determines the shape and types of groups according to the organisational policies and strategies. These groups are normally formed and facilitated by a professional social worker using professional skills and techniques to help people deal and cope with their problems. Social group work always calls for a professional worker from outside the group.

On a professional level, there are different definitions of group work as espoused by different authors. Some authors refer to group work as **social group work** and others refer to it simply as **group work**. Social group work is normally the professional term for the work done by social workers in groups. The following are some of the definitions:

Toseland and Rivas (2009:12) define group work as "a goal directed activity with small treatment and task groups aimed at meeting socio-emotional needs and accomplishing tasks. This activity is directed to individual members of the group and to the group as a whole within a system of service delivery."

Group work can also be defined as a method of working with people in groups for the development of skills, personal growth and development through self-reflection, the enhancement of social functioning, the achievement of socially desirable goals and the accomplishment of tasks. It is based on the knowledge of people's needs for each other and their interdependence. Group work is a method of reducing or eliminating obstacles that negatively impact on members' social interactions thus preventing the accomplishment of socially undesirable goals. Group work provides a context in which people influence and help one another to facilitate **change** at personal, group, organisational and community level. This happens through the process of reciprocal interaction, provision of mutual support and integration of solutions (see Figure 7.1).

Figure 7.1: Together we can improve our situation; together we shall succeed

In simple terms, a social group work is when two or more people are brought together by a social worker to satisfy a particular need. All these people have a common interest and need that may be satisfied through group intervention. People come to the group with different views, perceptions and emotions (see Figure 7.2). It is the role of the group leader together with group members to channel these emotions into workable solutions that will benefit all.

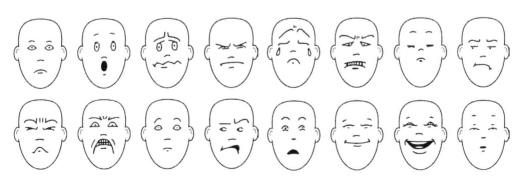

Figure 7.2: Examples of different emotions

STOP AND REFLECT

1   Look at the faces above. Can you identify the emotions?
2   Write a story about each face.
3   Can you relate any face to your own circumstances?
4   It is assumed that by now you have an understanding of what social group work is. If that is true, go back to the case study at the beginning of the chapter and determine why the social worker deemed it necessary to put mothers of children abusing drugs and alcohol in a group.

7.3   Why social workers make use of groups

Before outlining reasons why social workers make use of groups, it is important to emphasise that group work is one of the basic methods of social work. The other two methods are case work and community work. (Case work and community work are discussed in detail in Chapters 6 and 8.) Group work cuts across the other two methods. For example, a **community worker** makes use of groups to reach the larger community, or a community worker may work with task groups or social action groups to bring about desired changes within an organisation or within a community. A community worker may also establish different committees in the community, or may work with a group of women in income generating projects.

A **case worker** can utilise the group approach to deal with a number of clients experiencing similar problems. For example, in our case study above, the social worker deemed it necessary to run a group with mothers whose children abuse drugs and alcohol. These are mothers who came to the social worker as individual clients and were dealt with on a one-on-one basis (case work). The number of clients, with a similar problem of drug abuse, made it possible for the social worker to start a group. You can also refer to a family as a group of people.

The question "Why a group?" may be asked. The following are the reasons why social workers use groups:

- Groups provide opportunities for socialisation, alleviate isolation, and provide a platform to serve various clients simultaneously, and can expand insight and perceptions as people reflect on their interactions with others (Segal, Gerdes & Steiner, 2007:163).
- A group is a vehicle of growth and change. This is achieved through sharing knowledge, views and experiences. Through the use of activities, members get to interact and work together to bring about psychosocial competence.
- Group members have an opportunity to identify with others. There is value in a person knowing that he or she is not alone in a situation.
- Through interaction and communication, group members develop a sense of belonging as they continue to identify with one another.
- Integration of solutions is the cornerstone of groups.
- In groups, members have the opportunity to disclose their problems and concerns (in a safe environment) in an effort to develop coping skills.
- In groups, members work towards self-help and helping others.
- Groups provide members with a sense of belonging.

7.4 The benefits that members enjoy from groups

In groups, members enjoy a number of benefits as they interact and integrate solutions to their problems. It is in these groups that members have an opportunity to practise newly learned behaviour within the safe environment of the group. Outlined below are some of the benefits that members enjoy in a group.

- Collectivity: Group members work collectively on an issue and participate in decision-making.
- Mutual aid: As people interact and communicate in a group, mutual aid develops. Mutual aid is based on the concept of *ubuntu* where interdependence becomes an everyday affair and where each group member provides and equally receives help and support from other group members. It is a true African gesture based on the concept of *letsema*, commonly known as voluntarism, where different people come together to offer assistance to those in need of help. The rationale for cultivating mutual aid in the group is based on the following propositions:
  - > Members have assets, opinions, perspectives, information, expertise, and experiences that can be tapped into to help others in the group.
  - > Helping others helps the helper – a concept so typical of African communities.
  - > Some ideas and inputs are better absorbed and better understood when they come from peers rather than the worker. This can be referred to as peer pressure used in a positive manner. The best model is someone who has walked the road before.
- Generalisation: Being in a group provides group members with the opportunity to generalise their problems and to understand that their situation is not worse off compared to others. This gives members hope and the will to forge through difficult situations. Through generalisations, members feel they are not alone, and therefore develop courage and the sense that they will also triumph.

❓ STOP AND REFLECT

Consider the group members in the opening case study and answer the following questions.
1 Why do you think they agreed to join the group?
2 What and how do you think they will benefit from the group?
3 From your own personal experiences, think of one group you belong, or have belonged, to and indicate which of the above benefits you enjoyed. Explain why and how.

7.5 Group membership

All group membership must be voluntary. This means members need to join groups out of their own free will without being coerced into joining them. Voluntary membership improves participation, because each and every member feels that he or she is joining for a purpose.

The reasons why group membership must be voluntary are:
- to encourage willingness to participate
- to make members feel comfortable to disclose their problems
- to build a spirit of team work or an alliance of individuals who need each other's support
- to encourage a sense of belonging so central to our existence.

There are, however, other situations where members are coerced or forced to be part of a social worker's group. These are groups in which clients may be pressured to seek services as a result of the legal system. These are groups that take place in controlled institutions where it is mandatory for people to be part of the group, because the institution makes group membership part of a programme that members need to be affiliated to. These groups are normally referred to as "social control groups" (Garvin, 1981:247) and are found in areas such as correctional services, where an offender is required to attend a therapeutic group before he or she can be considered for parole. In this case, a group member joins the group because he wants to fulfil a stated requirement and not because he wants to be in the group. Other examples may be groups in a psychiatric clinic, hospital or rehabilitation centre. In a rehabilitation centre, group membership may be prescribed as part of a healing programme. This is normally referred to as involuntary membership. The involuntary client can be understood as someone who joins the group not out of his free will, but joins because he is pressured by some force he cannot resist.

Group members who are compelled to join groups present with resistance. In most instances, they are not willing to participate, and become suspicious of the group leader. They have difficulty expressing themselves or opening up to other group members and, at times, become destructive in a group. Regular attendance to group sessions is affected as members show little or no commitment to the group. Goal achievement may not be reached.

7.5.1   Dealing with involuntary group membership

Being an involuntary member comes with challenges for the member as well as the group leader. For the member, there is suspicion and lack of trust; and for the group leader, there is extra effort required to convince the members about the benefits of being in the group. The fact that members are mandated to be in a group calls for special recognition and acknowledgement of members by the group leader. To win the trust and acceptance of the group, the group leader must:

- make sure that group members understand why they are in a group (continuous reassurance is paramount)
- involve members in all decision-making to make them feel that they own the group
- show unconditional positive regard for each of the members
- allow members self-determination and respect them irrespective of their attitudes
- assure them of confidentiality at all times
- build trust.

EXAMPLE 7.1

A group leader is dealing with a group of offenders in a correctional service facility. This is a discussion during the group's first session.

Group leader: I am happy that you have made time to come to the group. I am looking forward to working with you over the next two months.

Kagiso: Well, do we have a choice? We were told to join the group whether we like it or not.

Thabo: I think it's just for them to know what we think about this place. You are one of them, and therefore we do not feel safe talking to you.

Group leader: I have carefully listened to your concerns about being in the group. I am aware that the organisation requires you to be in the group. But, I want you to understand that being in the group will hopefully benefit you, because you will have an opportunity to share your frustrations and concerns.

Thato:	For you to go tell them what we say?
Group leader:	I sense that you all do not trust me and are afraid that I will tell authorities what you say and do in the group. My position here is as a social worker. I am here for you, and to listen to you to make this group worthwhile. This is your group. You are going to determine for yourselves how to drive it. I believe we all have something to contribute towards helping one another. More importantly, everything we do or say in the group will be treated as confidential.

(Most of the group members are nodding their heads.)

Thabo:	We are pleased that you are not going to tell them. Our paroles are coming up in the next six months, and we do not want anything to jeopardise them.
Group leader:	You seem to be looking forward to leaving this place, and I equally do not want anything to disturb your wishes. This therefore means we are going to work together to make this group a success.

(The group leader goes on to explain the group process to the group members.)

The group members, though coerced to join the group, are now more willing to trust the group leader and to participate in the group.

 STOP AND REFLECT

Reflect on the above example and answer the following questions.
1 Was membership of this group voluntary or involuntary? If you choose involuntary, explain why?
2 Explain what the group leader did to win the confidence of the group members?
3 Why is voluntary membership important in social group work?

7.6 Types of groups

Social work groups come in different shapes and sizes depending on the organisation's policy mandate and focus.

Groups may be **short term** and **closed**, or **open** and **long term**.

Short term groups are groups with limited life span. For example, a group may run for eight sessions and thereafter terminate. Termination of these groups is planned from the first stage of the group development. Throughout the group process, members are continuously reminded of termination. Such groups normally have maintained membership in that they start and end with same number of members, and are referred to as closed groups. Once the group has started, no new members are allowed to join. Short term closed groups develop a high sense of cohesion since members get attached to each other. Self-disclosure is also high due to the level of cohesion. (However, since these groups are voluntary, people may also leave as and when they please.)

Long term groups are groups that run indefinitely. Members join and leave as and when they want to. This means group members are able to join the group at any stage of the group development process, and can terminate intermittently. Membership of such groups is open as members come and go. Compared to short term closed groups, termination is normally not planned, but determined by the needs of the individual members. Such groups may be facilitated by a professional social worker, but eventually may turn out to be self-help groups, as members take total control of the group. Though mutual aid, support and cohesion may exist, self-disclosure remains low.

The determination of whether a group is open, long term or closed and short term depends on the purpose and rational of the group. For example, a group of cancer patients helping each other cope with cancer can be an open group where new members join the group from time to time. Such groups may eventually end up as self-help groups as members continue to offer support to one another. Closed groups are normally short term because they have limited life span. An example of a short term group is a group of mothers with children abusing drugs where the group worker works with mothers for a limited period of time, for example eight sessions, after which the group terminates. In short term closed groups, new members are not allowed to join once the group has started.

7.6.1   Treatment and task groups

Social work groups are further divided into two main categories: treatment and task groups.

7.6.1.1   Treatment groups

Treatment groups are those groups that are formed to satisfy the socio-emotional needs of the group members. This means, members in treatment groups join for the purpose of satisfying a particular need, such as support, education, therapy, growth and socialisation (Toseland & Rivas, 2009:21).

In treatment groups, members are bonded together because of their similar needs and their desire to seek help.

To facilitate development of treatment groups, the following issues are important:
- The group leader allocates roles to individual group members as the group develops. Members are expected to fulfil the roles allocated to them. Roles are equally distributed depending on each individual member's capabilities and potential as well as the task at hand and are of course not imposed on members. Common roles allocated to members may include, for example: group leader, secretary, refreshment organiser, venue organiser and treasurer.
- Communication is greatly encouraged. Communication is normally open as members are continuously encouraged to interact with one another.
- The procedures during meetings or sessions are flexible to encourage reciprocal interaction and self-disclosure.

7.6.1.2   Task groups

Task groups are formed to accomplish a particular task or mandate on behalf of a vulnerable group, community or organisation, for example a group of influential people in the community coming together to teach gardening skills to disadvantaged women. Unlike treatment groups, members in task groups do not join to satisfy their individual socio-emotional needs, but the needs of a broader community or organisation. The following is typical of task groups:
- Though interaction is encouraged to achieve the goal or mandate, self-disclosure is not encouraged. Communication here is normally directed to the leader who controls the group to maintain order, and communication is based purely on the mandate or product to be achieved.
- Procedures during group sessions are more formalised, as there is a tendency to follow an agreed upon agenda.
- Role allocation is based on the task at hand and may depend on the position a particular member is holding within the community or organisation.
- The bond is created through the need to accomplish a mandate. As they work together to achieve their objectives, members automatically develop a bond.

- Task groups normally comprise of members with the necessary expertise and resources and a desire to help communities or organisations (Toseland & Rivas, 2009:17).

Figure 7.3: This is a group of people who identified the need for physically disabled people to be taught different skills, such as writing and reading

7.7 Stages of group development

In this section, students will be introduced to the stages of group development to create an understanding of how groups evolve over time. Students are encouraged to consult other group work recommended books, such as Toseland and Rivas (2009) for more detailed information.

Groups develop through different stages from the first stage to the stage of termination. As they develop, changes take place which may contribute positively or negatively to the group process. What actually changes in the group is the interaction and communication, which are the basic processes in the group. Without interaction and communication, group development cannot take place. This explains why interaction and communication are said to be the basic group processes. It must however be understood that the stages of group development are a probability and not a fact.

The following are the stages that a group is anticipated to go through. It is important to understand that the stages of group development are a probability and not a prediction.

7.7.1 Pre-group stage

This is the stage when the group worker recruits members and solicits for consent to join the group. It is the role of the worker at this stage to explain the purpose of the group to prospective members so that they make informed decisions. The group worker also outlines his or her expectations of the group. Prospective members are given an opportunity to ask questions for clarification. At this stage, the social worker may recruit members through:
- using pamphlets
- putting notices and posters on boards
- doing individual or focus group interviews
- using social media, clinics, churches and NGOs
- personal contact.

In recruiting members, the social worker must have specific criteria to direct his or her selection of members. It is important that members are selected according to specific characteristics or criteria in order for all members to feel comfortable in the group. This will however be dictated by the type and purpose of the group.

EXAMPLE 7.2

Look at Figure 7.4.

Figure 7.4: An example of a diverse group

It is evident that the group composition in Figure 7.4 may not contribute positively to the group development. The selection of members comprises tall, heavy, robust members that may threaten smaller bodied members. Secondly, a mixture of adults and children may not be appropriate due to differences in stages of development and accompanying interests.

This may result in members looking at themselves as individuals and not part of the whole group. Looking at this picture, one can see individualism, as each member is doing what she or he likes and the younger members look confused and scared. Interaction and communication in this group may pose a serious challenge due to a lack of common interest and homogeneity in the group.

7.7.2 Beginning stage

This is the first stage of the group's development. Members come together for the first time as group members. This is also the stage when a group leader introduces him- or herself to the members, and the members introduce themselves to one another. Ground rules and norms are set to control the behaviour of members. It is also during this stage that the group leader explains the purpose of the group to all the group members. Goals are discussed and a consensus is reached. The group may agree on long- and short-term goals, depending on the type of group. A group contract may be entered into to facilitate goal achievement. A contract in this sense is an agreement between the group worker and the group as a whole on how the group will be conducted. This may include practical considerations, such as the time of group sessions, venue, regular attendance, punctuality and respect for one another. Confidentiality and respect for all members are emphasised. Group sanctions are also discussed to encourage members to conform to the norms. It is at this stage that the group agrees on the number of sessions to be held, so as to prepare members for the ultimate termination of the group.

This stage is characterised by:

- low group consciousness because members are still finding themselves in the group and are therefore fearful and cautious, as they consider themselves different individuals and not part of the group
- low levels of interaction and communication
- members trying to find their place in the group
- no sense of self-disclosure.

The functions of the group leader at this stage are to:

- explain once more the purpose of the group
- discuss the values of confidentiality, respect, non-judgemental attitudes, and self-determination
- facilitate the setting of the goals, norms and standards
- direct the group towards goal achievement
- inform members of termination.

7.7.3 The second stage

This is called the transition stage. This is the time when the group members move from a stage of non-membership to a stage of real membership. During this stage, members try to gain acceptance from the leader and compete for recognition. There is more interaction and communication as compared to the first stage. A sense of togetherness begins to emerge, as group members develop a liking for one another. Conflict may arise as members try to assert themselves, and sub-groups develop. (See the discussion on sub-groups in the section on group processes.)

This stage is characterised by:

- improved interaction and communication
- development of sub-groups
- an emergence of conflict
- evidence of lobbying and competition
- jockeying for attention and acknowledgement.

The functions of the group leader at this stage are to:

- reinforce the purpose, norms and standards
- work towards conflict resolution
- facilitate interaction and communication
- allocate roles
- deal with sub-groups that emerge
- deal with disruptive competition.

7.7.4   The third stage

This stage is also referred to as the working stage. At this stage, the group is regarded as being fully functional, as members regard themselves as part of the group. Members no longer experience feelings of 'us' and 'them'. Members experience a sense of 'we', and cohesion is at its peak. There is high commitment to achieving the goals of the group. Members are fulfilling roles allocated to them, and self-disclosure is very high as members identify with one another and there is a generalisation of feelings. This is the stage when members work towards the resolution of their problems and the integration of solutions is rife.

This stage is characterised by:

- cohesion and we feeling
- a high sense of self-disclosure
- active participation
- a high level of interaction and communication
- generalisation and identification
- development of mutual aid.

Mutual aid in groups goes further than just the exchange of support, because it is conceptualised as a multi-dimensional helping relationship, which includes the sharing of intimate information, a feeling of need for one another, needing to use each other, developing intrinsic bonds among members, creating a sense of being in the same boat, developing a universal perspective, developing mutual support and mutual demand (including confrontation), rehearsing new skills in the safe environment, individual problem solving, and the strength in numbers phenomenon.

The functions of the group leader at this stage are to:

- move out of the central position
- help the group to focus on its mandate
- direct communication and interaction
- regulate excessive self-disclosure that may negatively impact on the development of the group.

7.7.5   Termination

This is the last stage of group development. It is normally anticipated that by this stage, group members will have reached their goals and will be ready to be weaned off the group. Termination simply means the group's life is ending and members are no longer going to meet as a group, though they may continue meeting as individuals since relationships have been established.

In a practical sense, there are two types of termination, namely planned and unplanned termination.

Planned termination is when a group terminates at the time that was agreed upon during the beginning stage. For example, if the group agreed to have ten sessions, it simply means the tenth session is the last session in which members meet as a group. Throughout the sessions, members need to be reminded about termination since termination is a process and not an end in itself. This process helps members to work towards achieving the goals by the set time and to work on their feelings regarding separation.

Unplanned termination is when the group terminates before the set time that was agreed upon at the beginning stage. Several factors may contribute to unplanned termination, such as a lack of participation resulting in little or no progress, continued absenteeism, the group not serving the original goals and purpose, the group leader leaving the agency or the area, or the group leader terminating his or her employment.

This stage is characterised by:
- a relaxation of the norms and standards
- ambivalent feelings towards being separated from the group
- members starting to view themselves as individuals
- maintaining and generalising the change efforts
- an evaluation of the group process.

The functions of the group leader at this stage are to:
- help members to deal with feelings of termination, especially in situations where the group developed close relationships
- direct the evaluation of the group process
- help members to reduce dependence on the group
- help members to maintain and generalise the change effort
- refer members who may still need assistance to other resources or groups.

Students are encouraged to view the stages of group development as a probability and not a fact. This is because of the different dynamics that may play out in various groups. For example, not all groups go through all the stages. In a case where members have already established good relationships before the start of the group, the group may not experience all the characteristics of the beginning stage, and such groups may plunge directly into the second stage or even the working stage. In other instances, groups may vacillate between stages. For example, a group may be in the third stage, but revert back to the previous stage. The regression may be due to some of the following factors: sensitivity to the topic under discussion, the worker's negative attitude, members not fulfilling their roles, and members judging each other and thus affecting interaction due to a fear of being judged or labelled.

 STOP AND REFLECT

Go back to the case study at the beginning of this chapter and answer the following questions to test your understanding of the subject matter.

1 Read the definitions of group work. Explain how these definitions relate to the case study.
2 Is a group worker different form a social worker?
3 What do you think mothers will gain from the group?
4 In your view, are groups static? Substantiate your answer with information from the chapter.
5 How would you classify this group: is it a task or treatment group? Give reasons for your choice.
6 After going through this chapter, what are your views on using group work as a method of intervention in social work practice?

7.8 Group processes

Group processes are the changes that take place in a group. As groups develop, group processes change and thus contribute to the characteristics of the different stages of group development. Group processes influence the behaviour of group members. They can facilitate group development or retard the progress in the group. The climate or atmosphere that prevails in the group can have an impact on the group processes. For example, if the group leader has a tendency to impose his or her ideas and decisions on group members, group members may feel uncomfortable, and therefore decide not to participate in any group activities. This may also have a psychological impact on members in that they may feel their contributions are not taken seriously. Group processes are sometimes referred to as group dynamics.

7.8.1 Interaction and communication

Interaction and communication are the basic group processes resulting in the development of other processes. Without interaction and communication, the group can certainly not develop. Interaction and communication are the ways members communicate with one another, and communication can be verbal or non-verbal. Through these two basic processes, group members develop an understanding of each other and identify with other group members, resulting in the emergence of a system of collectivity.

It is the role of the group worker to facilitate interaction and communication in the group. The following are different techniques group workers use to facilitate interaction and communication

- Different forms of activities: These could be singing a song together that all members can relate to, or pairing members to talk to each other about themselves and then each member reporting back to the group about what they learned.
- Ice-breakers: These can include, for example, a group leader taking the lead in introducing him- or herself, or telling members a short funny story to help them relax.
- Round robin: The group leader can encourage members to introduce themselves one at a time according to the group's seating arrangement.
- Using a model: These can include, for example, using someone who has been in a group before to talk to members about his or her experiences in a group. This should be a person who is similar to the group members, so for a group of teenagers, a teenager would serve as the best model.

The use of values, such as respect for the group and individual members, allowing self-determination and purposeful expression of feelings, and assuring members of confidentiality are all essential in facilitating interaction and communication.

7.8.2 Roles and status

To facilitate group development, group members are sometimes allocated roles to perform on behalf of the group. Role allocation happens as the group develops. It is important for a group worker to recognise and acknowledge the capacity and potential of different group members before allocating roles. This will help to improve members' self-confidence, as they will be capable of performing the roles allocated to them. Roles are normally associated with the status a member holds in the group. For example, if a group member is allocated the role of keeping the group's records, the status he holds in the group is that of a scribe or secretary. It is the role of a group worker to assess how members perform their roles and to acknowledge them for a job well done. Roles are one of the ways group workers use to facilitate active participation in the group. It is also the role of the group worker to see to it that roles are evenly spread across all members of the group.

7.8.3 Sub-groups

Sub-groups are a division of small groups that develop within a larger group based on similar points of view, and mutual feelings of attraction.

Sub-groups are inevitable in groups and sometimes become a source of conflict. As members get to know one another, they develop attractions to each other. Cliques also develop depending on personal interests, acquaintances, or areas of proximity. Sub-groups have a role in facilitating interaction and communication provided their energy is directed towards enhancing positive group development. Such sub-groups can be used as a model for other sub-groups. It is, however, very important to assess the development of sub-groups in order to direct their energy in a positive way that will benefit all group members. Sub-groups that have a negative impact on group development need to be discouraged through the use of confrontation, allocating roles to the group, involving members in a discussion to share their views, or involving them in decision-making processes. It is common for sub-groups to protest and behave inappropriately if they feel marginalised or not listened to. Furthermore, inappropriate group activities, or activities imposed on members, may activate the development of negative sub-groups.

EXAMPLE 7.3

A group leader facilitates a group of 11 pregnant teenagers in a nearby local clinic.

The teenagers are from the same township, and some have attended the same school for some years.

There is a lot of gossip in the group about how other members dress or carry themselves in the group. Three members, who attended school together, tend to keep to themselves, and have a tendency to be disruptive in the group by giggling, whispering and talking indiscriminately using nasty words. Three other members from the same area of the township stick together, come in and leave together and are always willing to actively participate in group activities.

The former sub-group does not contribute positively to the group's development. This has an impact on the communication and interaction in the group, as other members do not feel comfortable expressing themselves for fear of being laughed at or gossiped about.

 STOP AND REFLECT

If you were a social worker facilitating this group, how would you deal with the situation of sub-groups? Discuss this with your fellow students and find ways of dealing with the two sub-groups.

Advantages of sub-groups
- They may enhance the quality of interaction and communication within the whole group.
- Work oriented sub-groups may enhance general performance within the group.
- They may serve as positive models to other group members.
- They may reduce individual independence on the whole group as a system.

Disadvantages of sub-groups
- They may fragment the group effort. A group is expected to work together as a team. If sub-groups are many and not constructive, the whole purpose of forming the group may be defeated.
- Sub-groups may establish scales of social distance since sub-groups have a tendency to keep to themselves, and sometimes ignore the rest of the group.
- They may have a tendency to diminish general group performance.

- They may cause conflicts, which may retard the development of the group.
- Unhealthy competition among different sub-groups may result in group stagnation and feelings of rejection.

7.8.4 Group influence

As members interact and start to identify with one another, they automatically develop influence on each other. This is normally the development of mutual aid and generalisation. Members begin to imitate, or do as others do. Group influence, like sub-groups, can have a positive or negative impact on the development of the group. The group leader has a role of assessing this influence and making sure that other members are not coerced into doing anything against their will.

7.8.5 Cohesion

Cohesion is the development of the 'we' feeling in the group. At this stage, members look at themselves as members of the group and interaction and communication is at its optimum state. They refer to the group as 'our' group. A strong bond develops in the group, and members become dependent on the group. Cohesion is characteristic of the third stage of group development as indicated above. At this stage, self-disclosure is high, there is active participation, members work on their problems, and integration of solutions becomes paramount.

7.8.6 Group climate

Group climate is the emotional state of group members. It is determined by the level of satisfaction and contentment of group members. It depends on the atmosphere that prevails here and now. Group climate changes from stage to stage and can be affected by different variables, such as the topic under discussion, members' emotions, lack of positive emotional expression, the attitude of the group worker, and members failing to fulfil their roles. As indicated above, the level of communication and interaction can positively influence the group climate or vice versa.

7.8.7 Norms and standards

Norms are developed in the group and set standards for members' behaviour, or specify proper group behaviour. A group cannot develop if there is no order, or members do as they wish. Norms are normally developed during the first stage of group development, but are bound to change as the group progresses. This therefore explains that norms are not static. Norms are developed by the group members themselves. For norms to be effective and acknowledged, they must be accepted by the majority of group members. This is very important because norms have an element of conformity, and it is easy for members to conform if they are part and parcel of the development of norms. Norms therefore command conformity, because there is normally strong pressure to comply and in some cases there are harsh penalties for violating norms.

Norms direct the movement of the group, including issues, such as respecting one another, confidentiality, listening when others talk, allowing members purposeful expression of self, no discrimination of group members, and not imposing one's values on other members. As the group develops, norms, standards and values change to form the group culture, which binds members together to do things together. For example, as part of their values, members may decide to open all sessions with a prayer. The repeated use of prayer will eventually turn into a group culture.

7.8.8   Group culture

Group culture comprises rituals that members develop over time. It refers to values, beliefs, customs and traditions held in common by group members. Group culture emerges faster in homogeneous groups, because of similarities and identification with one another.

7.9   Conclusion

This chapter exposed you to social group work as one of the basic methods in social work. It started by giving you definitions of concepts and terms to facilitate your understanding of what group work is, and why social workers make use of groups in social work practice.

Different types of groups were explored and related to the group processes to indicate changes as they happen in groups from the beginning to termination.

Group work, as indicated above, can be used in different settings such as hospitals, correctional services, rehabilitation centres, and different forms of welfare organisations. It can be used for both rehabilitation and prevention purposes. It is a method that gives members the opportunity to share experiences, and it is based on the rationale that two heads are better than one. It uses members' strengths, assets, experiences and expertise to help one another. Integration of solutions is therefore prominent. Mutual aid and collectivity are characteristics of social group work.

End of chapter activity

Within your own community, form a group of people you have easy access to. This can be a group of children, friends, women or men etc. The purpose of the group should be for members to discuss general challenges they experience. Ethically, you are expected to inform them of your goal and not be pretentious.

You need a minimum of three people, and you are required to conduct a minimum of three group sessions. At the end of the group's sessions, assess if you were able to identify or observe the following:
1.   The development of the group stages
2.   The different group processes
3.   The roles you played at each stage
4.   The skills utilised.

This activity will give you an idea of how it feels to be a group leader. It will help you to understand the value of social group work as a method of intervention.

Key concepts

- **Group work** is a method of working with people in groups for skills development, personal growth through self-reflection, the enhancement of social functioning, the achievement of socially desirable goals and the accomplishment of tasks. It is based on the need that people have for each other and their interdependence.
- A **group worker** is a professional social worker who facilitates groups in social work practice for the benefit of members.

- **Group processes** are the changes that take place in a group. As a group develops, group processes change thus contributing to the characteristics of the different stages of the group development. Group processes influence the behaviour of group members. They can facilitate group development or retard the progress of the group.

References

1. GARVIN, C. 1981. *Contemporary group work.* USA: Prentice Hall.
2. McKENDRICK, B. 1987. *Introduction to social work in South Africa.* Pinetown: Owen Burgess Publishers.
3. SEGAL, E.A., GERDES, K.E. & STEINER, S. 2007. *An introduction to the profession of social work: becoming a change agent.* Brooks/Cole.
4. TOSELAND, R.W. & RIVAS, R.F. 2009. *An introduction to group work practice.* Boston: Allyn and Bacon.

Community work: A social work method

Mimie Sesoko

By the end of this chapter, you should be able to:

✓ outline the history of community work and the community centred approach

✓ define the concepts 'community' and 'development'

✓ define and demonstrate an understanding of the difference between community work and community development

✓ demonstrate an understanding of community development values and principles

✓ define the community development approaches

✓ define the role of social worker in community development processes

✓ define and identify the different role-players in community development processes.

 Bogolo village

Bogolo Action Group was formed after the local municipality failed to respond to the service delivery demands of the Bogolo community. This action group consisted of young women and men who work in the City of Tshwane. The group's aim was to challenge government on behalf of the village, as they felt they had a strong network of working people who could take time off to demand services from government at the provincial offices of the different departments. The village was 150 km from the city, so most of these young people stayed in town. The initiative was led by Mr Tate, a teacher by profession, who felt that since the government was slow to service their community, they could intervene from the city. At the village, other community leaders coordinated the work. This was a great strategy for the Bogolo community, as they were looking to address development from both inside and outside the village. The plan was to strengthen development and to encourage young people to participate in changing Bogolo village. Mr Tate also felt that since they were employed, educated and informed of a lot of things, they could be resourceful to the village.

Mr Tate arranged several meetings in the city to support the community back home in Bogolo village. Approximately 100 young professionals, who work in the city and are from Bogolo village, attended the first three meetings. Before the action group was formed, the people who were invited to the city meetings had different opinions regarding how to address the Bogolo village problems from outside the village. The following were the three community groups that emerged:

1 The **first group** felt they did not need to do anything, and wanted to wait for government to come to them, as they were taxpayers. They did not want to take the lead to drive community service delivery, but wanted the government officials to do their work.

2 The **second group** wanted to take a radical step to challenge the government and force officials to deliver the services. They wanted the community to continue protesting for service delivery.

3 The **third group** was the Bogolo Action Group. They were now an established group in the city that engaged the different government departments on the future of Bogolo village. They collected funds to address some of the short-term needs while at the same time they consulted with the private sector in the City of Tshwane for funding. The Bogolo Action Group coordinated development work in the city to speed up the village development process.

The case study 8.1 demonstrates that in a community setting, people differ in their way of thinking and handling situations. Members of one group may share an opinion on and understanding of a situation that that differs from members of another group's in same community. In a community setting, perceptions and experiences do differ. People will group themselves according to the way they want problems or situations to be addressed. The case study also suggests that there may be more than one solution to a problem. Furthermore, it demonstrates that some people may see challenges in a situation, while others may view the same problem as an opportunity to influence change.

8.1   Introduction

People in communities live together over many years in different settings. They handle simple and complex challenges as a collective. The settings may be rural, urban or informal settlements. Problems and challenges are not always easy for people living in a community to handle without someone helping them to tackle them. In social work, social workers are guided by theory, skills, values, principles, ethical standards and norms to facilitate a process of change. In some cases, the setting is not a geographical area like Bogolo or the City of Tshwane. It may be a group of community members working together towards a common goal, such as a rural women's farmer association. In the case of Bogolo village, the action group and the community leaders can be supported by a social worker, referred to as community worker, to address their challenges as a collective. In this chapter, we will look at how social workers in their capacity as community workers address community needs and concerns.

The chapter examines the concepts 'community', 'community work' and 'community development'. It briefly outlines the history of community work and community development. The chapter also covers the processes followed in addressing community issues, the role of the social worker as community work facilitator and the roles of other community development practitioners. The chapter also outlines the different principles, values and approaches applied in community development processes.

 STOP AND REFLECT

1 In your own words, define the concept 'community'.
2 Have you been involved in community processes in your own community, or any other community setting? If so:
    a What was your role?
    b What were the outcomes of your involvement?
    c What were the benefits?
    d What were the challenges?
3 Reflect on the following example sentences to help you understand the different ways in which the concept 'community' may be understood:
    a A group of high school teachers are talking about the school soccer team. They refer to the learners who support the team as a 'community of soccer supporters'.
    b Economists from the same business sector are referred to as the 'economist business community'.
    c Five countries in Europe are referred to as the 'European community'.
    d The people in Moutse village are referred to as the 'Moutse community'.
    e Hockey players from Soweto competing in America are referred to as South Africans from the 'Soweto hockey community'.
    f Union workers on a strike are being referred to as workers from the 'Cosatu community'.

ACTIVITY

Read the conversation between Pinky and Sophy in Figure 8.1. In a group, briefly discuss your views on what is said. Each group member must get a chance to share her or his interpretation of the concept 'community'.

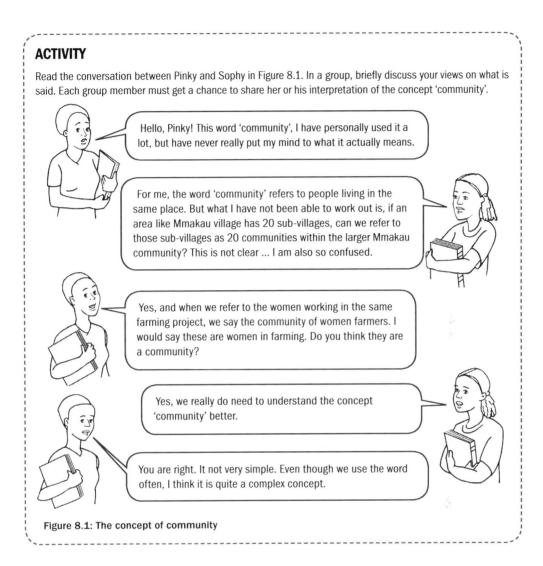

Hello, Pinky! This word 'community', I have personally used it a lot, but have never really put my mind to what it actually means.

For me, the word 'community' refers to people living in the same place. But what I have not been able to work out is, if an area like Mmakau village has 20 sub-villages, can we refer to those sub-villages as 20 communities within the larger Mmakau community? This is not clear … I am also so confused.

Yes, and when we refer to the women working in the same farming project, we say the community of women farmers. I would say these are women in farming. Do you think they are a community?

Yes, we really do need to understand the concept 'community' better.

You are right. It not very simple. Even though we use the word often, I think it is quite a complex concept.

Figure 8.1: The concept of community

According to Hawtin, Hughes, Percy-Smith and Foreman (1994:33), the term 'community' is very difficult to define as its usage has become so pervasive in everyday language. They see 'community' as referring to geographical areas or localities, such as a single street, a ward, a neighbourhood, a village, and a town, and a group of people. They further indicate that a community may have other common bonds that can create a sense of belonging, for example a shared problem such as a medical condition or disability, a shared working environment, or members of the same church or political group.

Clarke (1973:32) defines 'community' in the following four ways:

1. Community as a locality refers to a community of place.
2. Community as a social structure refers to the social relation between and among groups of people.
3. Community as a social activity refers to a group of people performing specific tasks.
4. Community as a sentiment refers to a sense of solidarity and common attitude towards a specific concern or task.

8.2 The concept 'community' defined

The concept 'community' is further defined as follows by other authors:

- Swanepoel and de Beer (2006:43) define 'community' as a grouping of people who reside in a specific locality and exercise some degree of local autonomy in organising their social life in such a way that they can, from that locality, satisfy the full range of their daily needs.
- Banks, Butcher, Henderson and Robertson (2003:34) define 'community' as a group of people who come together and perceive common needs and problems, acquire a sense of identity, and have a common set of objectives.
- Schenck, Nel and Louw (2010:7) define 'community' as perceptions and experiences of people in a particular space that are continuously changing. It may mean how people in a group experience their social reality at a given time.

In summary, these authors view 'community' as:

- a social relationship among people
- a group with shared interests and concerns
- a group with a particular function or activity
- people who live in the same place with common needs, problems, and concerns.

8.3 Community work as a method of social work

To differentiate community work from the other social work methods one can simply state that when dealing with individual cases, social workers utilise the case work method; and when working with a group of people with a common problem social workers utilise the group work method. For example, if a social worker is working with a family, the social worker will handle the family as one unit, but use the same space for group counselling with the members of the same family. If a social worker works with three or more families in similar situations in the same setting. it may be an opportunity to apply the community work process.

EXAMPLE 8.1

Ten Soweto foster parents are given a parenting course by a social worker who has specialised in community work. The social worker trains the ten women to become the champions of the parenting course as part of Child Welfare's train the trainer (TOT) programme. These ten foster parents then establish a foster care parenting support system in Soweto. This then becomes a community work programme offering support to foster care parents. It also becomes a chain of training. The ten women are then allocated to regions in Soweto to support foster care parenting. The social worker continues to supervise the ten champions to support other foster care parents. The social workers have started a community work programme for child welfare. This example shows that one can start working with just ten people in a group and grow the programme to work with the large community of Soweto. Community work, therefore, covers a large area and social workers handle a large number of people through the TOT programme.

So how do we define 'community work'? There are various definitions.

Evens (1974:12) defines 'community work' as a method that is primarily concerned with forms of collective action to the environment. He further indicates that in community work there is an inter-relationship between people and social change agents whereby people and the providers of services bring about a more comfortable fit.

Henderson (as cited in Beckett, 2006:94) defines community work as the methods and skills used to work with people around a shared interest or concern. At the core of the methods and skills is the idea of organising and helping people to come together to form an autonomous group. He further emphasises that community work is not about experts doing things for people or groups, but about promoting the development of organised activity by the community itself to either create its own resources to meet its needs, or to campaign to bring in resources from outside (by challenging local councils to provide proper services).

Henderson and Thomas (2013:2) use community work interchangeably with neighbourhood work, which refers to direct face-to-face work with local people who form groups or networks to tackle a need or problem they have identified to give support to each other and to provide services to people in the area.

Considering the definitions above, it is very clear that the concept 'community' is used differently in different settings. It is a concept that is used to refer to people in a specific setting and with a specific relationship. What is critical is for the social worker to understand how people on the ground are grouped and how they work together. We learned that when a group of people comes together to address a specific need they can be referred to as a community. Community members do achieve more in working together.

EXAMPLE 8.2

A social worker enters a rural community to work with a group of women farmers who have established a cooperative. The cooperative was struggling to generate income, as there were differences among members. The members did not want to confront their differences, as they indicated that their aim was not to talk about their issues but to make money. They were interested in getting financial support from their funders. They wanted the social worker to identify markets for them to sell their goods. They simply wanted specific support services from the social worker and nothing else. The social worker's approach when entering the community was different from what they had expected. She was guided by her training and wanted to follow her community work theory, which emphasises that in facilitating change in communities the social worker must:

- apply a developmental, grassroots, bottom-up approach in working with members of the community (this means to listen rather than instruct)
- get to know the community, their leaders, their resources, their history, the indigenous knowledge etc. (community profiling)
- apply his or her social work values (such as respect, acceptance, individualism and self-determination) to facilitate change in the community
- engage community members and help them drive their own development process
- move at the community pace and not decide for communities
- empower communities and not use a top-down approach.

🔖 STOP AND REFLECT

1 How do you think the cooperative would grow if the social worker simply gave them the money they wanted?
2 What do you think would happen to this money, considering that the community had no idea how to plan their activities?
3 What do you think would happen a few months down the line when the funds dry up?
4 Do you know of any stories where such funding was provided to cooperatives or organisations that were not trained to drive their own development? Is so, share the stories with your fellow students.

In Example 8.2, the social worker could not simply provide funding and expect the cooperative members to have a sustainable project or business. He or she needed to know more about how the cooperative was established and its history (including its strengths and weaknesses). The social worker would then need to build a relationship so he or she can facilitate a process of change in the cooperative setting. The social worker was therefore guided by her theory. She was able to:

- explore with the members their specific business goals, aims, and common vision
- facilitate change in the cooperative and help each member of the cooperative to identify his or her strengths and the strengths of the group members as a collective
- deal with their perceived needs and experiences
- address their differences before she could deal with the money matters
- empower the community to approach the different departments of trade and industry that support cooperatives
- allow the cooperative members to take a leading role in approaching the different stakeholders for help.

The facilitation process requires time, perseverance, patience and trust from both the social worker and the community. It can be very challenging for communities, as this process does not give them the immediate resources that they want. In most cases, communities will request resources from the social worker without going through the above facilitation process. Henderson and Thomas (2013:15) state that to build community capacity the community worker must develop the confidence and skills of local people and strengthen local organisations' network channels for growth. In this case study, the social worker needed to be smart in the way she applied her facilitation skills. She tapped into her network system in the government and private sector and allowed the cooperative members to approach the funders. The social worker needed to know who to refer the cooperative members to in government for them to get the right assistance. To open more doors for the community to get help from the private sector and government, she needed to study her environment and build strong partnerships. Therefore, there is the need for social workers to know the environments in which they operate for them to be effective.

It is recommended that social workers develop a balance between their social and economic knowledge and skills. If they work in communities that require knowledge on business, such as women farmers, women hawkers, and community members who want to start small businesses, they must understand how micro-credit programmes operate, including cooperatives. It can be challenging for social workers who only know welfare work to support the larger community as the needs in poverty stricken areas are so big and broad. Social workers in practice need to know how to deal with macro-businesses and not just understand small income-generating projects. It is also necessary for social workers to familiarise themselves with new developments in South Africa and learn about how other departments operate. For example, social workers need to understand how cooperatives are formed and how to facilitate interaction between the business sector and small businesses. They also need to also familiarise themselves with the funding structures and models of different organisations, such as the Department of Agriculture (which funds women and young farmers), National Youth Development Agencies (NYDA) and International Foundations like W.K. Kellogg and Ford Foundation programmes. Furthermore, it is important to understand the funding system in the private sector, as many programmes in non-governmental organisations (NGOs) are funded through social responsibility in the private sector.

In South Africa, the demand for government services has increased, especially in poor communities. This has changed the community work approach as more organisations are established to specifically address the demands of the larger society. Organisations have established programmes that address the specific needs of communities. Therefore the above consultation method of getting to know the community and moving at their pace may not be applicable where service delivery demands are very high. The next section addresses the roles social workers play in the changing arena within the South African community.

8.4 From community work to the community-centred approach

Social workers in South Africa are increasingly trained to practise different social work methods within the setting of the organisation in which they are employed. The majority of social workers employed in both government and non-governmental organisations use what Weyers (2011:9) refers to as the community-centred approach. This means they provide services to the vulnerable and needy individuals, groups, families and communities as part of a service delivery method. According to Weyers (2011:9) social workers in organisations provide programmes that are already set up by the organisations. In some cases these programmes are guided by funding organisations (in the government or private sector). This approach is mainly service focused. Evens (1974:14) refers to this kind of service model as a provider base and consumer base approach. The provider base is when the organisation provides social and community services with an emphasis on matching the services provided with the needs of the population. The consumer base is when services are supplied according to consumers' requests.

 Case Study 8.2 Dinokana NGO

Dinokana is a national non-governmental organisation with a mission to provide services to orphans and vulnerable children (OVC) and families affected by HIV and Aids. The organisation received R5 million from the United States Agency for International Development (USAID) for prevention work and for the OVC programme. The operations director submitted a funding proposal for three years and these funds were to promote HIV peer education programmes, including Men as Partners (MAP) programmes, which address gender-based violence, and OVC programmes.

The role of the social workers employed in the organisation was to provide one-on-one counselling to the youth and families, and to address the issues related to children and HIV and Aids. As part of their job description, the social workers had to ensure that the volunteers established Child Care forums (CCFs) to support OVC. The programme's reporting structure required that the social workers report on the following:

- The total number of children who received food parcels
- The total number of children who attended Kids Clubs
- The total number of children who received school uniforms
- The total number of children receiving psychosocial support
- The total number of new Child Care Forums established
- The total number of family visits.

This is a national programme and the social workers are employed in nine provinces. Dinokana has an internal monitoring and evaluation division that trains and assists social workers to monitor progress in Kids Clubs to generate monthly and quarterly reports for USAID.

STOP AND REFLECT

1 In your own words describe the difference between community work and the community-centred approach.

2 What do you think are the advantages and disadvantages of community work and the community-centred approach?

3 The following statements are practitioners' views on their organisations' performances. Reflect on them:

  a In my organisation we are ready to service communities. We provide food parcels every month.

  b Other NGOs use community work methods. They cannot engage communities to do programmes that address food security, because they don't have funding.

  c In my organisation, we deliver services very quickly. We don't delay.

  d Our church programme is donor driven, as we do what funders tell us.

  e Funding for programmes is now specific and not generalised, as funders want to see the results that were promised.

4 If you were the social worker at Dinokana NGO, and wanted communities to drive their own development with their leaders, how would you propose to address the community's needs?

5 Describe what it means for a social worker to help facilitate change in communities.

6 What approaches would you implement in dealing with communities to facilitate change at their pace.

7 Communities need service delivery. How would you assist communities to achieve a balance between driving their own development while receiving services from government or NGOs?

8.5   The concept 'development' defined

Development is a process, which brings about change and growth. If a country is developing it means that it lacks in certain areas, such as economic, political, human development, human resource, social, industrial and technological areas. These sectors are assessed for for a country to be classified as developed, developing or under-developed.

Since the colonial era, development has evolved. The concept 'development' is very common in the global arena, as each country is classified as developed, developing or under-developed. This classification positions a country in the global market as a First World (developed) country or Third World (under-developed or developing) country. According to Hope and Timmel (2007:13), between 1950 and 1980 development was mainly defined in terms of the country's economic position. They further explain that the different phases of the development era between these years largely looked at the economy of the country and measured the effectiveness of the development in terms of the increase in Gross National Product (GDP), which mainly considers the wealth of the country. Taylor (1994:60) states that the key function of development is to improve community capacity building and ensure that communities are able to prioritise and plan for their own development.

8.5.1   Evolution of community development approaches in South Africa

South Africa is part of the global community, so the changes that occur in the international arena have for many years affected development at grassroots level. The history of under-development in the country was influenced by a number of historical events (which will be summarised in the next section to facilitate an understanding of why communities are under-developed). This background will show how community development, as a method of intervention, has evolved.

During the agrarian era, South Africa was a farming community and the community members were all equal as they were guided by traditional systems that encouraged sharing.

Men were hunters and women took care of their family households and worked as subsistence farmers. Colonialism, industrialisation and apartheid changed the community processes. With the introduction of industrialisation, men migrated to the cities to work in the mines. The development of rural communities was affected, as women had to learn new ways of surviving. Some were employed by white farmers who produced for the global market. Commercial farming was for white farmers. This was the beginning of urbanisation and under-development in South Africa. Case study 8.3 gives a brief outline of the history of development in South Africa.

My granny, Gogo Molemo, tells me that in 1950 there were powerful countries in the north. These were countries in Europe who colonised Africa. These countries claimed they discovered Africa even though people were already living in Africa. They took over the control of countries in Africa, such as Ghana, Kenya and Cameroon. So some African countries, known as colonised countries, were under the strong leadership of these well-developed countries. Africa, Asia and South America were colonised by the British, the French and the Americans. In South Africa, people fought wars against the British and the Dutch. Then the Afrikaans community took over the control of South Africa.

I know something about these powerful countries. What I know is that two powerful institutions were established: the World Bank (WB) and the International Monetary Fund (IMF). They were based in America. My granddad told me that these institutions were established to develop the least developed countries (LCD) in Africa. To do this, they loaned governments money for development. The under-developed countries then had to pay back the loans at high interest rates. The under-developed countries used the funds to build infrastructure and to run their own governments. Then, to pay back the loans, communities were charged taxes. So governments in the least developed countries generated income for developed countries. This did not empower communities.

I also know from history books that different companies in America and Europe formed what is referred to as multi-nationals to do business in developing countries. The profits were for them and not for the local communities where they did business.

Now things have changed. Apartheid is no more, and we are to lead our own communities to develop infrastructure, business, health facilities and a lot more. Our local municipalities use a method of participation, through the Integrated Development Plan (IDP), for communities to express how they want the government to help them develop their local economy and infrastructure.

STOP AND REFLECT

1   What is your view of Gogo Molemo's story about developed countries and their development approach?
2   What do you know about the World Bank (WB) and International Monetary Fund (IMF)? Describe their role in the development arena?
3   What is the Integrated Development Plan (IDP)?
4   If you were to lead an under-developed country's development process, how would you engage communities at grassroots level?

8.6 Community development: A multi-disciplinary and multi-levelled intervention

Campfens (1997:25) defines community development as a process by which community members create an organisational structure for collective action with respect to decision-making and leadership training. The structure created will be utilised to facilitate needs identification and resources to bring about change in the community.

According to a United Nations report (as cited in Jones, 1977:7), the term 'community development' has come into international usage to refer to the process by which the efforts of the people are united with those of government authorities to improve the economic, social and cultural condition of communities, to integrate these communities into the life of the nation and to enable them to contribute fully to national progress.

Community development may be viewed as a means of mobilising communities to join state or institutional initiatives that aim to alleviate poverty, solve social problems, strengthen families, foster democracy and achieve modernisation and socioeconomic development. The integrated service delivery model document of the Department of Social Development (2005:9) states that with the shift from the social development approach a new cadre of community or social development workers were introduced to focus on community development.

Social workers have over the years utilised the community work method to facilitate community participation. Many were involved in helping communities' established micro- projects. Some of these projects never started; others have survived. In some cases the government was the main employer and funded those projects as part of the war on poverty. With the new dispensation, social workers joined private and business sectors, churches, traditional institutions, non-governmental organisations, and community based organisations, including different government departments and municipalities. These organisations employ other community practitioners from different fields, such as health, agriculture, education, religion, and psychology. The practitioners are referred to as community development practitioners. Since the setting has a variety of practitioners from different fields it therefore opens up opportunities to apply multi-disciplinary intervention at different settings and levels. Social workers can therefore participate in a programme that requires a team of practitioners from different fields.

8.7 Community development and social development in South Africa

In 1994, the social development and community development approaches were adopted as the welfare model for the new democratic South Africa. This approach is discussed in detail in Chapter 3 of this book. The *White Paper for Social Welfare (1997)* states that South Africans are called upon to participate in the development of an equitable, people-centred, democratic and appropriate social welfare system. The goal of developmental social welfare is a humane, peaceful, just and caring society, which will uphold welfare rights, facilitate the meeting of basic human needs, release people's creative energies, help people achieve their aspirations, build human capacity and self-reliance, and participate fully in all spheres of social, economic and political life.

Therefore, in South Africa, community development as a process is not only utilised by social workers, it is practised by farmers, health practitioners, sociologists and educators. According to the Budapest Declaration (2004:2), community development is seen by different practitioners as a way of strengthening civil society and prioritising the actions of communities. In utilising community development as an approach, the capacity of people as active citizens will be strengthened. It therefore plays an important role in supporting active democracy at community levels. The Department of Social Development's Integrated service delivery report states (2005:16) that community development is dynamic, multi-sectoral and multi-disciplinary in nature and has the following focus areas:

- Facilitation of community development processes
- Development of people and community-based programmes
- Facilitation of capacity-building and economic empowerment programmes.

 Case Study 8.4 Mafefe

This is a story of a group of social workers who worked for the Rural Advice Centre (RAC), which is an NGO operating in rural settings. The RAC employed a group of engineers, economists, and health, agricultural, and finance specialists, and social workers to work in a multi-disciplinary team. The opportunity to utilise this approach started in Mafefe. The village of Mafefe had a water system problem, as the rivers were polluted with asbestos because of mine dumps. This was a sensitive issue, as the mines where closed, but the after effect of the dumping caused problems. People suffered from cancer and some died from this disease. A multi-disciplinary team approach was critical as the community needed help with health, environmental, finance and human development issues. The health team was invited to assess the health status of the community. The civil engineers looked at the rivers and the water system as it was affecting the villagers. The agricultural specialists looked at the effect of the asbestos and food security matters. The finance team assisted in putting together a financial model to assess the cost of cleaning the polluted water system. The social workers looked at the human development aspect, which involved assessing who should work in each team and the capacity building needs, helping with counselling those who lost their families due to cancer, and helping to facilitate participation from all angles. The social workers were central to the team, as they needed to identify the feelings, concerns and experiences of the members of the larger community as they were experiencing pain and fear. The leadership wanted solutions for all the problems in the village. It was critical for them to also understand the roles of the different team members and how they would interact with the villagers. The leaders and the community members owned the development process as they wanted change and wanted to drive the process. Through a consultative process, schools and churches were identified as the first places to start creating awareness of the dangers of asbestos and to teach learners, women, and all the members of the community about the polluted water. The engineers, with a group of older men, were tasked with identifying new, unpolluted water springs at the top of the mountain for the community to use. The community of farmers and the team of agricultural specialists also went out to identify land for the community to plough and plant vegetables closer to the new spring. Everything came together as the community members began to understand their roles and share the knowledge gained from different team meetings. The social workers were able to engage the traditional leaders and community members, and the different teams from the Rural Advice Centre worked together to achieve a common goal of addressing the wellbeing of Mafefe.

8.8 The core values and principles of community development

Community development processes, like individual and group therapy, are guided by values and principles. These guidelines help to facilitate community change or development processes. Authors and organisations have different ways of looking at them. There are generic and common ways or steps that facilitators of change in community settings follow. Values and principles are tested and applied in many situations and settings where community interaction or development took place. This section highlights some of the values and principles one can apply in different community development situations and settings. These community development values and principles are:

1. **Participation of community members:** This means inclusivity – not excluding members when engaging with community issues and needs. Lessons learned is that participation leads to success. If people are left out, not consulted and not involved, in most cases projects or community activities fail. Participation is very important from the beginning during the initial decision-making processes up to when projects or programmes are established and implemented.
2. Growth and development are also referred to by some authors as **empowerment**: Any development process should lead to growth or should aim to empower individuals, groups or communities. The role of the facilitators of change must be to empower communities to lead their own development. It means that for change to occur or for community members to measure their success, focus should be on growth and development which is empowerment.
3. **Collaboration, cooperation, team work and partnership:** These concepts are used interchangeably. In all the processes of engaging communities in their own development, what is key in cooperation is team work and collaboration. Success can mostly be achieved through collective involvement. Community development should lead to strengthening the cooperation of the different members of the society. The facilitator's role is to help members to utilise their skills, knowledge and capabilities in community projects or programs.
4. **Problem-solving:** In community processes, be it in dealing with groups of women, men, children, youth or any other grouping, the people must be involved in addressing their own needs and problems. This value and principle of problem-solving through the involvement of community members teach us that people must drive their own development and should not be seen as the recipients of services or support without their full involvement.

The following section summarises the four common values as outlined above and gives examples of how they can be applied in community work processes.

8.8.1 Participatory democracy

The core values, as stated above, put more emphasis on community ownership, participative democracy, empowerment, partnership and collaboration. It is very clear that for community development processes to be effective, people must be consulted at all levels. As it is sometimes impossible for the larger population to be involved, representatives from all sectors need to be elected or appointed. This must be done in a democratic and participatory manner. All sectors of the community must be informed and be allowed to participate in the community development processes in communities. Representatives from groups of men, women, the youth, church leaders, professionals, the young and old, and poor and rich are all very important in community processes. A process of selection or elections must be consultative to make sure that no one is left out. All sectors or groups must be involved and no one must be discriminated against.

8.8.2 Empowerment

Growth is expected in a village or in communities. Hence the importance of facilitating empowerment processes at all levels. Communities need to be empowered in many areas of their development stages. Empowerment can come in different shapes and forms. It can be through strengthening existing programmes within communities or supporting new initiatives. Despite the many challenges communities encounter, life moves on as communities learn from one another and initiate new ideas. Each community has its own strengths and innovative ways. It is important for the practitioners on the ground to identify these initiatives so they can be strengthened through funding, capacity building, and in some cases through mentoring programmes. Women selling vetkoek on street corners is an initiative that is growing, as we find these women selling vetkoek on almost every street corner in town. They have established their own card box shops. This initiative can be further developed to become a franchise. This is how businesses such as KFC started. They started small and grew locally and internationally. The same model can be developed. We need people to look at these groups of women and develop a business model to empower them.

8.8.3 Partnership, cooperation and collaboration

All stakeholders must strive towards working together. Public and private partnerships must be encouraged for stronger collaboration to take place at a community level. In cases where micro-projects are supported on a small scale, partners with government departments can lead to communities developing far more sustainable and larger programmes, for example communities that are engaged in infrastructure programmes established to create jobs for the unemployed youth. In this case the government can provide project funding and materials, while the private sector invests in capacity building for youth to acquire relevant skills to perform jobs. So at a community level, we need the business sector and the government to work together with community leaders to bring change that is driven by community structures. Cooperation of community members and their leaders is especially important. Also collaboration of different political groups working in the same village or community is critical.

8.8.4 Problem solving

Problem solving as a community development value is critical, as it focuses on the understanding that all problems can be solved if the community acquires problem-solving skills. No problem is too difficult if the community looks at problems together as a collective. Once the first problem is solved, the next one can also be solved by community members as a collective. Community members have the potential to grow and continuously develop this skill. The above example of the Mafefe village illustrates how even the most complex problems can be solved: community members were able to identify new streams to avoid using the polluted water.

8.9 Community development approaches

The three different community development approaches are discussed below.

8.9.1 The top-down approach

The top-down approach to community development takes place when government or authorities, or any other organisation besides the community or the target beneficiary, initiates the development activity. In this approach, the community or the target beneficiary does not participate in decision making. Decisions are made regarding a community without the community's contribution. Communities are told what to do and everything is managed by government or a promoter. The government or the promoter of the development initiative conducts the planning while the community members remain passive.

8.9.2 The bottom-up or grassroots approach

The bottom-up approach sees people as the drivers of their own development. This section will cover three theories that focus on the strength of the people and how they can drive their own development. As previously discussed, development phases have reached an era that focuses on participatory development and emphasises the development process as people driven with community members taking charge of their own development. The following are examples of people-centered, bottom-up approaches.

8.9.2.1 Carl Rogers' person-centred approach

Rogers has formulated theories on the person and his or her behaviour, perceptions and experiences. The concept of self is important in these theories. The guidance the theories provide is for the community practitioner to develop an understanding of the people they work with in a community. It also emphasises that the practitioner should respect the community's self-determination and create an environment that will allow the community members to participate in the decision-making process. The community practitioner should therefore believe that the community has the potential to grow and develop. The community has the ability to discover its own experiences and strengths, so the practitioner must work from the community's frame of reference (Rogers, 1977:67).

8.9.2.2 The asset-based community development approach (ABCD)

The asset-based community development approach was developed by Kretzmann and McKnight (2012:172). It is also referred to as the strength based approach, as it focuses on the strength of the community and not the problem or the needs. It encourages community practitioners to create space for the community to appreciate what they have by assessing their own strengths. It is true that even in the midst of many challenges, communities posses many assets, such as social assets, the skills individuals possess, associations, churches, schools, cultural groups, networks, and strong family ties. The community is rich in social assets that can be utilised for their benefit (refer to the case study on Bogolo village). Community members need to recognise and appreciate their strengths as a starting point. In the strength based approach, civil societies, community network groupings, such as stockvels and church groups, can be utilised to benefit the community. **Appreciative interviewing** can be used to help communities identify their strengths.

According to Kretzmann and Mcknight (2012:171) the following are some of the steps facilitators can use to facilitate change:

Appreciative interviewing
- Start talking to people informally about their past achievements when working together as a community.
- Focus conversations by suggesting specific topics.
- Help community members to analyse their successes by facilitating group discussions.

Community analysis of success

- Encourage people to discover the local reasons for success that can help them understand how to create successful community development initiatives in future.
- After conducting many appreciative interviews, bring community members together to do a collective analysis of their past successes.
- Encourage deeper analysis and find out the reasons for their success.

Positive deviance

- Let the community assist in identifying individuals, families or groups that are above average.
- Encourage community members to identify specific behaviours and circumstances that explain the success.
- Discuss how this behaviour could be replicated.

These are the steps community practitioners can follow using the ABCD facilitation method:
- Build purposeful relationships.
- Motivate community members.
- Let the Communities identify assets and opportunities within the community by:
    > mapping individual and group skills and capacities
    > mapping assets of local institutions
    > mapping physical assets and natural resources
    > identifying economic opportunities.
- Help them link and mobilise these assets.
- Help them develop an action plan.
- Let them identify the sustainability plan and processes.

 STOP AND REFLECT

Using the asset-based community development approach, as described above, think about the squatter camp or informal settlement community in your neighbourhood or visit one close by. (If you live in one, use your experience.)

1   Describe a squatter camp or informal settlement. (You can also interview someone from a squatter camp.)
2   If there are development projects in the squatter camp or informal settlement, briefly describe a project that you like, visited or read about.
3   Describe how you would use the asset-based community development approach to support this project.
4   List four community assets, from the squatter camp or informal settlement, for each of the three categories in the table below.

Categories	List of assets
Economic	
Human resources	
Physical	

8.9.2.3   The role of social worker in community development bottom-up processes

Based on the above approaches, the role of social workers in communities is to facilitate a process of change which is community driven. A community driven process is a process whereby communities drive their own development and change. The community facilitators need to create a space for community members to define their own destination and the process of bringing change. This will bring socioeconomic change to the community and the familes who live in it.

American Society for Training Development (2008:13) defines a facilitator as a person who has no decision-making authority within a group, but who guides the group to work together more effectively to create synergy, to generate new ideas, and to gain consensus and agreement. The social worker plays a role of a change agent and community facilitator within different settings. The settings include government departments, the private sector, non- governmental organisations (NGOs), and faith-based and community-based organisations (CBOs).

8.9.3   The partnership approach

The third approach involves partnerships in which external stakeholders, including government, play a supportive role as facilitators and/or consultants (Geddes, 2005:14). In this approach, community members initiate and also play an active role in the development process. There are a number of organisations that work in communities to support change. These can therefore be referred to as stakeholders. They consist of the private sector, national NGOs, international NGOs and government departments, including municipalities at local government. These organisations can form strong partnerships with communities to facilitate joint-venture programmes. As Geddes (2003:29) states, partnerships are supposed to nurture community-driven processes, replace competition and unlock resources, ideas and energy for the benefit of the community. These partnerships, if well structured, can be effective and bring about collaborative advantages, such as:

- releasing synergy
- exchanging information and ideas
- improving decision making
- integrating provision across sectors and services
- allowing holistic strategic approaches to develop for the benefit of communities.

The challenge is that not every partner is ready to share space with others, hence the problems of duplication and power struggles. These problems confuse community-driven processes in the development arena. These are the struggles communities face in community development processes worldwide. In South Africa, communities are still learning how to drive their own processes as social development as a new paradigm shift is still unfolding.

8.10   Conclusion

In this chapter we examined the concepts 'community' and 'development', development phases, community work and community development. The history of community work as a social work method was outlined to facilitate an understanding of how this method has evolved over the years. Community development includes other fields, such as health, agriculture and education, and social workers find themselves having to apply this method as they work in different sectors. Community development approaches outline the values and principles at different levels. The case studies provide an opportunity to apply the knowledge acquired from the chapter and to reflect on the learning process.

End of chapter questions

Use the knowledge you have acquired from this chapter to answer the following questions.

1. If you were appointed as a social worker to facilitate a process of change in Bogolo village, which approach would you use? Briefly explain the process and approach you would utilise, and describe your role and responsibilities in the process.
2. Explain the difference between the top-down and bottom-up approaches.
3. How does the Dinokana NGO case study fit with Weyers's definition of the Community Centred Approach?
4. Compare the approach used in the Gogo Molemo case study to the approach used in the Dinokana NGO case study.
5. What is the difference between community work and community development?
6. Why are the Carl Rogers and ABCD approaches referred to as people-centred approaches?
7. What is meant by multi-disciplinary and multi-levels in community development?
8. Based on your involvement with communities, are there other role-players involved in the development arena? Who are they?
9. It is critical for facilitators to know and respect the community development values when working with communities. Explain why and give examples of how they should be applied.

Key concepts

- **Community** refers to a geographical area and/or a functional group, for example the community of Mafefe, women farmers and men in the army.
- **Development** is a facilitated process of change, which leads to growth. For example: Youth in a village participating in a computer training programme learn about new technology. This is a development process for them.
- **Community work** is one of the social work methods that allows communities to drive their own development. For example: A social worker building a relationship in which she engages a group of rural women in a micro-project.
- The **community centred-approach** is a service-focused community approach. For example: A social worker is employed by a community-based organisation to only help children with muscular dystrophy. Her role is to only use the play therapy method and nothing else.
- **Community development** is an integrated development approach, which can be implemented using a multi-disciplinary team. The community drives the development process. For example: A team of specialists from a local NGO working with community leaders, the youth, women and men to address health, environmental, financial and educational challenges in a community-driven programme.

References

1. AMERICAN SOCIETY FOR TRAINING AND DEVELOPMENT. 2008. *10 steps to successful facilitator.* Baltimore, Maryland: Victor Graphics Inc.
2. BANKS, S., BUTCHER, F., HENDERSON, P. & ROBERTSON, J. 2003. *Managing community practice, principles, policies and procedures.* Great Britain: The Policy Press.
3. BECKETT, C. 2006. *Essential theory for social work practice.* London: Sage Publishing.
4. CAMPFENS, H. 1997. *Community development around the world.* Toronto: University of Toronto Press.
5. CLARKE, D.B. 1973. The concept of community: a re-examination. *Sociological Review,* 21(3):32–37.
6. DEPARTMENT OF SOCIAL DEVELOPMENT. 1997. *White paper for social welfare.* Pretoria: Government Printers.
7. DEPARTMENT OF SOCIAL DEVELOPMENT. 2005. *Integrated service delivery model: towards improved social services social development.* South Africa: Department of Social Development.
8. EVENS, P. 1974. *Community work theory and practice.* Oxford: Alistair Shornach Ltd.
9. GEDDES, M. 2005. *Making public private partnership work: building relationships and understanding culture.* England: Gower Publishing Ltd.
10. HAWTIN, M., HUGHES, G. PERCY-SMITH, J. & FOREMAN, A. 1994. *Community profiling auditing social needs.* Bellingham: Open University Press.
11. HENDERSON, P. & THOMAS, D. 2013. *Skills in neighbourhood work.* Padstow, Great Britain: T.J. International Ltd.
12. HOPE, A. & TIMMEL, S. 2007. *Training for transformation: a handbook for community work Book 3.* Bourton, UK: Intermediate Technology Publication Ltd.
13. JONES, D. 1977. *Community work in the United Kingdom: integrating social work method.* London: Allen Unwinswick N.J.
14. KRETZMANN, J.P. & McKNIGHT, J.L. 2012. *Mapping community capacity.* New Brunswick: Rutgers University Press.
15. ROGERS, C.R. 1977. *Carl Rogers on personal power: inner strength and its revolutionary impact.* London: Constable.
16. SCHENCK, R., NEL, H. & LOUW, H. 2010. *Introduction to participating community practice.* Pretoria: Unisa Press.
17. SCOTTISH COMMUNITY DEVELOPMENT CENTRE. 2014. *The Budapest declaration.* 2004. [Online]. Available: http://www.scdc.org.uk/media/resources/documents/budapestdeclaration4683d.pdf [19 May 2014]
18. SCOTTISH COMMUNITY DEVELOPMENT CENTRE. 2014. *What is community development?* [Online]. Available: http://www.scdc.org.uk/who/what-is-community-development/ [6 March 2014]
19. SWANEPOEL, H. & DE BEER, F. 2006. *Community development: break the cycle of poverty.* Cape Town: Juta & Co. Ltd.
20. TAYLOR, V. 1994. *National social welfare development plan: working towards basic welfare rights for all.* South Africa: University of the Western Cape Press.
21. WEYERS, M.L. 2011. *The theory and practice of community work: a Southern African perspective.* 2nd ed. Potchefstroom: Keurkopie.

Chapter 9
Fields of social practice

Chapter 10
Employment settings for social workers

Fields of social practice

Peter Schultz

CHAPTER OUTCOMES

By the end of this chapter, you should be able to:

✓ identify and describe the different fields in which social work is involved

✓ explain the role of the social worker in each field

✓ understand the circumstances and needs of the clients in each field

✓ explain the obstacles and difficulties encountered by social workers and clients in each field

✓ identify other role-players in the different fields

✓ refer to the relevant Acts in the fields

✓ mention all the sectors where social workers can work.

 Case Study 9.1 Johanna

Johanna is a social worker who has just completed her studies. She finds herself employed by a community-based organisation. This organisation specifically focuses on working with poverty-stricken families, which include families who have very little and/or irregular income, families living in predominantly squatter areas, and families struggling with substance abuse, domestic violence and child neglect.

She was requested to assist a six-year-old boy who had run away from home and had been living on the streets for the past five months. The boy is timid, and is intimidated and abused sexually by older street children, yet he is more afraid to go back home than remain on the streets.

Johanna went to meet this boy on a street corner where he used to hang out. She explained who she was and enquired about his wellbeing and his circumstances. He became extremely tense, and to prove to his friends that he was well, he denied having any problems.

Returning to the office, Johanna was unsure of what to do next. What would you advise Johanna to do in this situation?

There are various factors to be considered when making this decision. They include the following:

• Johanna requires supervision and guidance.

• She may obtain background information about the boy, such as where the boy originally came from, why he ran away, and what the circumstances at home were.

• Johanna may also determine whether there are any projects in the community that reach out to street children and work with them.

• Johanna may decide to also pay attention to all the children on the street, and to first build a relationship with them instead of focusing on one child only.

• Johanna may also want to make contact with the local authorities to find out if the areas are earmarked for any future developments, such as housing, sport and recreation facilities.

9.1 Introduction

Due to the fact that people experience difficulties in all life phases and life areas, social work by default needs to address the needs and circumstances of people from birth, through childhood, adolescence, adulthood, ageing until death. People can be healthy, less-abled or sick. Some suffer loss, become addicted and/or commit crime. Then there are people who get married, divorced, neglect children, or lose their jobs. There is literally no life area in which social work has no role to play.

The purpose of this chapter is to give students an overview of the profession by describing the different fields in more detail. These fields are divided up into the following categories: health care, child care, family care, addiction, trauma and bereavement support.

9.2 Health care

9.2.1 HIV and AIDS, tuberculosis (TB) and sexually transmitted diseases (STDs)

After completing this section, you should be able to define, understand and explain HIV, AIDS, TB and STDs. You should also be able to place these within the South African context and have a clear understanding of the role of the social worker in counselling and supporting people living with these diseases.

9.2.1.1 HIV and AIDS

HIV is the abbreviation for the human immunodeficiency virus. It is transmitted through blood, semen and vaginal fluids. It uses the CD4 cells, which coordinate the body's immune system, to replicate itself, and as the amount of HIV increases, the number of CD4 cells drop, weakening the immune system.

AIDS is the acronym for acquired immune deficiency syndrome. It is acquired as it enters the body through a virus (HIV). It is not inherited and can, in most cases, be prevented. Immunity is the body's natural ability to defend itself against infection and disease. Deficiency reflects the condition where the immune system of the body is no longer able to defend itself against infections. Syndrome refers to a collection of specific signs and symptoms occurring simultaneously, which characterise a particular pathological condition.

AIDS is, in fact, not a specific disease or illness, but actually reflects a number of different conditions due to the inability of the body to defend itself against passing infections. It is perhaps better described as an opportunistic disease syndrome.

9.2.1.2 Tuberculosis

Tuberculosis, or TB, is a fairly common and often lethal infectious disease, which is usually found in the lungs. TB bacteria are spread by transmission of respiratory fluids through the air. Symptoms of TB include a chronic cough with blood spots in the sputum, fever, night sweats and weight loss. Determining whether a person has latent TB relies on skin and blood tests.

Treatment of TB is generally complex and requires long-term administration of multiple antibiotics as well as sometimes screening and treating social contacts. Treatment is currently complicated with a growing number of patients showing resistance to antibiotics. This phenomenon is called multiple drug-resistant tuberculosis (MDR-TB).

9.2.1.3   Sexually transmitted diseases (STDs)

STDs, or venereal diseases as they are also known, are transmitted by vaginal, anal or oral sex with someone who already has an STD. The germ-causing STD is carried in semen, vaginal fluid and blood. There are about 25 known types of STDs of which most are curable. Many people, however, do not even know they have an STD as they show no symptoms. Symptoms can include heavy discharge, swelling, rash, sores or redness near the sex organs, tiredness, vomiting, diarrhoea, swollen glands and sore muscles.

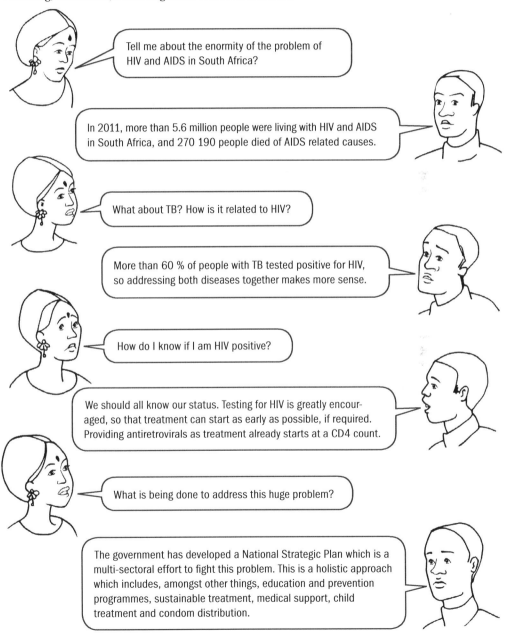

Figure 9.1: Discussing HIV and AIDS, TB and STDs

Although almost all activities regarding HIV and AIDS, TB and STDs are state driven, especially by the Department of Health and the Department of Social Development, there are a number of key role-players and organisations involved. These organisations include various private initiatives, NGOs and children's homes, the Treatment Action Campaign (TAC), medical practitioners and the media (South African Government, 2000:30).

Social workers become involved, either as an employee of the state or NGO, in education, prevention and a therapeutic capacity. In terms of therapy, social workers primarily play a supportive and practical role with both client and family. They are supportive in dealing with various feelings, including hopelessness, guilt, self-blame and depression; and practical in motivating clients to look after their health and planning for their future in spite of their disease.

Case Study 9.2 Thomas

Thomas is a 31-year-old man working as a technician at a factory in Pretoria. He has just heard that his girl-friend, who has been living with him for the past year, is pregnant. He is seeking advice from a social worker. Two weeks ago, during an HIV testing campaign at work, he was notified that he is HIV-positive. He does not want to disclose this to his girlfriend, as he is afraid that he may lose her as she tested negative a year ago before they became involved. He also does not want to disclose that he has a relationship with somebody else, which he started six months ago.

How do you think this situation could be addressed?

One of the ways situation can be addressed is as follows:

- In dealing with the problem, professional counselling is required to assist Thomas in working through the traumatic news. This deals extensively with his feelings first.
- During a second session, the social worker can sit with him and look at his responsibilities more logically. This will focus on the practical situation and the time he would like to deal with it.
- Practical situations that need addressing include the status and situation of his girlfriend and unborn child, attending to his own health and wellbeing, having another relationship in addition to his pregnant girlfriend, as well as issues of honesty and transparency.

 STOP AND REFLECT

1 What is your opinion of people living with HIV disclosing their status? Explain your opinion. Clarify who you think needs to know a person's HIV status, and explain possible consequences of such disclosure.
2 Do you think enough is being done in terms of awareness to help teenagers and the youth with decisions about their sexual life? What type of information needs to be conveyed and how do you recommend it be dealt with?
3 How can social workers support the families of those struggling with life-threatening diseases?

9.2.2 Mental health

It is important that the reader of this section has a clear understanding of what mental health and mental illness entails. Furthermore, the reader must be able to understand the role of the social worker in assisting persons with mental problems, and identify role-players in the field.

Although the concept of mental health may be differently defined along cultural, religious, personal and/or professional terms, it generally reflects a state of wellbeing – the ability to enjoy life and contribute to the lives of others. A mental disorder (or mental health problem) on the other hand, could be regarded as an inability to enjoy life. This could be caused by disease, abuse, trauma, poverty, political violence or suppression as well as the deterioration of, or ongoing, conflicting values. Mental disorders can take many forms. More well-known mental problems include, for example, depression, anxiety disorders and schizophrenia (Kendrick & Simon, 2008:180).

South Africa has a high incidence of mental disorders. Most of these problems seem to be caused by sociopolitical factors and economic inequality. Other factors include genetic predisposition, a high incidence of substance abuse and drug trafficking, family violence and abuse as well as a lack of treatment resources.

The role of the social worker in working with mental health issues cuts across all three methods of social work. Individual intervention sessions are important to assist the client in working through his or her feelings and thinking about his condition, specifically from a strength based perspective. It is important to make a thorough assessment of his or her situation, as this will determine whether the social worker will refer him or her to a hospital or clinic if it is serious, or whether he or she can be assisted within his or her community. The assessment will furthermore assist the social worker in making decisions about how the other family members will be informed and assisted.

Due to increasingly stressful life circumstances and demands on individuals and families, social workers also have a role in mental health awareness and mental health promotion. Information groups in schools or industry can be very helpful in this regard. Skills training, including stress and anger management, decision making and problem solving in groups, empowers those affected by it.

Other role-players in the field of mental health include psychologists and psychiatrists, nursing staff at hospitals and clinics, occupational therapists and general practitioners. Working together with these other role-players and cooperating with organisations dealing with mental health as well as involving clients in attending support groups, can be helpful in assisting clients to live a meaningful life.

 Case Study 9.3 **Sipho**

Sipho is seven years old. He was born with cerebral palsy and his biological father left his mother because he found Sipho to be a financial and emotional burden, as he could not relate to him and interact with him. Sipho has an older sister who is 11 years old and very close to him. Their mother is the only breadwinner and their aunt, who helped take care of Sipho, has become ill and can no longer look after him. The facility assisting children with disabilities in the nearest town, about 60 kilometres away, closed down due to insufficient funds.

As a student, what do you think a social worker should include in an action plan to assist this family and how would you go about it? In your reflection on this situation, the following can be taken into consideration:

- Any action for his family to be considered must involve the mother of the child as well as include Sipho, the aunt who looked after him and his 11-year-old sister.
- In drawing up an action plan, it is important that the social worker considers that it is not only the client who needs assistance, but the whole family. This is important, and even though many of the problems are not directly related to Sipho's condition, an action plan will play a role in determining how to assist him and his family.
- Factors to be considered include Sipho's condition with all its implications socially, emotionally and mentally, the fact that Sipho is of school-going age, the relationship with Sipho's sister who is close to him, the family's finances, accessibility to resources and lack of transport.

> **STOP AND REFLECT**
>
> 1 How can we determine when somebody is no longer responsible for their actions?
> 2 Is it better to keep mentally ill people in the community or should they be institutionalised?
> 3 Is the family responsible for the behaviour of the mentally ill? If not, who should be responsible?
> 4 Discuss with a fellow student, colleague or friend whether mental illnesses are a culturally sensitive issue and whether they are therefore perceived and dealt with differently.
> 5 Why do you think there is prejudice against persons struggling with mental illness?
> 6 Do mentally ill people have rights according to our Constitution? If yes, what are they?

9.2.3 Disabilities

In this section, the reader is introduced to various disabilities, including physical disabilities, hearing loss and blindness. The needs of each of the groups will be discussed, and different role-players in each field will be identified. Finally the role of the social worker will be described as it pertains to each disability.

Figure 9.2: Collage of international symbols for various disabilities

Physical disability refers to a condition where the mobility of a person is interrupted due to limited functioning of one or more limbs or organs (Conti-Becker, Doralp, Fayed, Kean, Lenucha, Leyshon, Mersich, Robbins & Doyle, 2007:281). The cause of the disability may be congenital or acquired, and the disability impacts the individual and his or her family and social life. The different disabilities are numerous and can be defined in various ways. They include, amongst others, people with paraplegia or quadriplegia, people with cerebral palsy, people who are hearing or visually impaired, people with epilepsy and people with Down syndrome.

The needs of people with disabilities are very different in terms of movement and access. However, a greater need of people with disabilities is to be respected and accepted as a person of value. Disabled people are often stigmatised based on their physical appearance and competence, which in turn leads to an avoidance of social interaction. They are sometimes referred to as handicapped, spastic, deformed, or paraplegic. These are nouns or adjectives referring to a condition and not a person and they lead to the devaluation of a person.

In order to counter the prejudices many people may have, disabled people have come together and compiled a Disability Rights Charter of South Africa in which they have noted 18 articles covering aspects of non-discrimination, education, employment, housing, sport, etc. This three-page document highlights how they should be treated on the same footing as able-bodied persons and that they must have access and opportunities similar to people who do not have a disability (Disabled People South Africa, 2014).

With the change of government in 1994, a new Policy on Disability was developed, by the Department of Social Development, addressing all matters regarding people with disabilities. It is the responsibility of this department to address all issues relating to disabilities and integrate service delivery on an equal footing as able-bodied people.

Role-players in service delivery directly include the Departments of Social Development, Basic Education, Labour and Health. The needs of the disabled are expressed via a national council called Disabled People South Africa (DPSA). In addition, various NGOs, societies, sports bodies and academic institutions play a vital role in supporting and promoting the needs of disabled people.

 Case Study 9.4 **Mandla**

Persons with disabilities constantly have to battle with the prejudices of many able-bodied people. Mandla was born blind and went to a special school for the visually impaired. He matriculated and went on to study at Unisa where he obtained a degree in law. He and his family were very excited at his graduation, but a year later Mandla became disheartened as he was merely doing administrative work in the law firm where he was employed. In spite of trying to convince the senior lawyers, who own the firm, that he is more than able to handle legal cases, he was not allowed to do so. His mother approached a social worker for advice.

Firstly, the social worker attended to the mother's feelings, as she was very emotional and angry about the situation. After the debriefing, the social worker explored with the mother different ways of addressing Mandla's problem, and also involving Mandla in the matter. Towards the end of the session, they agreed on the following:

- To inform Mandla of the social work session and share what was discussed in terms of possible options
- To find visually impaired lawyers in other firms who have successfully handled legal cases in court
- To find colleagues who are not prejudiced in order to assist him in strengthening his case
- To encourage Mandla to discuss his situation to help him to deal with his frustrations
- To help Mandla prepare to take up the matter with the senior lawyers (by means of role-play)
- To convince Mandla's superiors to give him a case, under the supervision of a senior partner in the firm, to prove that he can adequately manage certain court cases in spite of his disability.

Social workers play a key role in their work with disabled persons. It is important that they deal with any prejudices they themselves may have and learn as much as possible about the specific disability of the persons they work with. This is helpful in understanding the limitations the specific disability may bring with it. Once this is done, all the other requirements of successful social work can be applied.

 STOP AND REFLECT

1 Persons who are either born deaf or born blind have their own unique difficulties to overcome. Describe some of the difficulties you think these two groups of people have to deal with.

2 The word handicapped is negative and derogatory. Do you agree with this statement? If you do agree, what better word can be used? Explain why. Discuss this statement with fellow students and colleagues of different cultural groups.

3 Discuss the concept disability with somebody who is less-abled or disabled.

4 Children living with disabilities should attend special schools rather than be mainstreamed at ordinary government schools. Do you agree with this statement? Explain why.

5 Why do you think people are prejudiced towards less-abled people?

9.3 Child care

Child care and welfare services to children can probably be regarded as historically one of the first activities of social work practice. There has always been concern for children who are ill-treated, neglected and abused, for the very reason that they are vulnerable in an adult-dominated world.

In the past, the focus has been on the child in need of care. In recent years it has shifted more towards the role and coping of the family. Even the new South African Children's Act stresses the role of parents in providing emotionally and materially for children in need of care. In spite of this shift in emphasis, children and families fall within the larger socioeconomic context of South African society and children often become the culprits or victims when things go wrong.

In this section, various aspects of family life and related issues are discussed, including child care, foster care, adoption, street children and child-headed households. Reference is made to the different Acts and regulations as well as children's rights. Finally the role of the social worker in child care will be discussed.

9.3.1 Child abuse

Child abuse can take various forms, but it is usually the result of problems in the family or community. Children do not choose to be abused and are therefore not primarily responsible for the abuse. Parental substance abuse, divorce or separation, domestic violence, unemployment etc. all negatively impact on a child.

Abuse can make up various forms. Verbal abuse is probably the most common form of abuse and can be sporadic or ongoing. It takes place in the form of yelling, insulting, threatening or causing embarrassment. This form of abuse can occur when a child is alone or in public. Verbal abuse is often accompanied by non-verbal actions, such as unreasonable grounding of children, excessive punishment and even excessive possessiveness. Another form of child abuse is sexual abuse: when a child is forced to participate in unwanted sexual activities, including performing a sexual act, masturbation, watching pornography or being subjected to making pornographic material. Another form of abuse is withholding finances, clothing, food, medication or shelter by locking the child out of the house.

The role of the social worker in these situations is to consider what is in the best interests of the child and implement statutory actions when it is warranted. This may include the moving of the child or children to a place of safety, either in a children's home, or with a family or a foster parent.

 STOP AND REFLECT

1 Abused children are scarred for life, if they do not receive professional help. Do you agree with this statement? Explain why.
2 Adults who abuse children should receive life-long sentences in jail. Do you agree with this statement? Explain why.
3 Do you agree that children growing up in poverty can be seen as abused? Discuss this issue with a fellow student or colleague.

9.3.2 Street children

Street children are children who live on the city or town streets. Most of these children do have homes, but have run away from home due to adverse living conditions including abuse. A minority of street children are those who are born from parents living on the streets.

Street children vary in age from about five years old to adulthood. They usually form groups in which they protect each other and manage to adjust well to conditions on the street, generally begging at robots, parking cars and often becoming involved in criminal activities, such as pick pocketing and robbing or stealing from cars. All of these children use drugs to cope with the harsh circumstances they have to face. They do not attend school and the longer they remain living on the streets, the less likely it is for them to cooperate and return home, or be placed in a children's facility or with foster parents. Assisting children in returning to school and overcoming substance abuse are two very important factors in reintegrating children back into their communities.

9.3.3 Child-headed households

The AIDS epidemic has led to an increase in orphaned children, bringing with it a new form of family structure, namely households headed by children. This situation places the child heading the household in a difficult role in a number of ways; having a dual role of child and adult and being an "adult" without the legal authority to take this responsibility.

According to the Children's Amendment Act, Act 35 of 2005, children may not be in charge of a household or another child in the household until they have reached the age of 16 years and then, only at that time, there must be a mentor attached to the child and household, to support and assist the child. Mentors may supervise more than one child-headed household, but not more than 12 children heading up these households, to ensure effective support and supervision.

The mentor is responsible for the collection and administration of grants and mentors may not make decisions for the children, but rather consult with the child at the head of the household and the other children, according to their age and responsibility. The child heading the household takes all the day-to-day decisions relating to the household and the children in the household.

9.3.4 Foster care

Children may be placed in foster care at the order of the Children's Court. This has to be an adult or adults whose circumstances and suitability to take on this responsibility have been investigated by a social worker. When the Commissioner of Child Welfare has made this order, foster parents will receive a foster grant to enable them to provide for the child. Foster children are also entitled to free medical care and education at the state's expense.

When a child becomes 18 years of age, the foster care order and foster grant ends, unless the child needs more time to complete his or her school education. A special application has to be made for this through a social worker. Social workers usually monitor foster care placements in order to ensure that the child has adjusted to the foster family and that the family is managing with the child.

9.3.5 Adoption

Adoption, as is the case with foster care, can be regarded as a form of substitute care when parents are unable or unwilling to take responsibility for the child. Unlike foster care, adoption is a permanent arrangement in which parents' rights are terminated by the court. The need for adoption in South Africa increased with the onset of the HIV and AIDS pandemic, because parents could no longer care for their children or passed away.

 Case Study 9.5 **Peter's family**

Peter is five years old and born from a South African mother and an Indian father. His home environment is noted for its continuous arguments between his parents due to their cultural differences, specifically when it comes to raising Peter who is an only child. Peter's mother wants to work, as the family is struggling financially, but his father will not allow this, as he feels she should be looking after Peter who has started to act out due to the constant tension and arguments.

A neighbour informed a social worker about the noisy arguments and her concern for Peter. After meeting with the parents, the social worker found that Peter was not directly or deliberately being abused or neglected or in any physical danger. In this case, she motivated the parents to attend marriage counselling sessions for three months after which she will again meet with them to determine whether any progress was made. She chose on the least severe intervention first, after which other measures can be considered if warranted.

CHILDREN'S ACT

This Act makes provision for the needs of children and considers various aspects affecting them in order to act in the best interests of the child. The following two issues are highlighted:

• **Protection issues**

In South Africa today, it is compulsory to report all acts of child abuse. According to the Children's Act, Act 35 of 2005, any person who is in a profession or occupation, which has regular contact with a child, must report the assumed abuse when encountered. This includes all medical workers, social workers, teachers, ministers of religion, traditional leaders, and staff and volunteers at care facilities. The alleged abuse has to be reported to the South African Police Service, social workers employed by the state, or child welfare located in or working in the area.

• Guardianship

Guardianship of children is usually vested in both biological parents of the child while they are married. In most circumstances, if the parents are not married, guardianship primarily lies with the mother and the biological father can apply for guardianship should he so wish. If the mother is single and herself still a child, guardianship rests with her mother, which is the child's maternal grandmother. Guardians of children make crucial decisions about children, including those related to serious medical procedures and operations, applications for passports and travel outside of the country, marriage (if the child is between the age of 16 and 18), as well as a child's property and assets.

In a situation where parents separate or divorce, guardianship will usually remain with both parents, unless the High Court, which is the upper guardian of all children, decides otherwise. In a situation where children become orphaned, the High Court becomes the guardian of those children unless the parent or parents have assigned guardianship to another person before their death.

STOP AND REFLECT

1 It is often said that the Children's Act only provides for a certain sector of South African society, as it is inaccessible to most of the citizens particularly in matters of divorce. What is your experience of this situation?
2 Can you think of and describe situations where guardianship should rather go to the biological father instead of the mother?

9.4 Family care

9.4.1 Domestic violence

The Domestic Violence Act, Act 116 of 1998, regulates domestic violence. The aim of the Act is to assist vulnerable people in a domestic relationship who become victims of violence, by issuing protection orders and dealing with all matters related to this.

Figure 9.3: An example of domestic violence

The Act refers to a domestic relationship as any marriage relationship (whether between people of the same or opposite sex), including marriage according to any law, custom or religion, as well as people who are dating, engaged, or are living together, as well as family members who are related by blood, marriage or adoption who are or who recently stayed together in the same home.

According to the Act, domestic violence can include any of the following actions and/ or threats.

- **Physical abuse:** This includes, for example, any slapping, kicking, choking, pushing, biting, holding, or threats to carry out these acts.
- **Sexual abuse:** This is when sex is forced on a partner who does not want to, or agree to, have sex in a certain way.
- **Verbal abuse:** This includes name-calling, shouting, swearing, blaming, insulting and verbal humiliation.
- **Economic abuse:** This includes not allowing the partner to work, refusing to give money, taking money earned by the partner, and refusing to pay for household needs.
- **Emotional abuse:** This includes controlling all aspects of a partner's life in terms of where the person goes, what is said, how the person dresses, etc. It also includes all forms of disrespectful and humiliating behaviour, twisting of words, lying, cheating and unreasonable jealousy and suspicions. If non-compliant, the partner is punished by silent or abrupt behaviour (including breaking property or belongings) to force the partner into submission.

If you, as the abused, experience any of the following in your partner, you may want to review the relationship and seek help or consider ending it altogether. The abusive person has no insight into or control over this behaviour. He or she will not admit that he or she is wrong and will blame it on anything or anyone. He or she will blame it on his or her childhood or circumstances and generally avoid seeking help at all costs. In many instances the abuser is a survivor of child-hood, or another form of, abuse and for this reason he or she will choose someone who is vulnerable and easy to control in order to act out his or her aggression.

Domestic abusive behaviour usually is cyclical in nature as it changes from intimidation, aggression and abuse to being apologetic and loving after the abuse, and promising that it will never happen again. After a period of calm, the mood boils up again to another round of aggression and abuse.

People caught up in a domestic violent relationship, may choose to do one of the following actions (or inactions).

- **Not doing anything:** Often the victim of abuse is too scared to do anything as further violence may occur. The person may also have lost all faith in him- or herself and may feel that he or she deserves the abuse. He or she may at times feel sorry for the abuser and hope that things will eventually get better if he or she manages his or her behaviour better and does not anger the abuser. Many women are financially dependent on their abusing partners and cannot leave. Whatever the reason, doing nothing will not bring about any change.
- **Going to the police or phoning them to assist:** Irrespective of when and where the abuse takes place, the police are informed on how they can assist and the rules indicating this are written down at the different police stations. They include:
  > protecting the victim and children
  > helping to find a place of safety if required, or providing names of organisations that can assist
  > assisting the victim and children to see a doctor if required
  > assisting with laying a case if required.
- **Applying for a protection order:** Any person who has been abused may apply for a protection order at a court. This is done on a prescribed form (Form 2) and can be brought to court by the complainant or any other person, including a counsellor, health service provider, SAPS member, or social worker etc., who acts on behalf of the complainant with his or her written consent.
- **Getting legal help** for divorce or maintenance.

9.4.2 Marriage counselling / Couples counselling

It is generally acknowledged that marriage requires a definition in the broader sense of the word, due to different perceptions, expectations and needs of people individually and within specific cultures. Marriage includes a relationship in the traditional sense of the word, as well as two people living together (or cohabiting) for any period of time, from the same or opposite sex. For this reason, marriage counselling is more appropriately referred to as couples counselling.

Marriage counselling can be placed on a continuum in terms of its level of intervention. This includes premarital counselling for couples who decide to marry, marriage guidance for couples to prepare them for the stages and developments in the relationship, marriage enrichment for couples who want to improve their relationship and marriage counselling where specific ther-apeutic inputs are required to help couples cope with difficulties experienced within their relationship. Finally, provision is made for divorce counselling when the persons involved decide to end the relationship or realise that the relationship cannot continue.

Marriage counselling, in essence, addresses relationship issues. These issues include all matters of discomfort or tension identified by the two individuals, attitudes towards each other, problems in communication, expectations, disappointments, hurtful interactions and differences of opinion. The aim is to assist the couples to acquire a better understanding of themselves and their partners in order to interact more constructively.

 Case Study 9.6 Chriswell and Miriam

Chriswell and Miriam have been married for three years and have two children, a girl Mandy who is seven years old, and a boy Joel who is five years old. Chriswell was born and grew up in Malawi, but came to Tshwane ten years ago in order to find work. He found work as a waiter at a restaurant where he met Miriam who moved to Tshwane from Upington eight years ago to also find work.

When they met up with each other, their relationship was very strong. However, since the birth of Mandy, they became anxious as arguments about how the child should be raised caused much tension. Chriswell, who comes from a very conservative and religious background, was strict and controlling, while Miriam, who was Afrikaans speaking, grew up in an environment in which parents mostly left children to be with friends as the whole community looked after them. Arguments would vary from where Mandy should sleep, how often she should be fed, church and cultural issues, marriage as well as working hours.

Both Chriswell and Miriam wanted the relationship to work and two years after Joel was born they agreed to marry. They attended parenting groups provided by the social worker and were adamant to make the relationship work. These group sessions helped them understand and embrace their differences, improved their communication, decision-making and crisis-management skills and enabled them to reach agreement and compromises in raising Mandy.

9.4.3   Divorce

Divorce is the term which indicates that a relationship has come to an end, and by implication refers to the two married people continuing with their lives separately. Although divorce seems to indicate a specific action, it is in fact a process which develops over a period of time and consists of different elements within a relationship.

It is seldom that both individuals in the marriage jointly and suddenly reach a point where they simultaneously decide that the relationship is over. Often one of the partners may still care for the other person and may rather opt for marriage counselling as a last attempt to salvage the relationship.

Before a relationship reaches the stage of divorce, there is usually a point where one or both partners start to become emotionally removed or detached from the other person. This is portrayed by a loss of trust, affection and respect, often leading to feelings of rejection and failure and reactions of anger. However, when the stage of divorce is eventually reached, one or both partners have become resentful which complicates any and all other arrangements around the divorce, including agreements on where to stay, financial settlements, the children in terms of contact and care and the distribution of possessions, especially in terms of what is needed and/or acquired by both parties together.

9.4.3.1   Parent education, mediation and parenting plans

The Children's Act will always try and cater to the best interests of the child. Even in its terminology, the Act has become more user friendly and replaced words such as "parental authority" with "parental rights and responsibilities", "custody" with "care" and "contact" with the word "access".

Training parents in assisting their children through the divorce is probably the most important mechanism of change. Parenting education teaches parents how divorce affects children and parents, and how to consider the emotional and developmental needs of children in terms of their age, temperament and all aspects of attachment. At the same time, parents are empowered in terms of their knowledge and decision-making with regard to what is best for their children. The aim of the training is to cultivate resilience within children in working through the trauma of their parents' divorce.

In the course of divorce, provision is made for mediation, which is a voluntary process in which parents, with the assistance of a trained and impartial third party, discuss their differences and disputes with the aim of finding some form of agreement between the divorcing parents. As is the case with parent education, mediation is an empowering transaction through which parents are assisted to form a future working relationship with each other, while acknowledging and considering the needs of the child during and after the divorce.

Parenting plans are agreements between parents in which they agree on how they will contribute to the care and wellbeing of their children. They aim to assist parents in developing a meaningful environment for their children when they as parents are no longer living together, while considering the relationship between the parents and the relationship they each have with the children. It includes aspects of care and contact, responsibilities, expenses of the children and ways to handle disagreements about the children.

9.4.3.2 The role of the social worker

The role of a social worker in divorce matters is always therapeutic and should never become legal or technical. Under relatively normal circumstances, children have a right to a meaningful relationship with both parents. However, in all divorce matters, there is a lot of hurt and disappointment and due to this being very emotional, parents who divorce are usually not very logical about their situation. Social workers involved in these situations need to be impartial, understanding and fair with all affected while the legal matters are dealt with by other professionals.

 Case Study 9.7 **John**

John is four years old. He is the only child born from a 19-year-old substance abusing father and a 20-year-old mother. They have been married for one year as a means of trying to keep the relationship together for the sake of the child. John's paternal grandparents stay in the Eastern Cape, while his maternal grandmother stays with them in the house while his mother works at a restaurant to provide some income for the family.

John has lately been experiencing difficulty in sleeping and often wets his bed. He sleeps in a room with his grandmother and they seldom leave the house. His mother has irregular working hours, while his father is always out with friends and under the influence of drugs when arriving back home. His parents are regularly involved in violent arguments which John witnesses.

Having read this case study, discuss with fellow students or colleagues what you believe is in the best interests of John.

 STOP AND REFLECT

1 Should both parents be involved in the life of their children until they reach adulthood?
2 How can we motivate constructive involvement of parents in their children's lives?
3 How does divorce impact on society at large?

9.4.4 Youth

In this section, emphasis is placed on the youth, the underlying issues they struggle with and how they adapt to their environments. Reference will be made to youth in conflict with the law, relevant Acts and the role of the social worker in working with the youth.

It is commonly agreed that we live in a constantly changing world; advances in technology are probably the biggest contributor to these changes as they affect all people socially, emotionally and morally. Although children and youth are regarded as resilient and probably better equipped to deal with the constant change we experience, they lack the problem-solving skills and decision-making capacity to constructively manage their worlds. The result of this is commonly perceived in destructive acting out behaviour. Safodien (as cited in Nicholas, Rautenbach & Maistry, 2011:251) refers to daily reports in the media highlighting the involvement of children/youth in violent crimes such as murder, rape and robbery, indicating that it is an area of concern.

9.4.4.1 Youth in conflict with the law

Figure 9.4: Youth in conflict with the law

In the South African Constitution it clearly states that the "best interest of the child" should always be considered (Section 28(2)). This not only applies to a situation in which the child is the victim of abuse, but also to a situation in which the child is the perpetrator. This is in line with international developments and agreements and specifically led to the compiling of the Child Justice Act, Act 75 of 2007, which clearly distinguishes young people from adults.

According to South African legislation, children under the age of seven cannot discern between right and wrong and are therefore not held responsible for criminal activity. Children between seven and 13 can, in certain circumstances, be liable for criminal prosecution, and children older than 14 can in cases be held responsible for criminal offences according to the relevant Act.

There are various specific risk factors related to why young people become involved in criminal behaviour.

These factors may include an unstable family and social circumstances, drug abuse, peer pressure and abuse by adult criminals who involve young people in crime.

In 2008, the National Assembly of the South African government adopted the Child Justice Act into law. This Act has set out a number of objectives, including amongst other things, protecting the rights of children according to the Constitution, reinforcing children's respect for human rights, restorative justice responses, special programmes to break the cycle of crime, and interdepartmental networking to ensure a holistic approach in addressing the problem as well as upholding the policy issues set out in the Act.

9.4.4.2 Role of the social worker

The role of the Social Worker, in most cases, is performed as a state employee, and a facilitator networking with various other role-players. These role-players include state departments including the SAPS, Social Development, Home Affairs, Correctional Services, Basic Education, Justice and Constitutional Development, the National Prosecuting Authority, the non-government sector and civil society.

Social workers become involved in the various sectors of the Act, including capacity building within this system, the assessment of children and the drawing up of reports with recommendations on their findings, the management of children placed under probation, involvement in the diversion and alternative sentencing programmes, as well as prevention and education programmes. Their role is primarily founded within the Department of Social Development.

ACTS AND DOCUMENTATION

There are a number of Acts which are considered when it comes to legal matters affecting children and youth. They include the:

- Children's Act, Act 35 of 2005
- Child Justice Act, Act No 75 of 2007
- Correctional Services Act, Act 111 of 1998
- Criminal Procedure Act, Act 51 of 1977 as amended
- Probation Services Amendment Act, Act 35 of 2002.

 STOP AND REFLECT

1 At what age can children be held accountable for their actions, including criminal behaviour?
2 Which circumstances should be taken into account when assessing children who committed a crime?
3 How can victims of crime by a minor be compensated and who should be responsible for this restitution?
4 Reflect on the youth in your community. What are the critical issues they experience?

9.4.5 The elderly

The elderly are also referred to as older adults. Due to improved health care and medical practices, life expectancy is extended worldwide and more particularly in the developed regions of the world. Not only are people becoming older, but the number of older adults is also rapidly increasing. It is the aim of this section to help the reader formulate an idea of what old age entails and obtain some understanding of the needs of the elderly. The role of the social worker in the field of the elderly will also be explained.

Ageing brings with it many challenges, including retirement, deteriorating health, increasing financial short falls, loss of loved ones, independence and finding ongoing meaning and value in life (Ambrosino, Ambrosino, Heffernan & Shuttlesworth, 2012:341–360). The needs of this group of people vary, and depending on the income and community in which they live, different services will be considered. In most instances the social worker will help the elderly to address issues either as an individual or in a group. This intervention will include assistance and support in adjusting to the constant changes they have to face.

In South Africa the same trend of extended life expectancy and an increasing number of ageing persons is recorded. The economic difficulties experienced in a number of our more deprived and rural communities have brought with it a tendency for the elderly to look after their grand-children, while parents are working to make ends meet. On the other hand, many families are living on the pension of an elderly person, as this is the only source of income for the family. However, both these situations often lead to increased family tension and abuse of the elderly.

Social workers have historically been involved in assisting older adults in institutional care, and on an individual and family level, addressing specific personal problems including adapting to old age, securing resources, decision-making and loss. This responsibility has gradually moved to the community, while social work support is still provided or facilitated.

 Elderly

Mary is 73 years old and has lived in a small town all her live. Her children have moved to the city and she is the only family member left in her town. She broke her hip after falling at a shop. She is in hospital and her operation has resulted in complications. According to hospital staff, they have contacted her three children, but they can't help her. She has to go to her home, which is a shack without running water and electricity.

As a student, how do you think the social worker should conduct the interview? What steps will you advise him or her to take to address this problem situation?

 STOP AND REFLECT

1 Reflect on the aged in your community. What are the critical issues they have to address?
2 Discuss with fellow students or colleagues how you would like to be treated when you become an older adult.

9.5 Addiction

South Africa is perceived as having one of the highest incidences of alcohol and drug abuse in the world. Makhudu, regional chairman of the Gauteng Drug Action Committee (DAC) indicated that as much as 50 per cent of the youth in certain areas are sporadically abusing drugs. He continued by adding that the recovery rate for them is less than 10 per cent leaving high numbers of addicted youngsters roaming the streets.

The Central Drug Authority (CDA), by voice of the National Drug Master Plan (NDMP) 2013–2017, has in line with the Prevention and Treatment of Substance Abuse Act, Act 70 of 2008, acknowledged the increasing trend of substance abuse. Both documents emphasise an overall and holistic approach to addressing this problem, including providing education and prevention programmes, cooperating with law enforcement, increasing treatment options and clamping down on illegal substances.

This section will enable the reader to identify various defence mechanisms used by addicted people as well as explain the recovery and relapse processes in addiction. The reader should be able to understand the process of addiction as well as describe the effects of addiction in different life areas.

Addiction is a behavioural problem, characterised by the preoccupation of a substance and its use, and the loss of control once started, irrespective of the physical, psychological, social and spiritual consequences. Addiction is self-destructive by nature.

9.5.1   The process of addiction

The process of addiction generally follows a noticeable trend, namely consuming increased amounts of a substance over time, using substances more frequently, and/or starting to use stronger or additional substances to obtain the same effect they had when they initially started using. The abuse will gradually take on a fixed pattern from **normal** use to **risky** use, **problem** use and eventually **addiction**.

9.5.1.1   Normal/Responsible use

Alcohol: Normal drinking constitutes one to two drinks per hour, with a maximum of four drinks per occasion two to three times per week. It is controlled and does not follow a fixed pattern.

Other drugs: Normal use only applies to legal drugs which are prescribed or bought over the counter and are used as prescribed or stated on the container.

9.5.1.2   Risky/Hazardous use

Alcohol: Risky/Hazardous use is when a person starts drinking for the effect it has. It is usually accompanied by a sporadic preoccupation with alcohol and an urgency to drink. The user experiences some ambivalence about drinking and will start making excuses to drink or for his or her behaviour afterwards.

Other drugs: Risky/Hazardous use applies to experimenting with any illegal drugs or using more than the prescribed or required legal drugs. It is also accompanied by ambivalence and making excuses for its use.

9.5.1.3   Problem use

Problem use applies to both alcohol and any other drugs. It includes the onset of social problems, as the person generally uses more of a substance than planned and efforts to stop using mostly fail. The person will start using secretly and become defensive, as he or she experiences increasing emotional and health problems.

9.5.1.4   Addiction

The addiction phase of use is recognised primarily by a loss of control over the use of a substance. The person continues using despite the harm it does and problems it causes in all life areas. It is also accompanied by emotional turmoil, and increased defensiveness and irritation, and eventually noticed by intense fears or anxiety, and ethical and physical breakdown. The end result of this can lead to death, either by overdose, suicide, accident or physical collapse.

The following section briefly explains the effects of drug addiction:

- Digestive system: The mouth, oesophagus, stomach, liver, pancreas, kidneys, intestines are all exposed to the physical component of the drug when used and one or more of these organs become damaged after long-term use or when high quantities of a drug is ingested.
- Circulatory system: The heart, due to increased blood pressure when stimulants are used, has to work harder than intended and becomes damaged.
- Nervous system: Due to drugs directly affecting the brain functioning, the whole nervous system of the body is inadvertently affected as reactions are either increased or decreased, depending on whether a stimulant or depressant has been used.

- Thinking patterns: Because drugs generally have an effect that makes the user feel good, he or she thinks more and more about the effects and eventually becomes preoccupied with its use and effect. The user eventually experiences a breakdown in relationships, due to the addiction, and over time becomes suspicious of others as he or she believes they want to prevent him or her from using the drugs.
- Feelings: Eventually, after a prolonged period of use or abuse, the feelings the addict experiences are all negative feelings in spite of the initial feeling of relaxation, high or wellbeing.
- Actions: Due to the addiction and consequent loss of control over the use of drugs, the addicted person becomes defensive and experience underlying self-destructive feelings.
- Relationships: All the addict's relationships, whether it is a marriage or cohabitation, with children or parents, become disturbed and eventually all trust and respect is broken down.
- Work: As the addiction worsens, behaviour at the workplace is characterised by absentee-ism, accidents, mistakes, missed deadlines and stressed relationships.
- Friendships: These change over time, as the addict becomes limited to his or her relation-ships with other using/abusing persons.
- Interest and involvement is neglected: Due to the preoccupation with the drug of addic-tion, the person spends less time following any other interests and hobbies.
- Religion: All spiritual activities are affected, including prayers, attendance of religious gatherings or readings of scriptures.

9.5.2   Defence mechanisms

All people use defence mechanisms from time to time when they are in some sort of trouble. For people with a substance abuse problem, using defences becomes a mode of their survival, since they cannot stop abusing the substance, even if they may want to. Some examples of defences include the following:

- **Aggression** (provocation, intimidation, emotional blackmail, threats): The purpose for using these types of defence mechanisms is to create fear in the other person by means of abusive and insulting words, a strong negative attitude or physical contact.
- **Projection** (blaming): As is the case with aggression, the substance abuser is, by implica-tion, not denying his or her use. In this case, the responsibility for his or her problem is passed on to the other person.
- **Rationalisation** (excuses, justifications, intellectualisation): In this instance, the sub-stance abuser is also not really denying that there is a problem, but giving reasons and explanations as to why the situation is the way it is, repressing the actual facts.
- **Minimisation**: When confronted, he or she attempts to make the situation less severe or serious, either by twisting the truth or making a joke / being light-hearted about it.
- **Manipulation** (promises): This defence mechanism is used by the substance abuser either as a peace offering, or to try and prove that the situation is under control.
- **Silence** (withdrawing): This defence mechanism is the total opposite of aggression. In this case, when the substance abuser is confronted about his or her use/abuse, there is no forthcoming response.
- **Avoidance**: In this case, the substance abuser avoids discussing his or her problem by physically not being present at home. Instead he or she will avoid going home and rather spend time with friends, at a bar, function or even at work. "Working late" usually becomes an excuse for not being at home.

- **Lies** (denial): Substance abuse, more particularly alcoholism, is often referred to as the disease of denial. However, by using any of the above-mentioned defences, the problem has not openly been denied. In this case, the abuser stubbornly refuses to admit that there is a problem, even if it means he or she openly lies about it. Should he or she admit to their problem, it means he or she must stop the use, which is something they may not yet be prepared or ready to do? As is the case with manipulation, the truth eventually comes out.

9.5.3 Recovery and relapse

As is the case with addiction, recovery also follows a process over time. There is no easy or quick way of restoring the damage caused by abuse and addiction.

Recovery usually starts when an addict recognises that he or she needs help and stops using. The person accepts and internalises being addicted, develops coping skills and changes his or her values about the substance. This is followed by a commitment to the recovery, obtaining a balanced lifestyle and eventually repairing relationships. Finally, by coping with the addiction on a day-to-day basis, an addiction-free lifestyle is obtained.

A relapse means that the person has changed the commitment made to sobriety. In some cases, the person will experiment to determine whether he or she is still addicted, or start using due to a crisis or complacency, but then immediately stops using. This is referred to as a slip.

Like addiction and recovery, relapse usually follows a specific pattern. This pattern is noted by the following:

- The addicted person returns to a high-risk lifestyle by gradually not taking care of him- or herself, allowing stressful emotions to influence his or her relationships, getting into conflict with loved ones and not attending support groups.
- He or she again becomes involved in addictive thinking, longing to escape painful emotions, painful memories, and stressful interactions.
- By not constructively dealing with negative emotions, he or she becomes continuously irritable and defensive, over-reacts to situations, and at times becomes depressed.
- Neglecting to deal with negative emotions causes him or her to lose emotional control, have poor judgment, not stick to commitment or resist destructive impulses.
- All of this builds up to a temptation to fall back on old or addictive behaviour patterns. As the person tries to control the addiction, old feelings surface and again become unmanageable.
- Relapse becomes an unavoidable result of this process.

 STOP AND REFLECT

1   Describe your understanding and experiences of persons abusing chemical substances.
2   Reflect on the substance abuse situation in your community. Discuss with fellow students or colleagues how this situation can be addressed.
3   Do you agree that addicted people are selfish and inconsiderate? Explain your opinion on this statement.
4   Addiction can be regarded as learned behaviour? Do you agree with this statement? Explain why.
5   It is often said, "Once addicted, always addicted". What is your opinion on this statement?

9.5.4   Substances of abuse

In this section, different substances of abuse as well as the impact of abuse on the community are explained. Relevant Acts and official documents addressing substance abuse, as well as the role of the social worker in this field, will be mentioned.

Substances are generally categorised based on their effects on the central nervous system. They include stimulants, depressants and hallucinogens. Sports drugs (steroids, amino acids, growth hormones, Erythropoietin (EPO)) have little effect on the central nervous system and therefore do not fit into any specific category. This does not imply, however, that they are harmless when used.

9.5.4.1   Stimulants

Stimulants are so called, because of their stimulating effect on the central nervous system. Psychologically, users feel more activated and aware of surrounding stimuli and can experience an emotional high and excitement. Physically, users generally experience increased alertness, a higher level of energy, increased heart rate, elevated blood pressure, and an increase in body temperature.

Certain substances, due to their chemical structures, will have a more potent effect than others and are therefore more dangerous than others, even when taken in smaller amounts. The way it is used (smoked, eaten or injected) also influences the severity of the effect a specific stimulant has on the user. Furthermore, one needs to understand that after every high, generally there comes a low or crash and users may become severely depressed.

9.5.4.2   Hallucinogens

Hallucinogens bring about a distortion of reality and include Lysergic acid diethylamide (LSD) (acid, trips, and micro dots), cannabis (dagga, grass, dope, and marijuana), magic mushrooms and ecstasy.

9.5.4.3   Depressants

Depressants depress the central nervous system, slowing down most of the brain's functions. They tend to be disinhibiting early on and in low doses as they depress inhibiting pathways. One will generally notice an increase in talkativeness and courage; conduct which is often confused with the effects of stimulants.

Many substance abusers may use a combination of stimulants or depressants with a hallucinogenic substance, of which a combination of dagga and mandrax as well as dagga and alcohol, is the most commonly used. Dagga is also often used with stimulants, such as TIK, to counteract unwanted effects.

Treatment of substance abuse can take a number of different forms, but is best addressed by a team, which includes a social worker, medical practitioner and support group. There are options of attending short-term or long-term inpatient treatment programmes, outpatient treatment programmes and support groups, to assist with addiction and related problems. Some of the programmes make provision for including family members in their treatment programmes.

The role of the social worker in these instances is to first make a proper assessment of the addiction and the impact on the family, including the number of times the substance abuser has been for treatment before, and his or her willingness to cooperate in his or her recovery. Based on the assessment, the social worker will decide with the family which option is more appropriate and facilitate the solution. Should the substance abuser be unwilling to address his or her addiction, the social worker will intervene as he or she would with any other family discord.

STOP AND REFLECT

1 Do you agree that the best solution to substance abuse is getting rid of drug dealers? Explain why.
2 People who abuse substances are weak. If they have enough willpower, they can stop using drugs. Do you agree with these statements? Discuss the statements with fellow students or colleagues.
3 Do you agree that the family influences whether the substance abuser remains sober after treatment? Explain why.

9.5.5 Other addictions

In this section, the aim is to assist the reader in identifying and explaining other types of addiction, give an overview of the consequences and treatment as well as discuss a team approach to the treatment of addictions.

Figure 9.5: Collage of different types of addictions

When we consider the process that addiction follows, it is not surprising to realise that any person may potentially be at risk of becoming addicted to almost anything. Addiction, by implication, usually starts off innocently but over time progresses to a point where a person eventually loses control over his or her urges in spite of the detrimental effects on all areas of life.

Despite the similarities in the processes of addiction and relapse, there is a clear difference in how we go about treating the different subjects. The different subjects recognised as addictions include the following:

9.5.5.1 Food and drinks

Addiction to food and drinks is generally perceived as compulsive behaviour and is referred to and diagnosed as binge eating disorder. There are many contributing factors to this disorder, including physiological, psychological, genetic and cultural factors. It follows a similar pattern to the addiction process.

9.5.5.2 Medication

This refers to legal medication obtained by means of a prescription or bought over the counter at a pharmacy or supermarket.

9.5.5.3   Gambling
Gambling is generally regarded as a socially acceptable activity. It is only when this activity gradually increases and consumes increasing amounts of time and money that it becomes problematic and is referred to as pathological gambling or addiction.

9.5.5.4   Sex addiction and pornography
Sexual development is a natural process in a human's body, bringing about biophysical changes. This development becomes complicated when society is not clear in terms of what constitutes a healthy desire and abnormal behaviour. Sexual arousal is accompanied by the release of pleasurable hormones called endorphins and dopamine, which give a feeling of excitement. The process of addiction applies when the initial limited pleasure seeking becomes more risky and eventually self-destructive.

9.5.5.5   Television, computer and video games
Today television could be perceived as the main source of entertainment, which is accessible to almost all people of all ages. Television, computers and games in themselves are not problematic, but when a person spends most of his or her time in front of the television, computer or video games, important physical and social activities are sacrificed. In addition to the so-called more innocent television programmes, the portrayal of violence and sex, and the use of foul language are constantly increasing.

9.5.5.6   Sport
Sport is a socially acceptable way of staying physically and emotionally healthy. However, sport addiction, also referred to as over-training syndrome, can occur when a person exercises so hard that there is no time for physiological recovery. In addition, the time spent on exercise is at the cost of social interaction, and can lead to eating disorders and medication problems. The preoccupation with exercise eventually also leads to psychological difficulties.

9.5.5.7   Attention/Acceptance
Being addicted to attention or acceptance stems from a fear of rejection and abandonment. The person denies their own needs and devotes his or her life to satisfy the needs of another person. This is also referred to as rescuing or codependence. The person generally has a low self-esteem and will literally do everything in his or her power to earn the other person's love or acceptance.

In terms of treatment, there are generally two schools of thought, namely abstaining from involvement with a subject, and controlling the involvement with a subject. The latter may seem a contradiction with the definition of addiction, but in the cases of eating and sex, total abstinence is impossible. Once a person loses control over using or doing something, he or she should therefore abstain, but persons with an eating or sex disorder cannot be expected to never eat or have sex again.

A team approach in treating addiction is vital as addiction is a biopsychosocial problem and all these areas need to be addressed individually and, at times, simultaneously. The social worker usually plays a facilitating role in getting the substance abuser into treatment, but also has to take on a supporting role when assisting the family members affected by the addiction. Other social workers may make up part of a professional team together with medical doctors, psychiatrists, psychologists, occupational and physical therapists as well as nursing staff treating the addicted person. There are social workers who provide education and prevention programmes while other social workers work in and with communities to form drug action committees and other community groups fighting drug abuse.

9.6 Trauma

The word trauma originated as a medical term and describes a sudden unexpected event, which disrupts homeostasis. It describes an injury rather than the process of an illness. This term is unfortunately used indiscriminately in the field of psychology, referring to almost any difficulty. Even in cases of severe difficulty, they are all grouped under the term trauma, as if the impact and or consequences of all traumas (for example rape, hi-jacking, terminal illness and bereavement) are similar. However, the reactions and complications do not all lead to Post-Traumatic Stress Disorder (PTSD), which is the result of trauma, but in fact, can lead to depression. Trauma may also lead to other complications, such as eating disorders and substance abuse.

Due to the high incidence of crime and violence in South Africa, including robberies, assaults and even serious car accidents, people are regularly traumatised, both by what they experience and what they see. These incidents, together with the consequences of corruption and the unwillingness or inability to address serious matters, leave many people with feelings of powerlessness and often despair. People are so exposed to traumatic incidences at an increasingly alarming rate that social workers have to learn how to deal with trauma.

9.6.1 Three types of trauma

1. **Critical incident trauma:** This is an event, which is shocking, sudden, and accompanied by intense fear. It is an unusual event and usually very threatening.
2. **Process trauma:** This situation is characterised by ongoing, slow, continuous, fearful and threatening events.
3. **Combination of critical incident and process trauma:** Examples of this type of trauma include rape and childhood sexual abuse. These situations are characterised by an internal struggle and feelings of shame in telling somebody and living with the consequences. This means that a Critical Incident Technique (CIT) goes over into a process trauma, with the latter becoming worse. Another example is when there is a critical incident during bereavement (process trauma). Police officers, war victims, soldiers coming back from an uncalled for war, like Vietnam, and boarder wars are often subjects of process traumas, as the social support structures fall away. Police officers are often disrespected externally and discarded internally by colleagues and superiors after experiencing trauma.

9.6.2 Normal reactions to trauma

- **Impact phase:** This phase is characterised by numbness and can last from a few minutes to some hours, even days after the incident. Everything is illogical and often even characterised by calmness before the fear kicks in, which is the primary stress response (fight, flight, freezing or surrender). The greatest needs, at this stage, are to be rescued and protected.
- **Recoil phase:** This phase, also known as the emotional phase, lasts from a day to approximately ten days. Emotional turmoil can be recognised by extreme nervousness, fear, anger, intrusion and a preoccupation with the event. If the subject has difficulty accepting this stage as a normal response to trauma, it can develop into PTSD.
- **Reorganising phase:** After two weeks, this phase, also called the rational phase, is reached. At this point, the person gradually regains control over his or her life and gets back into his or her usual routine. Feelings of intrusion may still surface from time to time, but generally speaking, his or her emotions are now more manageable. Should he or she remain in the victim mode, he or she will develop PTSD.

- **Recovery phase:** After about four weeks, there should be a gradual relief from symptoms of trauma and he or she will return to lead a more normal life. There are three phases of recovery, namely **victim** when the person experiences intense vulnerability, **survivor**, when the person feels different emotional turmoil and questions and finally **growth**, when the person moves on from this experience.
  Trauma can be defined as a shocking, unexpected incident that is experienced as intensely threatening and is associated with feelings of horror and/or extreme fear.
- **Loss of internal locus of control:** The impact of the traumatic incident may be lessened by some amount of control remaining. The loss of internal control implies the loss of autonomy, decision-making ability as well as a sense of mastery. The person feels intensely helpless and blank, almost like a baby again. This is why the person will in many cases wet him- or herself.
- **Loss of sense of coherence:** Coherence has to do with the ability to manage oneself and circumstances. It is an indication of how intact a person is with reality. In trauma, the perception of the world as a manageable and predictable place is removed. This is very subjective and should not be interfered with, as it is an internal struggle with which they have to deal.
- **Shattering of basic beliefs and assumptions:** All people have a basic set of beliefs based on life experiences and perceptions. Most people feel invulnerable, believing that negative things mostly happen to other people and do not affect them. Should something negative or traumatic happen, people will often come to the conclusion that things happen for a reason, rationalising the reasons for it happening and thus sustaining the belief that bad things do not really happen to them. Most people are able to distinguish between right and wrong, strengthening a belief that bad things happen to bad people, and because people perceive themselves as good, they believe bad things cannot happen to them. When they experience something traumatic, they feel shock and this affects their self-identity.

9.6.3   Needs of the trauma victim

- The first needs people experience after a traumatic event are the need for protection and safety. These needs are met by logically structuring and directing activities within the context of the event as well as receiving practical assistance.
- Reassurance is important during all three phases of trauma, merely the content differs:
  > Impact phase – you are safe now
  > Recoil phase – what you are experiencing is normal
  > Reorganising phase – you are effectively reintegrating yourself.
- Validation follows some time after the traumatic event and is a cortical cognitive process of addressing blame for the event and responsibility for the experience.
- At this stage there is a need for information and normalisation through trying to understand exactly how the event happened and how to deal with the experience of the event.
- Support from family, friends and colleagues is needed during all three phases.
- Victims need to be assisted in coping with reactions to trauma, including not sleeping, nightmares, intrusive thoughts, and reliving the event. Advice on how to cope, relaxation exercises, meditation, practical help, assistance with going back to work, and having somebody to stay with the victim, all aid the coping process.
- During the process of recovery, trauma victims need assistance in incorporating the trauma into their belief systems in order to get a sense of coherence.

The objective of trauma assistance is to facilitate a normal recovery process, by re-empowerment and restoring autonomy, as well as preventing the onset of PTSD and other complications.

9.6.4 Determinants of recovery

9.6.4.1 Pre-traumatic characteristics of the victim

There are a few factors in a person's life that influence the severity of the impact of a traumatic event. A history of psychiatric illness; 50 % of psychiatric disorders have a history of abuse during childhood, including sexual abuse, physical abuse and emotional neglect. Most psychological problems originate from a traumatic event and personality disorders have a history of PTSD. Having had a previous traumatic incident may make a person more vulnerable. However, continuous trauma, such as living in a township, may make a person become desensitised. Other stressors may determine how trauma is handled.

9.6.4.2 Characteristics of the event

There are different types of incidents which all have different effects. Rape in the case of women, and military combat in the case of men, are the two most severe forms of trauma. Other types of incidents include terrorism, criminal violence, and car accidents. Other characteristics include where the incident took place, how long the person was exposed to the trauma, and if somebody died, etc.

9.6.4.3 Characteristics of the recovery

One of the most important characteristics is the degree and timeframe of hyper-arousal. Social support and validation by significant people is found to be the most helpful and effective. Medical intervention, including benzodiazepines and sick leave, complicates the intervention as it disallows a normal reaction and slows down the gaining of control. It then becomes more difficult to reintegrate. There is also the added possibility of them becoming a habit. Trauma is a psychological, not a medical, problem. Furthermore, the availability of resources, such as money, transport, fitness, social support, and spirituality, can also make a positive contribution to resolving the trauma. Significant others are helpful if they: recognise that the traumatic incident was as bad as it was described to be, do not blame the victim, and react appropriately, more so with actions rather than words.

 STOP AND REFLECT

1 Reflect on a trauma you have experienced or witnessed. Discuss with a fellow student or colleague how you felt and how you managed it.
2 Do you agree that in certain cases people never recover from trauma? Explain why.

9.7 Bereavement counselling

This section will discuss aspects of loss and recovery as well as the role of the social worker in bereavement counselling.

As is the case with trauma counselling, dealing with grief is best addressed by being supportive and providing practical help. The following is a list of suggested interventions to assist somebody who is grieving:

- Nothing can erase or minimise the painful tragedy a person is facing. It may often be sufficient to just be a presence that the person can lean on when needed.
- Do not try to minimise the situation or make the person feel better. Being in a caring profession, social workers often hate to see somebody in pain. They may end up saying

things like, "I know how you feel" or "Perhaps it was for the best" in order to minimise the hurt. It never works with grief.

- Do not tell the person how to react or handle their emotions or situation. Simply let him or her understand that you support his or her decisions and will help in any way possible.
- While working through the grief process, many bereaved people report difficulty with decision making. Be a sounding board to help them think through decisions.
- Everyone grieves differently. Some will be fine and then experience their true grief a year later; others will grieve immediately. There are no timetables or rules. In some cases, a person is unable to overcome the loss.
- Remind the bereaved person to take care of him- or herself.
- Find a family member or friend to support the grieving person in practical ways, such as assisting with food that is already prepared or easy to prepare, helping with laundry, and watering plants. Prioritise these tasks. Help the bereaved complete as many tasks as possible. If there are many responsibilities, find one or more additional friends to support him or her (Noel & Blair, 2008:22–23).

9.8 Conclusion

Social work as a profession covers a variety of fields, both worldwide and in South Africa. It is a profession which needs to address various social issues on a micro-, meso- and macro-level. It requires cooperation of various stakeholders and other professions as well as volunteers.

It is important that social workers are well skilled in working with people on different levels and that they acquire knowledge in the areas of specialisation in order to provide a meaning-ful contribution that is of a high standard.

End of chapter questions

1. Does this chapter provide a sufficient overview of the different fields within which social workers can work?
2. Has this chapter allowed for new insights and are you better able to determine a field in which you would want to work?

Key concepts

- **Bereavement** is the process of dealing with grief and loss.
- **Paraplegia** is a state of physical impairment through the loss of two legs or two arms.
- **Quadriplegia** is a state of physical impairment due to the loss of both legs and both arms.
- **People with cerebral palsy** have a condition caused by brain damage around the time of birth. It is marked by lack of muscle control, especially in the limbs.
- **People who are hearing impaired** are in a state of total or partial hearing loss.
- **Visually impaired** people experience total or partial loss of sight or vision.
- **People with epilepsy** have a medical disorder involving episodes of irregular electrical discharge in the brain. It is characterised by the periodic sudden loss or impairment of consciousness, which is often accompanied by convulsions.
- **People with Down syndrome** have a genetic disorder characterised by a broad skull, blunt facial features, short stature, and learning difficulties. It is caused by the presence of an extra copy of a specific chromosome.

- **Recovery** usually starts when an addict recognises that he or she needs help and stops using. The person accepts and internalises being addicted, develops coping skills and changes his or her values about the substance.
- The word **trauma** originated as a medical term and describes a sudden unexpected event, which disrupts homeostasis. It describes an injury, rather than the process of an illness.
- **Addiction** is a behavioural problem, characterised by the preoccupation of a substance and its use, and the loss of control once started, irrespective of its physical, psychological, social and spiritual consequences. It is self-destructive by nature.
- Physical **disability** refers to a condition that interrupts the mobility of a person, due to limited functioning of one or more limbs or organs.
- The **elderly** refers to older adults. Ageing brings with it many challenges, including retirement, deteriorating health, increasing financial short falls, loss of loved ones and independence, and attempting to find ongoing meaning and value in life.
- **Foster care** is a form of substitute care when parents are temporarily unable or unwilling to take responsibility for the child.
- **Adoption** is a form of substitute care when parents are permanently unable or unwilling to take responsibility for the child.
- A **child-headed household** is a home that has a minor child as the head. This may be the result of an unforeseen circumstance or there may be no alternative option.
- **Guardians** of children make crucial decisions about children, including those related to serious medical procedures and operations, applications for passports and travel outside of the country, marriage (if the child is between the age of 16 and 18), as well as about a child's property and assets.
- A **mental disability** is an inability to enjoy life. It could be caused by disease, abuse, trauma, poverty, political violence or suppression as well as the deterioration of, or ongoing, conflicting values. A mental disorder can take many forms. More well-known mental problems include, for example, depression, anxiety disorders and schizophrenia.

References

1. AMBROSINO, R., AMBROSINO, R., HEFFERNAN, J. & SHUTTLESWORTH, G. 2012. *Social work and social welfare: an introduction.* 7th ed. Canada: Thomson Brooks.
2. CONTI-BECKER, A., DORALP, S., FAYED, N., KEAN, C., LENUCHA, R., LEYSHON, R., MERSICH, J., ROBBINS, S. & DOYLE, P.C. 2007. A comparison of the international classification of functioning, disability, and the health to the disability tax credit. *Canadian journal of occupational therapy,* 74:281–287.
3. DISABLED PEOPLE SOUTH AFRICA. 2014. *Disability rights charter of South Africa.* [Online]. Available: http://www.vut.ac.za/drop/disability/DISABILITY_RIGHTS_CHARTER.pdf [9 March 2015]
4. KENDRICK, T. & SIMON, C. 2008. Adult mental health assessment. *InnovAit,* 1(3):180–186.
5. NICHOLAS, L., RAUTENBACH, J. & MAISTRY, M. 2011. *Introduction to social work.* Johannesburg: Juta.
6. NOEL, B. & BLAIR, P.D. 2008. *I wasn't ready to say goodbye.* Illinois: Sourcebooks Inc.
7. SOUTH AFRICAN GOVERNMENT. 2000. HIV/AIDS/STD *Strategic Plan for South Africa: 2000-2005.* [Online]. Available: http://www.gov.za/sites/www.gov.za/files/aidsplan2000_0.pdf [9 March 2015]

Employment settings for social workers

Peter Schultz

CHAPTER OUTCOMES

By the end of this chapter, you should be able to:

✓ give an overview of the various settings, internationally and locally, in which a social worker can be employed

✓ reflect critically on each of the settings, including the various government departments and non-governmental organisations

✓ describe the role of social workers in Employee Assistance Programmes

✓ describe the role of social workers in private practice

✓ have a clear understanding of the role of social work in the South African legal system.

10.1 Introduction

In the beginning of the book, an overview of the scope of social work was provided. In addition, the National Planning Commission (2012:378) recognises that social services are "critical for improving social integration and human development", underlying the fact that all role-players in the various social work settings contribute in a coordinated way.

With the ongoing socioeconomic changes worldwide, as well as in South Africa, and the accompanying social insecurities caused by unemployment and poverty, substance abuse, trauma and family breakdown, social workers are continually in demand. The increasing demand for service delivery and community development makes social work a profession that can make a meaningful contribution.

Earlier in the book, we dealt with the various fields in social work, the skills required and methods used to bring about change. The section covers the areas where these skills can be applied, or more simply put, where you, once you are a qualified social worker, can go and work.

10.2 Social work internationally

Social Work as a profession has become broadly recognised, especially in Westernised countries, including Australia, Canada, Europe, Great Britain and North America. Both South Africa and India also have strong social work histories. Kuilema (2014:1) points out that the history of international social work has three distinct phases or "waves", namely at the end of the 19th century and beginning of the 20th century, the period after World War II, and the period that he refers to as the "rise of globalisation". He stresses that the profession must "regain a sense of urgency about international matters ...", recognising that there are problems no single country can address on its own.

With globalisation and increased technological advances and communication, international and intercontinental market and trade agreements, and the economic interdependency of countries, we are all affected by issues, such as poverty, health, the availability of energy and water, war, terrorism, an increase in the number of refugees, and drugs and human trafficking.

All these, and many more social issues, require social workers to work within the broader framework of the expanding global society in which we find ourselves today. It is especially the millions of vulnerable children affected by poverty and malnutrition, child labour, child trafficking, exploitation by combatants in war zones, AIDS orphans and child-headed households who require social work attention.

South Africa, as an international role-player and member of the so-called BRICS countries (Brazil, Russia, India, China and South Africa), is also affected by the socioeconomic trends of globalisation. In terms of the demands on our welfare system, we have been hit particularly hard by drug trafficking and immigration from our northern African neighbours as well as from South American countries. The impact of drug abuse has been felt more adversely in our communities, and the impact of immigration has severely pressurised the countries total infrastructure. These factors have affected the whole country in terms of health services, housing, schooling, employment, crime and economics. In addition they have placed demands on family life and religion, and integration into already established and sometimes hostile communities is difficult.

Considering the information provided by AfricaCheck (2013:5), the Department of Home Affairs received 185 198 applications for asylum in 2010, 87 020 applications in 2011 and in 2012 they received 85 058 applications. In total, an estimated 340 000 more people immigrated to South Africa in a period of three years. These people need to settle and utilise services and infrastructure that are not available.

 Joseph

Case Study 10.1

Joseph, a 25-year-old bookkeeper, has left the Congo due to the war. After losing two older brothers who opposed the government, he relocated to South Africa (four years ago) with his wife and three-year-old daughter.

Joseph and his family stayed in an RDP house. At first Joseph parked cars from 08:00 in the morning until 18:00 at night outside a retail store in a rural town in Northwest Province. He did not earn much from the tips provided by motorists, but they were enough to pay for accommodation and food.

Joseph approached the local office of the Department of Social Services. He reported that he could not enrol his daughter at the local primary school, as they said that because she was French speaking she would not benefit from the school. Furthermore, he was afraid of the increased xenophobia in the area where they stayed, which included threats to burn down the shops of the Somali people in order to get rid of all the foreigners. Joseph and his family have also been denied help twice at the local clinic, as the staff could not determine what they needed due to the language barrier. Joseph was the fifth person who reported these problems and fears to the Department of Social Services office.

The social worker at the office discussed these problems with the supervisor and branch manager. They decided to take the following measures to address the situation:
- To set up a meeting with the local town counsellor and community leaders to investigate and discuss the situation of the foreigners in the area
- To set up a meeting between the foreigners and local leaders to discuss problems they encounter and try and find solutions for them
- To approach the Department of Health and the Department of Education to determine how to accommodate people from other countries
- To find a French-speaking person who could teach French-speaking immigrants how to speak English
- To inform the local police and ward counsellors about the tension between the local residents and immigrants.

In spite of South Africa's increasing needs, many of our social workers move to First World countries, including Great Britain, Canada, Australia and New Zealand for better work opportunities and social circumstances, and more competitive salaries. The majority of these social workers are more experienced and qualified and so it is a great loss to our country. The welfare systems in Great Britain and the United States draw a strong parallel with the South African systems due to a shared welfare history. This history and the development of social work is covered in the curricula of South African Universities and Colleges, which makes the transition to these countries relatively easy. In addition to this, a number of these Western countries have business companies in South Africa that have EAP systems, which also make the transition of social work across boundaries fairly simple.

 Case Study 10.2 **Caroline**

Caroline, a 30-year-old social worker, with six years' experience in hospital social work, emigrated to England to work as social worker at a county hospital. After a thorough induction at the county hospital, it took Caroline almost four months to become comfortable with the hospital's policies and administrative requirements. Together with adapting to a new work environment, she also had to adapt to the English way of life and the weather. Fortunately, she had a strong support structure of other South Africans who had emigrated and settled in a nearby city.

 STOP AND REFLECT

1   Should you complete your social work studies, would you be willing or able to become involved with international issues, such as child care or immigration matters?
2   Would you be willing to go and work in an African country, such as Rwanda, the Central African Republic or the Congo, or a country, such as Malaysia, Sri Lanka or Brazil? In your reflection, consider the following:
   a   Orientating yourself within the foreign country in terms of the culture and language
   b   Becoming familiar with the country's welfare policies and structures
   c   Becoming familiar with the country's climate and way of life
   d   Becoming familiar with the health, housing, schooling and policing services
   e   Determining if there are support systems, such as other South Africans living there.

Xu (2006:690) points out that the future of international social work will be confronted with increasing multi-ethnic populations affected by global interdependence. It requires that social workers focus more on addressing matters of human rights, global justice and equality. Nadan (2014:8) agrees with Xu, stating that international social work is increasingly challenged in a world "characterised by growing diversity, intergroup tensions, and ethnic and political conflicts". This, interestingly enough, also holds true for social workers working locally in South Africa.

10.3   Social work and Employee Assistance Programmes in the business and private sector

Industrial social welfare and social work can be traced back to the turn of the 20th Century when it was applied primarily in American manufacturing companies. This intervention included corporate housing, boarding facilities, provision for needy families, medical care and child care facilities. With the advances in technology in the early 1900s, industries became more mechanised and the term industrial social work became referred to as occupational social work to provide more specialised services to the so-called troubled employee. This in turn made way for Employee Assistance Programmes (EAP), also known as Employee Wellness

Programmes, in the 1940s in America. These programmes were initially introduced to provide counselling and assistance to employees who had drinking problems. Over time, the EAPs began to include a wider range of work-related problems, such as financial and family problems, relocation, and retrenchment. This became known as the "broad brush" approach (Ambrosino, Ambrosino, Heffernan & Shuttlesworth, 2012:424). Employee Assistance Programmes were first introduced in South Africa at the Chamber of Mines in 1986. People everywhere are affected by incidents or situations that may result in a loss of concentration and making mistakes at work, and being late for or absent from work.

What types of problems do employees experience that warrant social work consultations?

Problems outside the workplace can affect an employee's work performance. These problems can include marital problems, substance abuse, problems in the family, relationships, loss or trauma and other personal problems.

But surely it is the employee's responsibility to address these issues?

Indeed it is, but that will require time off work, which is a loss to the company. In addition, there are problems caused within the workplace, including stress due to wrong placement, transfers, lack of training, workload and relationship problems with colleagues or superiors.

So who are all involved in EAPs?

Most of the EAPs consist of a multi-professional team, which includes medical and/or nursing staff, HR consultants and professional staff. Personal or workplace problems are usually referred to psychologists or social workers, as they require confidential, short-term, in-depth intervention.

Apart from individual intervention, what other services can the social worker offer the company?

Social workers are also involved in prevention, training and development programmes, either as facilitators or coordinators. These programmes cover a variety of topics including substance abuse, financial management, health issues, stress management, anger management and basic communication and social skills.

Figure 10.1: Social work and EAP programmes

With the emphasis on work performance in industry or business, professional help is often required to assist these people through their difficult situations. Irrespective of whether the problems are caused by factors at home or the workplace itself, the core functions of the EAPs are to enhance workplace effectiveness through the identification and resolution of these personal or work-related problems, as well as through topical information and prevention projects. In addition to this, training and development programmes, physical wellness, safety, marketing, networking, and evaluation of employees and the EAP have been included as part of the EAPs.

The role and place of EAPs in the public sector is no different to those functioning in the private sector and operate on exactly the same principles and legal requirements. According to the Evaluation of EAP in the Public Service report (Public Service Commission, 2006), EAPs within the South African Public Service focus on a variety of employee problems including "substance abuse and dependency, adaptation problems in the Public Service workplace, mental and personal relationship problems, dealing with disease and providing counselling." It was determined that the effectiveness of these programmes was strongly related to management commitment and leadership regarding EAP services.

Over the past three decades, social work has become an intricate part of EAPs in most of the major companies who run them. These programmes are accommodated in the public sector as well as in most national private companies. Social workers are often included in these programmes as part of bigger off-site brokerage companies or as private practitioners.

The relevant Acts to refer to are:
- Basic Conditions of Employment Act as amended (Act 10 of 2002)
- Employment Equity Act (Act 55 of 1998)
- Labour Relations Act (Act 66 of 1995)
- Occupational Health and Safety Act (Act 85 of 1993)

 Case Study 10.3 | **Mandla**

Mandla is 32 years old. He has been working for ABC, a company that manufactures of crates, since he completed matric 13 years ago. He started off as an Administrative Assistant and did various tasks, including the sorting and delivering of mail, shopping, filing and data capturing. He is a fast learner and was promoted to Administrative Officer three years later and is currently the Personal Assistant to the manager. He is married and has two children.

Over the past 12 to 18 months, Mandla has been late for work on a couple of occasions and has been absent on a few Mondays. The manager complained about him forgetting important appointments and recently confronted him about increasing oversights and mistakes. The manager referred him to the on-site social worker.

The social worker set up a meeting with Mandla. She explained to him that he was referred by his manager who was concerned about his absenteeism and work performance. Mandla was initially defensive and listed a number of reasons for his behaviour. The social worker did not confront Mandla at that stage, as she first needed to build a relationship with him. To build a relationship, she needed to acknowledge his difficulty first and ask him for suggestions to solve his problem.

Once an agreement was reached between Mandla and the social worker, feedback was given to Mandla's manager with his consent, as well as an agreed-upon plan of action if the problem were to recur. If a situation like this is caused by addiction or stress, it will happen again and the social worker would need to suggest further medical or professional help.

STOP AND REFLECT

1 How you would address substance abuse prevention and treatment in a work environment – consider:
   a Becoming familiar with the Prevention and Treatment of Substance Abuse Act as well as the Occupational Health and Safety Act
   b Becoming familiar with company disciplinary policies, company structures and company climate regarding substance abuse
   c Becoming familiar with testing for alcohol and other substances
   d Involving other role-players in the community for example SANCA and AA.
2 What aspects of social work intervention must be addressed in the induction of an employee who has relocated from Nigeria? In your reflection consider the following:
   a Company policies
   b Company climate regarding immigrants and whether other immigrants are already employed
   c Support structures accommodating immigrants
   d Language and cultural issues
3 If the employer pays you to see the employee, is it your responsibility to inform the employer of an employee's counselling session?

10.4 Social work in private practice: Brokers and private work

There are an increasing number of social workers who work privately, either for themselves or as members of an EAP brokerage company. The private practitioner or company is contracted by a business or the state to assist employees who experience personal or work-related problems, on the same basis as discussed in the previous section.

Social workers who practise privately carry a great responsibility in terms of their professional conduct and accountability. Not only do social workers who do counselling, in addition to their professional duties, need to be members of an association, such as the South African Association for Social Workers in Private Practice (SAASWIPP) or the National Association for Social Workers (NASW) to avoid isolation, but they also have the added responsibility of social work administration, which includes billing clients and keeping proper records of their income and expenditure.

Social work in private practice is very demanding and challenging. There is a general perception that social workers should work free of charge or at a lower professional rate than other professionals. Many medical aids do not pay for these services or set a limit to the fees payable towards social work sessions. Furthermore, social workers are not allowed to make a diagnosis of a client's problem. This prevents them from obtaining an ICD-10 code, which is required when claiming from medical aids.

To avoid many of these issues a private social worker encounters, it is more conducive for social workers to work for a brokerage company. These companies have contracts within various industries and provide a general professional service regarding the wellbeing of employees, including health care, legal care, financial advice, and psychological and social work services. When there is a need for social work services, the industry conveys this to the company concerned who then arranges a meeting between the social worker and the affected employee. The social worker reports back to the brokerage company and claims financially for services rendered. The company provides feedback to the industry of the services it provided.

Many private social workers prefer to make a living from short-term contract work at learning institutions, state departments or NGOs where they can become involved in the supervision of staff or students through policy or developmental programmes or providing training. This requires great skill in marketing to obtain such contracts. Social workers in private practice need to build up a strong network of professional partners and contacts with other organisations as clients often need to be referred.

Social workers in private practice are responsible for their own daily planning, including days set aside for training and leave days. They plan their own medical aid and insurance as well as indemnity in case a client sues him or her for a work-related issue. As social workers are solely responsible for providing for their own income, any day or time not working results in a a loss of income. The following are examples of how social workers in private practice manage their work.

Social worker A
- Fixed-term contract work at an NGO to supervise social workers and students: 8 hours per week
- Short-term contracts with two industries to provide EAP services: 8 hours per week
- Contract for training at a municipality on substance abuse in the workplace: 4 hours per week
- Private consultations at own office: 12 hours per week
- Administration including reports, files and invoices: 6 hours per week
- Group supervision with colleagues in private practice: 2 hours every second week

Social worker B
- Private consultations at own office: 24 hours per week
- Contract with brokerage company to provide EAP services: 6 hours per week
- Contract with community-based organisation for development and consultations: 6 hours per week
- Administration including reports, filing and invoicing: 6–8 hours per week

There are social workers in private practice who are involved in child care matters only, for example working with mediation, contact and care, parenting plans, and adoption; while others, for example, base their practices on working with addictions only. There are also social workers who provide full-time training sessions at companies, addressing staff development and skills training for personal development, and conflict and anger management courses.

The relevant Acts to refer to are:
- Basic Conditions of Employment Act as amended (Act 10 of 2002)
- Social Service Professions Act (Act 110 of 1978)

🗨 STOP AND REFLECT

1. Describe how you would deal with substance abuse as a private social worker. Consider the following:
   a. Involving the client's doctor (if required)
   b. The family members
   c. Support groups in the area
   d. Whether more intense treatment is required, including detoxification or in-patient treatment
   e. Drug testing.
2. How would you manage your finances as a private social worker? Consider the following:
   a. Invoicing for services rendered
   b. Payment expenditures
   c. Late payments or clients not paying at all
   d. Tax submissions
   e. Determining your salary
   f. Employing a bookkeeper.
3. What would you do if a client does not want certain information disclosed and the brokerage company does not want to pay you for the session unless the information is provided?

10.5 Social work in government

Currently, there are an increasing number of social work positions available in various government departments, particularly in the Department of Social Development. The Department of Social Development has a more general approach; but other departments have different settings and expectations in which social workers have to adapt. Social workers employed by these departments become more specialised in the various settings in which they find themselves.

10.5.1 The Department of Social Development

This department aims to provide a caring and integrated system of sustainable social development services that facilitate human development and improve the quality of life in partnership with implementing agents, such as state-funded institutions, non-governmental organisations, community-based organisations and faith-based organisations. It renders its services through three broad programmes, namely Social Security, Social Welfare and Community Development. Two branches, namely Integrated Development and Welfare Services, are involved in social work activities. The majority of the functions at the national office are primarily administrative in terms of developing programmes and policy, setting standards and monitoring services as well as interacting with organisations that are subsidised or funded by the department.

The provincial offices are more directly involved in social work activities by the provision of regional and district offices. The services provided by these offices include prevention programmes, rehabilitation, protection programmes, continuing care, mental health and addiction services. All services are integrated, coordinated and managed to maximise their benefits to society.

 Case Study 10.4 **Child abuse and neglect claim**

A 60-year-old grandmother is concerned about her two-year-old grandchild, who, in her opinion, is neglected and at times physically abused by his parents who, she claims, abuse drugs. She wants the child to be removed and placed in her care, as she has been looking after him since his birth.

The social worker dealing with this case must obtain as much information from the grandmother as possible, bearing in mind that the information may be biased. It is important that the consultation is followed up with a home visit, so that the social worker can consider where the family stays and what the circumstances are. The consultation with the parents must be done in the presence of the child, so that the interaction between the parents and the child can be observed. The social worker should obtain as much information as possible and determine if the family can first be assisted and supported before any intervention takes place (unless it is clear that the child is seriously neglected and abused). In case of neglect or abuse, the best interests of the child are considered and the social worker responds to this in terms of the appropriate Act.

10.5.2 The SA National Defence Force (the military)

The South African National Defence Force is made up of four different arms of service, namely the Army, the Air Force, the Navy and the Military Health Service. According to Kruger and van Breda (2001:947), the arm consisting of the Military Health Service renders a comprehensive service to employees and their families as well as the organisation itself, including, amongst other things, social work services that are both curative and preventative.

Functions of social workers strongly resemble that of EAPs when they deal with the personal problems of staff members, such as substance abuse, marital discord, financial difficulties and child abuse. For this purpose, case work and group work are implemented. Social workers are also involved in awareness sessions and skills development workshops to improve the psychosocial functioning of the military staff. They are furthermore involved in facilitating greater communication between the military system and families where the focus is on capacity building and support of families in dealing with work demands and military work conditions.

 STOP AND REFLECT

Elaborate on how you think a social worker could assist the spouse of a soldier who has been killed in an ambush while on duty, in a peace-keeping capacity, in an African state.

10.5.3 The Department of Health (hospitals)

Although the primary focus of this department is to provide for services regarding physical and mental wellbeing, it does make provision for social work services to a certain extent. The functions of social workers, who generally apply a holistic approach to health, are limited primarily to providing support to patients and their families. Work is also strongly based on interaction with other professionals, such as medical doctors, psychiatrists and nursing staff.

Although most social work services required by hospitals are referred to external private or state social workers, social workers involved with patients assist patients and their families in adapting socially and emotionally to their changed circumstances.

 Discharge of a disabled patient

The person for whom assistance is requested has just been discharged from hospital and is to go home. He lives in a rural area and was the only breadwinner in his family. He worked at a mine and provided for his mother, two sisters, wife and two children before he was involved in a car accident in which he lost both legs. He is now bound to a wheelchair.

The social worker involved in this case has to focus on:
- the emotional wellbeing of the client and his reintegration into his home and community
- assisting the family emotionally and providing knowledge and skills to adapt to the changed situation
- contacting the employer and/or union if he was a union member and negotiate compensation
- having regular follow-up visits to ensure that the family is coping with the changed circumstances
- ensuring that the client attends all follow-up medical appointments.

10.5.4 The South African Police Service

The South African Police Service has as vision to create a safe and secure environment for all who live in this country. It combats crime and brings criminals to justice and participates in actions to combat crime.

The objectives of social workers in the police department generally focus on three areas, namely to enhance employees' individual wellness, to enhance organisational wellness and to ensure a dynamic work-life balance and productivity. These objectives are encompassed in the Employee Health and Wellness Programme for all staff members.

Social work services are grouped into four interventions to achieve the objectives set out by this programme. The interventions make provision for individual and group sessions, which are therapeutic, and assist staff with personal problems, such as marital, relationship and family issues, addiction problems, and financial and adjustment difficulties. Individual and group sessions are also presented to enhance personal growth and development. These sessions also cover stress and anger management and provide information on relationship building, substance abuse and finances. Thirdly, work-person interventions are put in place to address all work-related issues, and finally, there are work-place interventions that focus on matters such as balance in work and personal life, policies, and productivity transfers.

 Case Study 10.6 **Patrick**

Patrick has requested a transfer from Mbombela to Mdantsane Police Station where his family is staying. He stated as motivation that his mother, who herself is terminally ill, has to take care of his frail father who is bedridden. The transfer committee requested the social worker to submit an assessment report on his home circumstances. It is the function of the social worker in such a situation to provide a confidential report, indicating an extensive, unbiased exploration of the situation.

The social worker arranged a meeting with Patrick as part of her assessment. She checked with him whether there were other ways he could address this problem (for example, if there were any other family members who were able to assist), how the transfer would solve the problem, if his parents both passed on, would he request to go back to Mbombela, and whether he had discussed his relocation with all the family members involved. The social worker also found out how long he had been in his current post and how his commander felt about his leaving.

Following this consultation, the social worker contacted a social worker in Mdantsane to verify the circumstances of Patrick's parents and the support they were receiving to cope. She then set up a meeting with Patrick's commander to verify how he felt and how the move would affect the unit. Finally, the social worker arranged a meeting with Patrick's spouse to determine how she felt about leaving and how their children would be affected. Once all the information was obtained, a report was compiled on all the evidence found. This report was accompanied by a covering letter with the social worker's recommendation and confirmation that the content was discussed with Patrick.

10.5.5 The Department of Correctional Services

Social workers in the employ of this department work with all categories of offenders, including children, young offenders, offenders with disabilities, the elderly as well as parolees and probationers.

Functions of social workers include the assessment of offenders, counselling and support services as well as crisis intervention. They are furthermore responsible for orientation and various life skills programmes on anger, substance abuse, marriage and the family. They are also responsible for facilitating the sexual offenders' treatment programme, an HIV and AIDS programme, a pre-release programme, and various awareness programmes on social issues.

All the primary and secondary social work methods are applied, including case work, group work, community work, and research and administration. In addition, they need to submit reports to Correctional Supervision and the Parole Board, network with NGOs and families in the process of the rehabilitation of the offender, and provide capacity building to professionals.

Inmates' release

A young social worker who has just started working in the department, after qualifying last year, is requested to contact the families of inmates who have completed 15-year sentences for rape and murder. The social worker is to prepare the families for the inmates' release in three months time. What are the challenges?

In such a situation, the social worker would have to make a thorough study of the files of the inmates who are being released. She or he would then need to check their visit sheets and arrange interviews with each inmate individually in order to establish their insight and progress as well as future aspirations once released from prison. He or she would then need to arrange a group session where general circumstances and expectations are discussed and even role-played. Issues discussed would include financial circumstances, finding work, fears, and reintegrating with family and socially into the community.

The social worker should contact a social workers in the areas where the inmates lived before going to prison. It is advisable that the process becomes a team approach instead of one social worker working to prepare both the inmates and their families in the community. Regular and frequent contact between the social workers will need to be maintained up until the release of the inmates.

10.5.6 The Department of Education (schools)

Educationists and social workers have long been aware of the role community and the environment plays in the schooling of children. South African communities have a strong historical link with apartheid, as do the different schooling systems that were controlled by the previous government. Schooling has been further complicated by systems developed after 1994.

Social workers at schools do not only have to deal with community-related issues, such as poverty, crime, a general lack of support at home, drug abuse and early pregnancy, but also with children who have behavioural difficulties and children who experience difficulties adapting to the school environment.

Children who struggle to adapt at school are those who come from disruptive communities or home circumstances, those who have difficulty learning, or those who struggle to adapt emotionally. Behavioural problems usually manifest in acting out behaviour or social and emotional withdrawal. These children are often referred to as naughty, difficult, unmotivated or attention-seeking children, as they are disruptive in class and/or cause problems during breaks or after school. Social work intervention can assist these learners in developing coping skills and with their general emotional wellbeing.

 Michelle

Michelle was often late for school. She was thin and often dirty when she arrived at school. Her teacher complained that Michelle, who is in Grade 7, was not paying attention in class and seldom did her homework. However, in previous years she was a good student and well-liked by her friends as well as her teachers. Lately, her aggressive and argumentative behaviour was noted and for this reason she was kept after school as a consequence of this behaviour. As her behaviour deteriorated, she was referred to the school social worker.

Upon investigating her circumstances, the social worker found that Michelle's father passed away and her mother started drinking and socialising with friends in the community who also drink a lot. Her mother often arrived home very late at night and sometimes early the next morning. Michelle, who is 12, has two younger brothers that she has had to take care of. She helped them with their homework after getting food from a neighbour who expected her to do household chores in return. Initially, she managed to cope, but as her mother's problem worsened, the neighbour became more demanding. Michelle struggled to keep up with all her responsibilities. The case was eventually referred to a social worker who managed to place the three children in foster care while her mother received help for her alcohol problem.

STOP AND REFLECT

1   If you could choose to work in a specific department, which one will you choose? Motivate your preference.
2   Do you think that social workers should be available in other departments, such as the Department of Home Affairs, which works with immigrants?
3   Can you think of any other departments in which social workers can play a role? Motivate your opinion.

10.6 Social work in non-governmental, faith-based and community-based organisations

It is noticeable from the history of welfare in South Africa, that both community-based and faith-based organisations have strongly influenced the development of non-governmental organisations and all three of these organisations have played a key role in the development of our welfare structure. These organisations developed from a specific need that was experienced in a particular area, for example housing, disability and addiction, and this drew community members, or members sharing a faith, together to address these situations. Initially, the assistance provided by these organisations included practical assistance and support and only later on made use of professional services. Originally, these efforts were run under the auspices of religious organisations and the people who became involved experienced an obligation to help the poor and disadvantaged people, or formed societies or associations made up of volunteers with a strong sense of altruism. Any income that was made or received by these organisations was ploughed back into the organisation to further assist those in need. A well-known example of such an organisation is the Salvation Army, which has various homes and treatment centres as well as disaster relief programmes in more than 188 countries worldwide.

Over time, these organisations needed to be coordinated as they expanded into other geographical areas or required more specialised assistance. Many of them became provincial and even national bodies, such as national councils, while others remained more localised. Examples of such organisations include the National Institute on Crime Prevention and Rehabilitation of Offenders (NICRO) and the South African National Council on Alcohol and Drug Dependency (SANCA).

As the welfare system, and social work in particular, developed and grew, organisations needed to become regulated, so standards of practice started to develop. In South Africa, as was the case in most Western countries, the government departments took over this responsibility. Unfortunately, in spite of the political era in South Africa, the voice of the non-governmental faith-based and community-based organisations as well as any other form of participatory governance has become silent, almost as if politicians choose not to hear it.

In spite of these trends currently being experienced in South Africa, the NGO sector, as well as the faith-based and community-based organisations, are generally perceived to be the places of work for social workers who prefer to specialise in an area of interest. These areas include working with children, the youth, the elderly, substance abuse, street children and the disabled.

 STOP AND REFLECT

Explain your understanding of the specific position of social work in the different settings covered in this section.

10.7 Social work and the South African legal system

After completing this section, you should be able to:
- have a clear understanding of the legal system in South Africa, including the different courts and their jurisdiction
- be familiar with the professional members who make up a legal system
- connect the legal system in South Africa to the social work profession and services
- be familiar with the Code of Ethics in social work.

This section explores the South African court system, the members of the legal system as well as the policies and Acts of legislation directly related to the profession of social work (see also Figure 10.3).

10.7.1 The South African legal system

In which court is a specific case heard and where does one appeal if one is not satisfied with a court's decision? The answer to these questions is determined by the jurisdiction of a specific court. Jurisdiction of a court is generally determined by two factors, namely the type of case (civil or criminal) brought to court and the geographical area in which a person stays or where a crime is committed.

SOUTH AFRICAN COURTS
- Constitutional Court
- Supreme Court of Appeal
- High Courts
- Magistrates' Courts
- Lower Courts

Figure 10.2: The South African courts and Lady Justice

- **The Constitutional Court**, which is situated in Johannesburg, is the highest court in all constitutional matters and consists of a Chief Justice and Deputy Chief Justice and nine other judges. It decides only on constitutional matters brought by any individual, association, interest group or organisation. At least eight judges hear a case and the decisions of the Constitutional Court bind all other courts.
- **The Supreme Court of Appeal**, based in Bloemfontein, is the highest court of appeal in all matters except constitutional matters. It consists of a president, deputy president and a number of appeal judges. It decides on any appeals, issues related to appeals and other matters referred to it, for both civil and criminal cases. It can impose any sentence and make any order.
- **The High Court** is based in different areas and is made up of 13 divisions which are geographically distributed, each with its own judge president and one or more deputy judge-presidents. It hears both civil and criminal cases and has the power to hear and determine appeals and reviews from all lower courts. Civil cases include claims of more than R100, 000.00 and the more serious criminal cases include murder, robbery, treason, serious fraud and cases with a probability of longer than 15 years imprisonment.

The areas of the divisions are as follows:
- Eastern Cape High Court – Bisho
- Eastern Cape High Court – Grahamstown
- Eastern Cape High Court – Mthatha
- Eastern Cape High Court – Port Elizabeth
- Free State High Court – Bloemfontein
- KwaZulu-Natal High Court – Durban
- KwaZulu-Natal High Court – Pietermaritzburg
- Limpopo High Court – Thohoyandou
- North Gauteng High Court – Pretoria
- North West High Court – Mmabatho
- Northern Cape High Court – Kimberley
- South Gauteng High Court – Johannesburg
- Western Cape High Court – Cape Town

- **Magistrates' Courts** are divided into district courts and regional courts and their jurisdiction is determined by legislation such as the Magistrates' Courts Act. They may not hear appeals or review cases.
- **Regional Courts** cover the geographical area of jurisdiction of several magisterial districts and they may hear both civil and criminal cases except high treason. They may also hear murder and rape cases, but sentencing is limited to life imprisonment or a fine not exceeding R300 000.00.
- **District Courts** are spread over almost three hundred different districts and hear both civil and criminal cases. Civil cases must not exceed claims of R100 000.00 and criminal cases must not exceed three years imprisonment. They also serve as a maintenance court and children's court for their area of jurisdiction.
- **Special Courts** are divided into Special Higher Courts and Special Lower Courts. Special Higher Courts have been instituted to deal with all aspects of specialised legislation, such as the Water Court, Labour Courts and Court of Income Tax Appeals, as well as Divorce Courts. Divorce matters no longer fall under the High Court.

Special Lower Courts include the following courts:
- **Children's Courts** make up part of the magistrates' courts for a particular district and the magistrate functions as a commissioner of child welfare. They deal with matters, such as adoption, protection of children from abuse or neglect and the protection of children in institutions.
- **Maintenance Courts** have been instituted as part of magistrates' courts to enforce procedures of maintenance orders. They hear complaints against parents who neglect their children or against divorced persons who fail to contribute financially towards their children where a court order is granted.
- **Small Claims Courts** hear disputes of individuals without legal representation of claims not exceeding R12 000.00.
- **Courts for Chiefs and Headmen** are courts where civil disputes with regard to indigenous African law are heard informally without representation, with no written record and no witnesses are required.

Why must social workers be familiar with the law and legal matters?

As social workers, we are likely to get in contact with various cases particularly in child care and divorce matters as well as matters relating to addiction, which may come before a court. For this reason we are likely to meet members of our judicial system who are members of the legal profession. It is important that we know who they are as well as the role each member plays within the legal system.

Which members of the judicial system can we expect to get into contact with?

Depending on whether a case comes before a high court or magisterial court, we may meet up with different legal persons. Advocates and attorneys, for instance, are legal practitioners who practice law in accordance with the requirements set out in the Attorneys Act (Act 53 of 1979) and the Admission of Advocates Act (Act 74 of 1964) and after applying for admission, are granted permission by the High Court to do so.

Are there any other legal persons we should be aware of?

Yes, let me introduce you to the most important people you need to know about:
Advocates are legal practitioners who usually argue a client's case in court. They are specialists in litigation.
Attorneys directly assist clients with all legal business, including legal advice, documentation and representing clients in court if required.
Judges are legal practitioners who independently and impartially preside in the constitutional court, court of appeal and the high courts.
Magistrates are legal representatives who work for the state in regional and district courts as well as specialist courts, presiding in child welfare and maintenance matters.
Public Prosecutors and State Advocates represent the state in legal matters, such as criminal law. They work under the control of the high court in each area.

Figure 10.3: Social work and the South African legal system

10.7.2 Policies and Acts related to the social work profession

There are various policies and Acts that social workers should be familiar with. However, it is vital that one policy and one Act, namely the White Paper on Social Welfare and the Social Services Professions Act, receive closer scrutiny.

Since 1994, a new Constitution for South Africa was inevitable. The Constitution of a country includes all the fundamental political principles that determine the way a country is governed. These policies are found in the laws, policies and programmes. Already in 1990, a multi-party negotiation process was started to negotiate an interim Constitution and in 1996 the new Constitution of South Africa was finally signed off by the then president, Nelson Mandela.

The *White Paper on Social Welfare (1997)* is regarded as the official policy for Social Welfare and all its clauses are supported within the Constitution and it is accepted as such by parliament. This document strongly focuses on social relief and assisting vulnerable groups of people in the country. It promotes an integrated and intersectoral approach to service delivery and clearly spells out a number of guidelines for intervention to be followed by all social service practitioners.

All professional people involved in the so-called helping professions, including doctors, nurses, psychiatrists, psychologists, social workers and therapists, should be registered with councils which oversee their professions. These councils set standards, in terms of what constitutes ethical behaviour, and promote ongoing training and development of its members in order to ensure good quality services.

Social Work has its own Act, namely the **Social Service Professions Act (Act 110 of 1978)**, which replaced the earlier Social Work Act. It makes provision for the South African Council for Social Service Professions (SACSSP), also referred to shortly as council. The council's main functions are to establish and regulate professional boards of the social service professions and provide for the registration of social workers and social auxiliary workers.

Social workers and social auxiliary workers, like many other helping professionals, have to comply with a number of legally determined requirements and obligations, deriving from common law, legislation, regulations and often from court decisions. In line with these obligations and based on the principles of human rights and social justice, a set of core values, with underlying ethical principles, has been put in place to serve as a guideline for the ethical conduct of social workers in South Africa. It also applies to social auxiliary workers.

Social workers and social auxiliary workers who do not comply with the Code of Ethics provided by the council may be accused of malpractice or unprofessional conduct. This behaviour can be heard by the council or, if very serious in civil or even criminal cases, in a court of law. Malpractice is defined by Cournoyer (2005:84) as the "... wilful or negligent behaviour by a professional person that violates the relevant Code of Ethics and professional standards of care that proves harmful to the client."

Specific regulations have been drafted by the council regarding the conduct of social workers and social auxiliary workers.

Regulations are set out in the Code of Ethics and include the following:
- Conduct that concerns the profession
- Conduct that concerns a client
- Conduct that concerns a colleague or other professional person
- Conduct that concerns an employer, a social service institution
- Conduct that concerns a community.

Appropriate conduct is described under each of these headings. Section 21(1) of the Social Service Professions Act (Act 110 of 1978) spells out in detail the acts or omissions which constitute unprofessional conduct by a social worker and social auxiliary worker.

Unethical behaviour

As a social worker you discussed with a colleague certain problems that you experienced with a client. You asked her for advice about a husband who is unfaithful and may have AIDS. His wife, who is pregnant, does not know about it and he does not want to tell her that he is having a relationship with a 16-year-old girl. Your colleague then discussed the matter with a friend who happens to know the expecting mother and informed her. The husband has now laid a complaint at the council.

The first lesson you must learn here is not to discuss any clients with colleagues. Names or any other identifying particulars should also not be disclosed. It may seem innocent to say that you merely wanted some advice from a colleague, who is also a good friend, but in this case it would be more advisable to have approached your supervisor. Secondly, your friend should not have discussed this with a personal friend of hers, as this is an extended breach of confidentiality. What complicates the situation even further is that a minor child is involved.

It is important to study the Social Service Professions Act or follow the website of the SACSSP to be clear about what constitutes unethical behaviour.

The White Paper on Social Welfare and the Social Service Professions Act are two documents that social workers and social auxiliary workers must be very well acquainted with.

Other relevant legislation and policy documents, with which they should familiarise themselves once they start working, include, amongst others, the following Acts:
- Aged Persons Act (Act 81 of 1967)
- Children's Act (Act 38 of 2005)
- Child Justice Act (Act 75 of 2008)
- Constitution of the RSA Act (Act 108 of 1996)
- Correctional Services Act (Act 111 of 1998)
- Criminals Procedures Act (Act 51 of 1977)
- Domestic Violence Act (Act 116 of 1998)
- Drugs and Drug Trafficking Act (Act 140 of 1992)
- Maintenance Act (Act 99 of 1998)
- Medicine and Related Substance Control Amendment Act (Act 59 of 2002)
- Mental Health Care Act (Act 17 of 2002)
- National Health Act (Act 61 of 2003)
- Prevention of and Treatment for Substance Abuse (Act 70 of 2008)
- South African Schools Act (Act 84 of 1996)
- Social Assistance Act (Act 59 of 1992)
- South African Police Service Act (Act 68 of 1995)
- Sterilisation Act (Act 44 of 1998)
- Termination of Pregnancy Act (Act 92 of 1996).

Further Acts to consider are:
- Access to Information Act (Act 2 of 2000)
- Basic Conditions of Employment Act as amended (Act 10 of 2002)
- Employment Equity Act (Act 55 of 1998)
- Labour Relations Act (Act 66 of 1995)
- Magistrate's Court Act (Act 32 of 1944)
- Non-profit Organisations Act (Act 71 of 1997)
- Occupational Health and Safety Act (Act 85 of 1993)
- Public Finance Management Act (Act 1 of 1999).

STOP AND REFLECT

1 How would you address unethical behaviour of a work colleague or fellow student? In your reflection familiarise yourself with the social work Code of Ethics.
2 In which social work setting would you prefer to work when completing your studies? Motivate your answer.
3 To which court would you take a father who physically abuses his wife and sexually abuses their minor daughter? How would you suggest a social worker should address this family situation?

10.8 Conclusion

The social work profession is much needed in different sectors and settings in South Africa. It is a versatile profession with many challenges and great responsibilities.

However, because of this versatility, it is possible for a social worker to choose and excel in a specific area. Social workers can choose to work with individuals, families, groups or communities. They can work with children, adults or the elderly, with disabled or able-bodied persons, in government departments, non-governmental organisations, in companies or privately.

However, whichever setting a social worker chooses to work in, it will require great integrity and conduct that is above reproach. Working with people is a great responsibility, as it can sometimes be as destructive as it is helpful. Social work is a profession that we can be proud of, as it is a team effort in which we create opportunities for many people to consider positive change and equip them to do so.

End of chapter questions

1. Does this chapter provide you with a sufficient overview of the different settings within which social workers can work?
2. Has this chapter provided new insights, and are you better able to determine the area in which you would like to work?
3. Do you have a better understanding of the South African legal system and how it functions?
4. Can you describe the place of social work within the legal system?

Key concepts

- **Brokers in social work** are persons who negotiate contracts between a company and a social worker to deliver specific social interventions.
- A **community-based organisation** is a group of people with a common background or with shared interests within a society who came together to form a body to address a specific problem in the society or community.
- The **Constitution** is a bill or statute, which describes the acceptable and legitimate conduct and processes of an organisation or country.
- **Employee Assistance Programmes** are formal short-term programmes of intervention to help an employee with a particular distress affecting his or her work performance.
- A **faith-based organisation** is a group of people from a particular religious belief or denomination that forms a body to address a specific problem in a community or at a regional or national level.

- A **non-governmental organisation (NGO)** is a body or organisation, registered with the government, addressing a specific welfare matter. It is reliant on state subsidy or public funds.
- **Private practice** is the independent practice of a profession whereby the professional person is paid for the services he or she delivers.

References

1. AFRICACHECK. 2013. *Is South Africa the largest recipient of asylum-seekers worldwide? The numbers don't add up* [Online]. Available: http://africacheck.org/reports/is-south-africa-the-largest-recipient-of-asylum-seekers-worldwide [9 October 2014] [Online]. Available: http://africacheck.org/reports/is-south-africa-the-largest-recipient-of-asylum-seekers-worldwide [9 October 2014]

2. AMBROSINO, R., AMBROSINO, R., HEFFERNAN, J. & SHUTTLESWORTH, G. 2012. *Social work and social welfare: an introduction.* 7th ed. Canada: Thomson Brooks.

3. COURNOYER, B.R. 2005. *The social work skills workbook.* 4th ed. Belmont, CA: Thompson Brooks/Cole.

4. DEPARTMENT OF SOCIAL DEVELOPMENT. 1997. *White paper for social welfare.* Pretoria: Government Printers.

5. KRUGER, A. & VAN BREDA, A.D. 2001. Military social work in the SANDF. *Military medicine,* 166(11):947–951.

6. KUILEMA, J. 2014. *Lessons from the first International Conference on Social Work.* [Online]. Available: http://isw.sagepub.com/content/early/2014/10/06/0020872814547438.full.pdf [7 October 2014]

7. NADAN, Y. 2014. *Rethinking 'cultural competence' in international social work.* [Online]. Available: http://isw.sagepub.com/content/early/2014/09/09/0020872814539986.full.pdf+html [7 October 2014]

8. NATIONAL PLANNING COMMISSION. 2012. *National Development Plan. 2030: Our future – make it work.* Pretoria: Department of the Presidency; National Planning Commission.

9. PUBLIC SERVICE COMMISSION. 2006. *Evaluation of EAP in the Public Service.* 2006. [Online]. Available: www.psc.gov.za [15 March 2015]

10. XU, Q. 2006. Defining international social work: a social service agency perspective. *International social work,* 49(6):679–692.

Index